The Novel Stage

TRANSITS:
LITERATURE, THOUGHT & CULTURE, 1650–1850

Series Editors
Kathryn Parker, University of Wisconsin—La Crosse
Miriam Wallace, New College of Florida

Transits is a series of scholarly monographs and edited volumes publishing beautiful and surprising work. Without ideological bias the series seeks transformative readings of the literary, artistic, cultural, and historical interconnections between Britain, Europe, the Far East, Oceania, and the Americas between the years 1650 and 1850, and as their implications extend down to the present time. In addition to literature, art and history, such "global" perspectives might entail considerations of time, space, nature, economics, politics, environment, gender, sex, race, bodies, and material culture, and might necessitate the development of new modes of critical imagination. At the same time, the series welcomes considerations of the local and the national, for original new work on particular writers and readers in particular places in time continues to be foundational to the discipline.

Since 2011, sixty-five *Transits* titles have been published or are in production.

Recent titles in the *Transits* series:

Romantic Automata: Exhibitions, Figures, Organisms
Michael Demson and Christopher R. Clason, eds.

Beside the Bard: Scottish Lowland Poetry in the Age of Burns
George S. Christian

The Novel Stage: Narrative Form from the Restoration to Jane Austen
Marcie Frank

The Imprisoned Traveler: Joseph Forsyth and Napoleon's Italy
Keith Crook

Fire on the Water: Sailors, Slaves, and Insurrection in Early American Literature, 1789–1886
Lenora Warren

Community and Solitude: New Essays on Johnson's Circle
Anthony W. Lee, ed.

The Global Wordsworth: Romanticism Out of Place
Katherine Bergren

Cultivating Peace: The Virgilian Georgic in English, 1650–1750
Melissa Schoenberger

Jane Austen and Comedy
Erin M. Goss, ed.

Intelligent Souls?: Feminist Orientalism in Eighteenth-Century English Literature
Samara Anne Cahill

The Printed Reader: Gender, Quixotism, and Textual Bodies in Eighteenth-Century Britain
Amelia Dale

For a full list of *Transits* titles go to https://www.bucknell.edu/script/upress/series.asp?id=33

The Novel Stage

NARRATIVE FORM FROM THE RESTORATION TO JANE AUSTEN

MARCIE FRANK

Bucknell | UNIVERSITY
UNIVERSITY | PRESS
LEWISBURG, PENNSYLVANIA

Library of Congress Cataloging-in-Publication Data

Names: Frank, Marcie, author.
Title: The novel stage : narrative form from the Restoration to Jane
   Austen / Marcie Frank.
Description: Lewisburg, Pennsylvania : Bucknell University Press,
   [2020] | Series: Transits : literature, thought & culture, 1650-1850 |
   Includes bibliographical references and index.
Identifiers: LCCN 2019016869 | ISBN 9781684481682 (cloth) |
   ISBN 9781684481675 (paperback) | ISBN 9781684481712 (pdf) |
   ISBN 9781684481699 (epub)
Subjects: LCSH: English literature—18th century—History and
   criticism—Theory, etc. | English drama—18th century—History
   and criticism—Theory, etc.
Classification: LCC PR441 .F73 2020 | DDC 822/.40939—dc23
LC record available at https://lccn.loc.gov/2019016869

A British Cataloging-in-Publication record for this book is available
from the British Library.

www.bucknell.edu/UniversityPress

Distributed worldwide by Rutgers University Press

Manufactured in the United States of America

To my mother, Esther Frank, with love

CONTENTS

Introduction   1

1 Genre, Media, and the Theory of the Novel   15

2 The Reform of the Rake from Rochester
   to Inchbald   43

3 Performing Reading in Richardson and Fielding   75

4 The Promise of Embarrassment: Frances Burney's
   Theater of Shame   97

5 Melodrama in Inchbald and Austen   125

   Coda: The Melodramatic Address   157

   Acknowledgments   167

   Notes   171

   Bibliography   199

   Index   215

The Novel Stage

IN APRIL 1792, ANNA LARPENT read Samuel Richardson's *Clarissa* for the second time and found "the stile prolix, the manners obsolete, yet surely it is wonderfully wrought."[1] In that same month she also read a Goldoni play; Thomas Holcroft's long novel *Anna St. Ives*; a new opera, *Just in Time*; Thomas Paine's *Rights of Man*; William Smellie's *Philosophy of Nature*; and the monthly digest of new books, the *Critical Review*. The seventeen-volume diary she kept between 1773 and 1828 offers a detailed portrait of a profuse and diverse reading practice that was certainly unusual for having been so extensively recorded. So was her direct involvement with the theater: she occasionally aided her husband, John Larpent, the chief inspector of plays in the Office of the Lord Chamberlain, in his duties of censoring new plays in manuscript before they were performed on the London stage. John Brewer has proposed that she can be regarded as an "exemplary modern reader": exemplary rather than heroic because even though Larpent's appetite for literature was large and her capacity to intervene in performance culture privileged, the generic range of her reading and her engagement with both printed and performed materials were common.[2]

Reading novels, play-going; rereading, attending the same play more than once; reading published plays, including those that were adapted from novels, and reading novels that adapted plays: apart from poetry, these were the most significant ways eighteenth-century audiences and their authors experienced literature.[3] Yet the dominant history of the novel has emphasized the ways it failed to fit into the extant categories and therefore remade literature in its own image. Our account of its singularity will be distorted if we fail to grasp its borrowings as well as departures from the other genres, particularly drama.

The novel stands in stark contrast to the theater insofar as it is experienced individually, at a self-determined pace in a proposed order from which it is possible to deviate at will (to skip, repeat, or jump ahead to the ending) and for a chosen amount of time, rather than collectively, sequentially, and at set hours. These are among the reasons that accounts of the novel, when they pay attention to drama, assume an opposition. But the differences between reading and attending a performance should not be allowed to overshadow the significance of reading drama in the long eighteenth century. Between solitary private reading and attending the public theater, moreover, a number of other intermediary possibilities existed that complicate the opposition, including reading aloud in the home or in semipublic clubs or public places like taverns and participating in amateur theatrical productions. When the novel and drama are understood as opposites, only some of their characteristics will be captured. If they came to be rivals, they did not start out that way.[4] Though they tend to be studied separately, and their histories demand different methods, they had much in common at the moment of the novel's emergence. *The Novel Stage* is a literary history of the novel that tracks the significance of the drama to its narrative form.

From Aphra Behn to Jane Austen, many writers of the period wrote novels and plays, and the novels of the most important few who did not—Defoe, Richardson, Sterne—were adapted for the stage. The modern form of the novel was legitimated in terms of the classic forms of drama. William Congreve's preface to *Incognita* (1692), Henry Fielding's preface to *Joseph Andrews* (1742) fifty years later, and Samuel Johnson's *Rambler* 4 (1750) almost another decade on used comedy to prop up prose fiction; in the postscript to the first edition, Samuel Richardson called *Clarissa* (1748) a "modern tragedy."[5] But the significance of the theater to the history of the novel was not simply that the older, more prestigious form fostered the newer one. Plays shaped readers' expectations of the kinds of experiences novels delivered and the ways novelists delivered them at every level. When, in a footnote, Richardson asked David Garrick to restore *King Lear*'s original ending, he assumed not only that the man of the theater would read his novel but also that his other readers would go to the theater. Fifty years later, Elizabeth Inchbald regularly reflected on the differences between reading plays and seeing them performed in her "Remarks" on the plays included "as acted" in the affordable anthology *The British Theater* (1806–1808).[6] Elements of her own plays attest to her understanding that her audience included novel readers. Theater was the default aesthetic experience of the long eighteenth century, and novels took their shape with reference to it; but novels also shaped plays, providing plots and perhaps also the impetus to increase the number of asides in the last third of the century in response to the access that narrators could supply to characters' minds. *The Novel Stage* observes a few of the ways drama registered the increasing importance of the novel but concentrates mainly on the influence of the theater on novels.

Novels provided readers with experiences of embodiment partly on the basis of a homology between reading and theatergoing that depicted reading as mental theater; partly on the basis of sociable reading, whose signs and cues abound in novels; and partly on the basis of other narrative techniques designed to enlist theatrical experience in their absorption.[7] The theatrical history of the novel thus problematizes the usual association of performance with embodiment and print with disembodiment, but it also recognizes the novel's contributions to hardening the relation between print and performance into a media opposition that, in turn, has helped to naturalize the novel's opposition to the stage. By giving a history of the first opposition and defamiliarizing the second, *The Novel Stage* collates the media of print and performance with the genres that crossed drama and prose fiction to give a new history of the novel.

Forty years ago, Michael Fried defined the aesthetics of eighteenth-century painting in terms of an opposition between absorption and theatricality, the latter understood as an aesthetic mode derived from the theater although not completely identified with it.[8] The novel and the theater map readily onto Fried's absorption and theatricality, but at the level of consumption, the opposition cannot be sustained. Once published, both novels and plays circulated through booksellers, circulating libraries, and book clubs. The Licensing Act of 1737 regulated the performance of plays on the patent stages but not their publication. Jan Fergus has shown that provincial readers of the second half of the eighteenth century in the Midlands may have preferred novels to plays but routinely consumed both.[9] *The Novel Stage*, in any case, is more interested in the level of production: it examines the influence of the experience of play-going, play-writing, and play-reading on the novel's narrative form in the hands of major novelists of the period: Aphra Behn, Samuel Richardson, Henry Fielding, Frances Burney, Elizabeth Inchbald, William Godwin, and Jane Austen. A symptomatic rather than an exhaustive study of the novel, *The Novel Stage* operates on the assumption that if the influence of the stage is so prominent in the novels at the center of the canon, it will surely be found also at the margins.

The story of the novel's relationship to the stage has begun to be told by eighteenth-century scholars. Useful accounts by Emily Hodgson Anderson, Ros Ballaster, Nora Nachumi, and Lisa Freeman nevertheless oppose the novel to the stage.[10] *The Novel Stage* takes its point of departure in the idea that, rather than rivals or opposites, the novel and drama were allies and collaborators; it forges an innovative way to study their relations at the intersection of media and genre that affects our understanding of both the canonical history of the novel and the modern organization of the literary field to which their collaborations contributed.

Wolfram Schmidgen has recognized that studies of the novel need to suspend the powerful association of the novel with modernization and can do so through the lens of genre, for genre studies "has embraced the assumption that all genres are already mixed."[11] In the history that the novel shared with the theater, however, the category of media intersected both with the category of genre and with specific genres themselves. Bookended chronologically and conceptually by two of the genres that traversed drama and the novel between 1680 and 1820, the comedy of manners and melodrama, and introduced briefly by a third, tragicomedy, *The Novel Stage* restores the novel to its position of one genre among others. Consequently, it gives a more unified account of its history and an enriched account of its form; because of its attention to media, it can also identify the contributions to the changing status of the genre concept in the organization of literature that other accounts of the novel have failed to provide when they treat it as sui generis or as that which incorporates or subsumes other genres.

Whereas the history of the novel given in *The Novel Stage* leaves plenty of its elements untouched, it fundamentally alters our sense of its aesthetics and therefore its accomplishments with three main consequences. First, by moving the novel away from an exclusively realist paradigm, it produces a more unified history of the genre that can accommodate some outliers both at its moment of emergence, such as Aphra Behn, and toward the end of the long eighteenth century, such as William Godwin and Elizabeth Inchbald, each of whose improbabilities, when they are not seen as incompetent, tend to get read primarily in political terms.

Scholarship on the novel grants realism a centrality that has supported a fixation on the category of character whose analysis has taken two adjacent directions: toward problems associated with "relatability," including the range of identities, and toward the representation of mental processes. *The Novel Stage* displaces realism not to minimize its significance but to bring other elements of novelistic representation into view, including the modulation of the reading experience by the incorporation of generic conventions familiar from the theater and a host of associated techniques to solicit (or refuse) moral judgment and manipulate distance and involvement. Extending the capacity of vicarious identification to go beyond humans to objects, ideas, and even authorial style, these sometimes serve and sometimes disrupt realism. The theatrical history of the novel thus unsettles the dominant interests in realism and character. By disclosing aspects of the novel that work beyond their grasp, *The Novel Stage* challenges the adequacy of these critical terms, proposing both to circumscribe their application and to supplement them.

Second, the achievements of Aphra Behn, Frances Burney, Elizabeth Inchbald, and Jane Austen are integrated alongside those of Richardson and Fielding instead of being set apart in a female genealogy. These women writers achieve a prominent place in *The Novel Stage* not because of any collation of gender and genre but because of their contributions to narrative form. In fact, the status of both the genre concept and the specific genres structuring *The Novel Stage* precludes any systematic association of genre and gender. If Burney fused Richardson and Fielding to narrate female development, Austen and Inchbald each used melodrama to modify the comedy of manners they inherited partly from Burney, thereby taking the female bildungsroman in different directions.

Third, since interpretation occurs at the intersection of the categories of genre and media, a new sense can emerge of how both worked together in both the formal history of the novel and the reorganization of the modern field of literature to which the novel, together with drama, contributed. Scholars of genre reform in the Romantic period who are interested in the modern organization of literature have had little to say about the theater, notwithstanding the fact that its relations to the novel made significant contributions to the displacement of the older organization of "Poetry" that had comfortably accommodated plays and not so comfortably novels.[12]

Along with the realism paradigm, *The Novel Stage* also displaces those narratives that identify the novel's aesthetic achievements as ones that it, and only it, can achieve. Ian Watt, Michael McKeon, Nancy Armstrong, and Catherine Gallagher have presented such accounts under the rubrics of formal realism, domesticity, or fictionality itself.[13] By highlighting instead both the novel's medium-specificity and its cross-generic and intermedial collaborations with the theater, this history of the novel can include those narratives that have proven inassimilable to the realist canon because they are too supernatural (i.e., Gothic), too didactic, or too invested in panoramic social itemization (e.g., later Burney) and overdetermination (e.g., Inchbald and Godwin), some of which have been consigned to an alternative genealogy of the Romantic novel, which has itself been granted a long prehistory that goes back to Walpole's *Castle of Otranto* (1764).[14]

Tragicomedy, the comedy of manners, melodrama: each emerged first onstage but then also came to be bound up significantly with the novel. Tragicomedy helped to shape the short prose fiction of Aphra Behn; it was a vehicle through which the social and aesthetic valences of tragedy and comedy were reconfigured and made available to the eighteenth-century novel, a genealogy I explore in the first part of chapter 1, "Genre, Media, and Theory of the Novel." The comedy of manners migrated from the Restoration stage to the novel over the course of the long eighteenth century, a process I track in chapter 2, "The Reform of the Rake from Rochester to Inchbald." The comedy of manners reached its apotheosis in Jane Austen, though the mark of the stage in her novels manifests itself in the terms of melodrama as well, as I establish in chapter 5, "Melodrama in Inchbald and Austen." Although the first melodrama is often identified as Pixérécourt's *Çoelina* (1801), translated almost immediately into English by Thomas Holcroft as the *Tale of Mystery* (1802), stage melodrama was conditioned by the Gothic novel—Coleridge even traced its roots back to Richardson's *Clarissa*.[15] A revisionary history of melodrama's emergence introduces its influence on the novels of Inchbald and Austen.

The Novel Stage takes advantage of the ways the history of the novel can benefit from theater studies, though it also respects their significant methodological differences. The distinction between theater and drama, between what is staged and what is read, has made performance and its histories subject to analysis in theater studies. Yet the interest in performance as a medium has served to separate drama from other literary genres; in a complementary fashion, novel studies has had eyes only for the medium of print. Despite our thoroughgoing sensitization to media since the digital turn, we have yet to acquire the most efficacious sense of its history or its interactions with terms such as "form" and "genre," which will enable its best application to literary analysis. The relations of the novel to the theater can provide another history of what John Guillory has called "the media concept," one that, by demanding its collation with the category of genre, produces a literary history of their intersection.[16]

Whereas the history of performance and the repertory itself are important to *The Novel Stage*, the relationship of print to performance should not automatically be understood as an opposition, as I have been suggesting. Although plays were largely read rather than seen in performance during the Interregnum, when the theaters were closed, there is no evidence that reading and seeing plays were understood as competing rather than mutually enhancing activities once the theaters reopened in 1660.[17] The contrasts that must have been observed between reading plays and seeing them performed were not commented on in print until the end of the eighteenth century. Indeed, "dramatize," according to the *OED*, only came into use in 1780–1783; by 1823, its meaning had been extended from putting into dramatic form to behaving melodramatically. As I argue in the second part of chapter 1, it was only at the end of the eighteenth century that the relation of print to performance came to be construed as a media opposition, a case I make on the basis of the history of printing plays and a brief reception of Shakespeare, who is often taken as a figure for English national culture.

The concept of the repertory is crucial to any understanding of the theater: it structured the experience of theater managers, actors, audience members, and authors alike and formed the backdrop to the Larpents' decisions. Long ago, Michael Booth argued that critics interested in drama will ignore the history of performance at their peril.[18] Furthermore, as Robert D. Hume has demonstrated, it is impossible to understand the history of the theater in the eighteenth century by focusing only on new plays, genres of plays, or the history of regulation, although all of these elements will enter into an understanding of the repertory.[19]

The repertory signifies the synchronic availability of all the plays it contained whose rotation of performances within and across the seasons and the years shaped revivals of old favorites, new stagings of older plays updated to reflect contemporary concerns, and new plays. The repertory has been theorized by Tracy Davis as that which permitted the elements of performance that were not recorded to be shared between performers and audiences and whose significance can thereby be captured.[20] For Diana Taylor, "the repertoire" is the concept that gives performance a history comparable, if not superior, to the print archive for its capacity to convey the politics of gesture.[21] Constituted by repetition and rotation, the repertory enables the detection of the differences between convention and innovation in performance and elsewhere and can thus provide an essential corrective to the dominant history of the novel, whose critics frequently have emphasized the novel's association with other novelties, including the news, newspapers, and other "novel objects," to emphasize its modernity.[22]

The history of the novel, like other historical scholarship, has gravitated toward "firsts," innovation, and novelty. Yet the repertory too was significantly invested in novelty. As Stuart Sherman has argued, the influence of the news on the theater was reciprocal: not only did the theater take up current events, but it also served as a content provider for newspapers, with notices and reviews helping to determine their daily rhythms.[23] Moreover, just as the news was important to the theatrical repertory, so too were novels, and not just because of their novelty: they provided plots and affected some other matters of dramatic presentation. The differences between dramatic and narrative form pushed the development of both in the genres they shared as much as did their similarities; as each discovered what it alone could do, each also discovered its capacity to provide versions of the experience of the other. In *The Novel Stage*, I build on the insights of theater history but depart from it methodologically. This is not an archival project, and I give more weight to drama theory, read drama, genre, and generic convention as I work with textual evidence that novelists were influenced not only by other novelists and that playwrights were influenced not only by other playwrights. I am interested in the shift from the conjunction, novels-and-drama, to the disjunction, novels-or-drama, as it reflected the changing relationship between the categories of genre and media in the organization of the literary field. Bringing out the tendency of the category of media to overshadow that of genre from the end of the eighteenth century into our own day, *The Novel Stage* explores instead ways for their being thought together.

Looking at the ways narrative form was influenced by the theater permits the discovery of a number of techniques that have not been described before. Critics have sometimes observed the novelistic incorporation of dramatic elements in scenes set at the theater, amateur theatricals, and the direct adaptation of elements such as *tableaux vivants*. But these have been depicted most often as signs of the theater's derogation when they could just as easily be read as signs of homage to and appropriations of the theater's powers. I add to the list of familiar theatrical elements others including Fielding's systematic use of letters as props, Burney's development of reversals of perspective that pivot 180 degrees as if on a proscenium, the equivalent of what film studies calls shot-reverse-shot but which has no name in the study of print narrative, Austen's use of the drawing room as a stage set, and Inchbald's use of the narrator to address characters directly, techniques that sometimes serve and sometimes disrupt realism. Our sense of novelistic aesthetics is distorted when its account is confined to realism or to the novel alone and even more so when the novel is signified by the critical fetish, free indirect discourse. I challenge this excessively streamlined account, disclosing the theatrical roots of free indirect discourse to recontextualize the technique among the other narrative innovations that the theater inspired in the novel. I also observe some of the effects novels had on plays, including the use of letters, asides, the ways sudden changes of heart were dramatized. Treating the novel's intersections with the theater prompts a new history of melodrama that demonstrates new connections and divergences between the comedy of manners, domestic fiction, female bildungsroman, and novels concerned with overdetermination.

Using the terms of both genre and media, *The Novel Stage* keeps one eye on the consequences for the modern organization of literature and the other on novelistic and dramatic techniques in a range of canonical novels and some plays. Invested neither in bringing together literature and its nonliterary contexts in order to disclose their ideological division of labor, as does the New Historicism, nor in an archive-oriented older historicism, this book instead produces a literary history by synthesizing the literature of the period and its scholarship, including archival scholarship, to reflect the contributions that the relations between the novel and the theater made to the modern conceptualization of literature, which gradually displaced the older dispensation of Poetry. I expose in order to move beyond an exclusive print orientation to capture the formal and technical contributions drama made to the narrative form of the novel.

Chapter 1, "Genre, Media, and Theory of the Novel," launches the chapters that follow by discussing the categories of genre and media separately in two sections apiece. The first of each takes specific examples as its focus, and the second extrapolates the implications in more abstract and general terms. An analysis of two pieces of short prose fiction by Aphra Behn that channeled tragicomedy, *Oroonoko* (1688) and *The Fair Jilt* (1688), can explain their narrative form more fully than other accounts. I thus introduce by example the contributions the genre concept made to the reorganization of the literary field over the course of the eigh-teenth century. As novels and plays, first treated more often with regard to their similarities, came to be treated more often with regard to their differences, the older Poetry was displaced by the more modern Literature. Genre, deployed along the axis of ancient/modern, had reigned supreme in Poetry; the suprageneric Litera-ture, by contrast, was structured by two new oppositions: serious/popular and print/performance. My discussion here is focused around melodrama, through which relations between the novel and the stage crystallized at the end of the period. Although stage melodrama had been informed in crucial ways by the Gothic novel, its status as multimedia spectacle, perhaps paradoxically, elicited attention to the medium-specific properties of performance as well as print. Stage directions in printed melodramas bring out the absence in reading that the plays supplied in performance: spectacular scenic effects and the almost perpetual simul-taneous musical accompaniment to speech. Both melodrama and the Gothic novel, moreover, were excluded from the domain of "serious" literature on the basis of their popularity.

Turning from genre to media, I provide an account of the relationship between print and performance as it emerged as a media opposition, which intro-duces a more general discussion of the place the media concept could occupy in literary studies if it included the medium of performance and was collated with the category of genre. This chapter thus provides the theoretical basis for the rest of the book, which pursues an integrated analysis of novels at the intersection of genre and media.

Chapter 2, "The Reform of the Rake from Rochester to Inchbald," finds in debates over the story of the rake's reform in print and performance a key prob-lematic that challenges the canonical accounts of novelistic realism and pursues at the same time the story of the migration of the comedy of manners from the stage to the novel. The reception of Gilbert Burnet's 1680 pamphlet reporting Rochester's deathbed conversion, the competing and complementary plays *Love's Last Shift* (1696) and *The Careless Husband* (1704) by Colley Cibber and *The Relapse* (1696) by Sir John Vanbrugh, and the 1740 *Pamela* controversy each debated the authenticity of the rake's conversion to virtue but put as much emphasis on its exemplarity as its credibility. The chapter concludes with a discussion of Elizabeth Inchbald's treatments of the rake's reform in her last original play, *Wives as They Were, Maids as They Are* (1797), and her first novel, *A Simple Story* (1791). Her hybrid writing at the end of the century displays the long-standing relationship between the novel and the drama on the cusp of their rearticulation.

The contributions of the *Pamela* controversy to the history of the novel are well known, but its recapitulation of the earlier debates clarifies the persistence of the moral imperative of aesthetic representation. The shared investment across drama and the novel in the impact or force of aesthetic form makes it impossible to assign the aesthetics of realism to the history of the novel alone. I do not here mean that realism should be applied to the stage but seek rather to identify some of its sources in drama. The theoretical and technical preoccupations with the representation of convincing reform shared across the theater and the novel, and debates about these matters within and across both, made it possible to separate questions of morality and poetic justice from questions of aesthetic presentation, including matters of credibility and verisimilitude, though these debates also clarify that this separation could not be permanently achieved. The perennial capacity of morality and aesthetics to collapse back into each other has not been explained in canonical accounts of the novel that presume the permanence of the distinction.

In Richardson, letters sometimes have the transformative effects on readers that they have on *Pamela*'s Mr. B. Some critics consider him to be a highly dramatic writer; for others, however, he is antitheatrical.[24] Neither characterization tells us much about the significance of the theater to the history of the novel unless their opposition is presumed. Although virtually every reader of Richardson has discussed the status of letters in his novels, no one has yet remarked on the role they play in Fielding, in both his plays and his novels. Fielding's treatment of letters reveals the reciprocal relations between the theater and the novel at the heart of the novel's history. Chapter 3, "Performing Reading in Richardson and Fielding," extends chapter 2's treatment of *Pamela*, *Shamela*, and *Joseph Andrews* (1742) by examining letters in dramatic adaptations of *Pamela* and *Clarissa* and scenes of performed reading in Fielding's play *The Letter Writers* (1731), as well as in *Joseph Andrews*, *Tom Jones* (1749), and *Amelia* (1751). Both authors' contributions to the history of the novel look different in this theatrical history of the novel: performed letters effectively expose the ways Richardson and Fielding each positioned readers differently and thus sharply contrast the immersive and interruptive styles of reading they each elicited.

Colley Cibber's appearances in this book are not confined to chapter 2's discussion of his dramatizations of the reform of the rake. He is also centrally important in chapter 4, "The Promise of Embarrassment: Frances Burney's Theater of Shame," which analyzes the novelistic incorporations of his play *The Provok'd Husband* (1728), one of the most popular plays of the eighteenth century, into a puppet show in Fielding's *Tom Jones* and the amateur theatricals in Burney's *The Wanderer* (1814). Indeed, provocation handily sums up Cibber's status in the period, for it captures his force as an entertainer and his effects on others. The combination of Cibber's shameless embrace of theatrical entertainments and an unselfconscious morality was what Alexander Pope came to excoriate in *The Dunciad* (1743): in portraying Cibber asleep in the Goddess Dulness's lap, Pope reversed the emblem of reform that Cibber had produced in the *Careless Husband*, at the climax of which the sleeping husband literally awakens to virtue. Fielding's treatment of Cibber in *The Author's Farce* (1730) had helped to inspire Pope's satire of Cibber, and Fielding extended the critique in *Tom Jones*. Pope's and Fielding's rejection of Cibber's shamelessness resonated with Burney; but their masculinist classicism was inaccessible to her, and she was more sympathetic to Cibber's bourgeois feminism.[25] A potent combination of shame and theatricality alternately inspired and provoked by Cibber sparks the heroine's development in each of Burney's four novels and structures readers' engagement with them.

Legible not only in *The Wanderer*, Cibber is present across Burney's oeuvre. His signature term, "provoke," and its variants appear forty times in *Evelina* (1778), which amounts to once in about every nineteen pages, and it occurs twenty to thirty times more frequently than in any other novel published that same year. The dynamics of Cibberian provocation drove Burney to abandon epistolary form after *Evelina* and to develop a number of innovative narrative techniques, including a use of free indirect discourse best understood in relation to theatrical asides and a 180-degree reversal of perspective that pivots on a proscenium, both of which crop up at moments of heightened embarrassment in *Cecilia* (1783), *Camilla* (1796), and *The Wanderer*. Distilled in narrative form, the connections that Burney expressed between shame and theatricality, however, are not merely biographical; instead they make a significant contribution to the history of the novel. Though standard histories of the novel often limit her importance to her influence on Austen, in *The Novel Stage*, Burney plays a central role. Her synthesis of Richardson and Fielding for the novel of female development, mediated through the theatrically inspired narrative innovations I examine in chapter 4, reached writers from across the political spectrum, including Elizabeth Inchbald, William Godwin, and Jane Austen. Chapter 5, "Melodrama in Inchbald and Austen," looks at the ways Inchbald and Austen (and to a lesser extent Godwin) used melodrama, as Burney did, to modify the comedy of manners in narrative.

An acute reader of Burney who reread *Cecilia* (1782) when he came to compose *Caleb Williams* (1794), Godwin had already published anonymously a faithful parody of a Burney novel in *The Herald of Literature* (1783–1784).[26] Burney's scenes of excruciating female confrontation influenced Godwin, though in *Caleb Williams*, he transposed them to men; *The Wanderer* was influenced in turn by his parodic depiction of a hostage-taking inspired by love. Like Burney's novels, Godwin's feature a remarkable amount of repetition. This way to register the pressures of social determination has frequently been associated with the Jacobin doctrine of necessity, for it expresses the subordination of characters to circumstances and signals that sequence is not always developmental but sometimes discrete, though not for that reason any less causal. Martin Meisel called this mode "serial discontinuity" and claimed it as a hallmark of melodrama.[27]

Linked to the stage in different ways than Burney's, Inchbald's *A Simple Story* also had a significant influence on *Caleb Williams*, even though Godwin's adaptation to the first-person perspective of the ways Inchbald subordinated characters to circumstance has functioned to obscure the nature of its debts to her and to the theater.[28] Austen, meanwhile, has often been characterized as antagonistic to the theater, even though she not only exploited the amateur theatricals in *Mansfield Park* to great effect but also depended on theatrical mise-en-scènes in *Sense and Sensibility* and *Persuasion*, through which her complex attitudes toward marriage were conveyed. As novels and plays came increasingly to be described with regard to their differences rather than their similarities, Inchbald and Austen took the novel of female development they inherited from Burney in different directions: the Jacobin novel of social determinism and the Austenian comedy of manners. Though they are rarely discussed together, chapter 5 explores the significance of the theater to both and recovers the set of narrative possibilities they shared notwithstanding their political differences.

A short coda, "The Melodramatic Address," tracks a technique that Inchbald adapted for the novel from melodrama to signal the pathos of ordinary characters subordinated to their circumstances, the narrator's direct address to a character who cannot hear, as it is taken up by Dickens, Trollope, and Hardy. The melodramatic address is used to open a view of an alternative future that remains unwritten but marks the boundaries of the particular fictional world in which it appears. Though necessarily incomplete, my sketch of the counterfictional mode produced by the melodramatic address indicates in one instance the persistent influence of the theater on the novel at the level of narrative form and identifies the pressures it exerts on contemporary accounts of the novel.

Walter Benjamin used both media and genre in a fashion that is most congenial to the basic argument of this book, that the narrative form of the novel was mediated by the theater in the eighteenth century, with significant implications for the modern organization of literature. In his great essay "The Storyteller," the novel could become the "earliest symptom of a process whose end is the decline of storytelling" because of its "essential dependence on the book," that is, print.[29] In "By the Fireside," an earlier essay only recently translated into English that took the opportunity of a review of a German translation of Arnold Bennett's *The Old Wives' Tale* (1908) to rehearse some of the later essay's most important claims, attention to media is more attenuated. Nevertheless, it yields a set of distinctions that are absent from the later essay for the experience of the genres: the reader of novels sits alone by the fire; the member of the audience at a play "subside[s] into the crowd and shares its response"; and the reader of poetry "is willing to turn into a partner and lend his voice to the poem."[30] Benjamin insisted on the mediation of generic differences, but he also recognized that the process of generic disambiguation was shaped by generic collaboration and interpenetration across media, and depended on the persistence of story.

The example of Benjamin attests to the fact that literary history need not be opposed to formalist analysis, as this book demonstrates with its investigation of a long arc of cross-genre and cross-media relations between the novel and the stage from 1680 to 1820. But with its focus on the narrative techniques that these intersections disclose, *The Novel Stage* presents just the tip of the iceberg of the complex relationship between the novel and the theater in the eighteenth century. Many other authors, including Delarivier Manley, Eliza Haywood, Tobias Smollett, Charlotte Lennox, and Maria Edgeworth, could have been included in my analysis, but a complete catalogue was not my goal, as it would have driven my argument in different directions. The full extent of the novel's influence on stage, moreover, is a matter that will best be determined by theater scholars. Other combinations of genre and media are possible in the multimedia literary history of the eighteenth century to which *The Novel Stage* belongs. In developing a rationale for working at the intersections of genre and media, however, *The Novel Stage* provides some terms necessary for such a literary history and illustrates a way to use them.

GENRE, MEDIA, AND THE THEORY OF THE NOVEL

QUINTESSENTIALLY MODERN, the novel was the first print-born genre of literature; epic, drama, and lyric were originally oral forms. Famously new, or "novel," it arrived late to the literary field that was identified throughout the Renaissance and eighteenth century as "Poetry." Its appearance began to destabilize an organization that relied on the neoclassical classifications of genre along the axis of ancient/modern.[1] By the beginning of the nineteenth century, the field of literary production became recognizable as the suprageneric "Literature," now dominated by other distinctions, including serious/popular and print/performance. In classic accounts of the novel, this backdrop motivates its identification with modernity itself, but because they blur its generic specificity by treating it as sui generis, or as incorporating or subsuming other genres, such accounts cannot understand its contributions to either the changing function of the category of genre or the axes along which literature was reorganized.[2] In these operations, the novel did not work alone; nor were its accomplishments due solely to print.

Theater, the default aesthetic experience of the long eighteenth century, brought genres including tragicomedy, the comedy of manners, and melodrama to life. Each of these genres helped to shape the novel; each was also reshaped not only as but also by prose narrative. Together, not only did the representational possibilities of the novel and the theater refine these genres; but, as they did so, they also realigned the genre system by helping to produce the two oppositions, serious/popular and print/performance, that granted media an emphasis retained to this day, even if the term "media" was not then in use. The historical relations of the novel to the theater loosen the novel's overly narrow identification with realism, making it possible to reframe its status as one genre among others, with consequences for the history of its emergence and our account of its formal characteristics. The relations between the categories of genre and media across the media of print and performance also help to determine the applicability of the media concept in literary analysis more generally.

The experience of theater included the reading, writing, and/or reading aloud of drama, and the attendance of (and/or participation in professional or amateur) performance; theater thereby offered a range of intermediations of engagement, both individual and collective, private and public, with literature. Going back to antiquity, meanwhile, drama had supplied the key terms—comedy and tragedy— for organizing the literary genres in Poetry, including those that were not performed. Though immersed in the earlier system, these terms were carried over and applied regularly to the novel; drama thus enables a reconsideration of the genre concept in the history of the novel. With theater's existence across the media of performance and print, and as a significant influence on the development of the novel, theater refines applications of the media concept to it. In fact, the novel's relation to the theater, including drama, requires a theorization of the intersections of genre and media.

The novel's great success has been crucial to its status as a supergenre, a status that has discouraged cross-genre and cross-media comparison. Its aesthetic value, moreover, has been located in its representational achievements in realism; being identified with realism has served further to obscure its status as one of many genres in the modern literary system. Recognizing, in order to suspend, the powerful association of the novel with modernization and observing that genre studies "has embraced the assumption that all genres are already mixed," Wolfram Schmidgen has called for "a fully historicized and theorized understanding of how mixture works" in the history of the novel.[3] By tethering the category of genre more firmly to that of media, the history of the novel's relation to the theater answers this call by prohibiting the media blindness, or exclusive orientation to print, that has dominated other accounts. Yet neither media-oriented work in scholarship in the history of the book nor new media theory has had much to do with genre, the former because its interests in print go beyond the bounds of literature, a category about which it also has had surprisingly little to say, and the latter because generic mediation has come to be subsumed under the category of media. Indeed, genre seems also to have been relegated to the back seat in a new formalism that privileges the single rubric of "form."[4] Histories of the novel, histories of the theater, and studies of their intersections, furthermore, have assumed an opposition of print to performance in which we see one of the ways genre's subsumption into media has been naturalized. In the intersection of genre and media, however, the history of the novel's relation to the theater discloses a crucial matrix in the modern organization of literature for which a literary history then becomes possible.

This chapter explores the concepts of genre and media by examining the problems their relationship can resolve as a way to introduce the more specific genre- and author-oriented chapters that follow. I begin with their specific convergence in Aphra Behn's use of tragicomedy in two pieces of her short prose fiction, a conjunction that lays bare the main reason the history of the novel has not properly incorporated her contributions: realism is not her aesthetic goal. Behn also introduces the key place occupied by women writers in the rest of this book. Tuning into the differences gender makes, especially to representations of marriage as a telos in female development in both novels and plays, I pay attention to, but do not segregate, a female and feminist literary tradition. Instead, Behn's channeling of tragicomedy for prose fiction introduces a more free-ranging discussion of the place of genre in the organization of literature as it changed over the course of the long eighteenth century. This place is best described when the default assumption that the novel was opposed to the theater is called into question; its consequences for writers across the board militate against the collation of genre with gender.

The more specific and more general discussions of genre in the first and second sections are followed in the third and fourth sections by a more specific and a more general discussion of media. The first explores the history of the relations between print and performance as it can be tracked through a brief reception of Shakespeare that exposes how they came to be understood as opposing terms. The second looks at what thinking the categories of genre and media together means for the literary history of the novel.

GENRE 1: BEHN AND TRAGICOMEDY

What will it take to consolidate Aphra Behn's place in literary history as the first novelist in English? Answering this question involves probing the intersections among the categories of genre, gender, media, and the history of the novel; it thus has heuristic value even if "firstness," tied too closely to the heroism of the individual literary career, ultimately cannot be a productive term in a literary history interested in the organization of literature as a system. In 1989, the feminist scholar Judith Kegan Gardiner advocated for granting the position of the first English novel to *Love-Letters between a Nobleman and His Sister* (1684), Behn's three-volume experiment with rendering a scandalous roman à clef in the epistolary style.[5] Sadly, however, it remains out of print. Canonical status was granted instead to the significantly shorter *Oroonoko* (1688).

Yet for all the attention *Oroonoko* has received, its narrative form has yet to be elucidated. Critics have persuasively analyzed Behn's use of the trope of "true history," her experimentation with the "as told to" features of prose romance and its function as political allegory, but it has not yet been recognized that in *Oroonoko*, as in some of her other short prose fiction, Behn channeled tragicomedy.[6] Behn had turned to prose fiction out of financial need in the 1680s when the collapse of theatrical competition led to a decline in new productions, but the importance of tragicomedy can be seen across her career. Her three earliest plays, *The Young King* (probably first performed in 1679), *The Forc'd Marriage* (1670), and *The Amorous Prince* (1671), were tragicomedies, as was her last play, *The Widdow Ranter* (1687 or 1688).[7] Both *Oroonoko* and *The Fair Jilt* (1688) are tragicomedies in the sense that they each contain two narrative lines that are harmonized differently, even if incompletely so, by being presented sequentially.

Whereas tragicomedy will not explain those features of Behn's prose that derive from romance, scandal chronicle, and journalistic political writing, on the basis of which other critics have situated her within the history of the novel, it proves to be the missing link that explains the level of coherence that these narratives do (or do not) obtain. Behn's contribution to the history of the novel is more readily comprehended in terms of intermediality than has been recognized in those histories of the genre that oppose the novel to the stage by default. For that reason, she demands a specific kind of literary history, one located at the intersection of genre and media that invites us, furthermore, to re-evaluate these categories as they have (or have not) been applied to the novel itself.[8]

In 1995, Catherine Gallagher made an important case for the signal contributions of women writers to the establishment of the literary marketplace. Women writers, she argued in *Nobody's Story*, were ideally positioned to represent virtual embodiment in fungible ways because as women, they had to negotiate the marriage market controlled by men.[9] Their bodies served as objects of exchange, which equipped them more readily to understand and innovate the textualization of embodiment on which the novel relies. Behn, who fashioned herself, or actually was, a widow, controlled the disposal of her own body, and her body of work, by the adoption of two authorial personae, the "newfangled whore" and the "author-monarch." As Gallagher's inaugural example, Behn was accorded two chapters, one for her plays and one for her prose fiction, with the latter focusing on *Oroonoko*.

Gallagher initially paid scrupulous attention to the different contributions the theater and the novel made to the literary marketplace. She applied the possibilities for actual embodied performance onstage to the virtual embodiment offered by print on the basis of Behn's sustained exploration of the conditions of female embodiment across her writing. Virtuality was critical to the novel's capacity to abstract from the referential real as it became "nobody's story." But as the novel developed into an increasingly sophisticated delivery system for realism, Gallagher moved the medium of performance into the metaphorical register despite its having been empowered at first by the literary relations between actual and virtual embodiment. After Behn, the significance, and signifying potential, of drama disappeared from her account even though the rest of her authors—Delarivier Manley, Frances Burney, Charlotte Lennox, and Maria Edgeworth—all wrote plays. The distinctive contributions that drama, read, written, or performed, made to the novel were thereby effaced, subsumed into a fictionality that was to be identified with the novel itself.[10]

With fictionality, Gallagher moved away from prose fiction or the novel as a genre, seeing it instead as a force field that registered the workings of capitalism in the joint registers of economic speculation and fictional representation, yet this move is costly to literary history.[11] It occludes the fictional status of literature in the other genres, including drama; perhaps more problematically, as an expansion of the novel, Gallagher's fictionality smuggles in realism, making it more central to literary analysis than it needs to be and at the expense of other representational or aesthetic goals—even those of some novels. Behn's aesthetic goal, however, was not realism. Critics struggle to account for the many improbable episodes in her fiction, including Isabella's murder of her two husbands in *History of the Nun*, Oroonoko's adventures hunting the tiger, the story that brings Prince Henrick to the monastery in *The Fair Jilt*, none of which can be reconciled with or assimilated to the novel form as it has been understood. Their place and function, however, are accommodated by tragicomedy. Recognizing in Behn's work the contributions of tragicomedy to narrative form thus launches a history of the novel whose generic development can be understood otherwise.

Michael McKeon's more recent treatment of Behn illustrates a different problem with the intersection of the novel and the categories of genre and media. He granted Behn's *Love Letters* a central place in *The Secret History of Domesticity* for two reasons: it offered a microcosm of his larger argument, that the separation of private matters from public ones is crucial to the creation of the category of modern knowledge; and it illustrated the transformation of the secret history into the domestic novel as the key epistemic and aesthetic achievement of the early modern period.[12] Though McKeon here made a sophisticated case for the significance of Behn to the history of the novel, his uptake of the secret history is not shared by other literary scholars who grant it a generic history of its own, one that overlaps, but is not perfectly congruent, with that of the novel.[13] This lack of agreement over the generic status of the secret history points to a deeper problem with

McKeon's application of the genre concept: his portrait of the secret history as handmaiden to the construction of the category of modern knowledge widened the scope of the argument he had made for the novel's generic subsumption of romance in *Origins of the English Novel*, by means of which it consolidated the aesthetics of realism. This widening exacerbated the loss of capacity to register the ongoing significance of generic distinction already present in his earlier history of the novel.[14]

Acutely attentive to the dynamics of subsumption, McKeon discussed tragicomedy in *The Secret History*, locating it among other mixed modes as a conflation of its elements, tragedy and comedy, that had been defined in opposition to each other. He portrayed it as a dialectical recapitulation that contributed to making private domestic matters into matters of public national significance but fell short of fully realizing the formal domestication delivered by the secret history.[15] This account of the features of tragicomedy independent of its orientation toward performance granted it a minor role in the media-blind forward march of the genres but suggested that the theater got left behind by history. Whereas in *The Secret History*, McKeon was interested in art in other media, notably painting and architecture, in his account of literature, there is only one genre, the (domestic) novel, and only one medium, print. McKeon thus obscured just how central tragicomedy's reconfiguration of the relations between comedy and tragedy was to the prose forms of the period. When the specific features of drama, either as a performance medium or as a genre, disappear, it can be readily assimilated to the novel (even if, often enough, it then gets construed as the novel's opposite). In neither formulation are its contributions fully accounted for, to the detriment of the history of the novel.

What was tragicomedy? Its popularity peaked and waned over the course of the seventeenth century. Even before its efflorescence, Sir Philip Sidney had called the hybrid form "mongrel" in his *Defence of Poetry*, where he decried the combination of kings and clowns on the Elizabethan stage, which perennially had failed to obey Aristotelian drama theory.[16] Tragicomedy came to be more strictly codified as the bringing together of plots as well as persons, as John Fletcher made clear in the note "To the Reader" appended to *The Faithful Shepherdess* (1609): "A tragi-comedy is not so called in respect of mirth and killing, but in respect it wants deaths, which is enough to make it no tragedy, yet brings some near it, which is enough to make it no comedy, which must be a representation of familiar people, with such kind of trouble as no life be questioned; so that a god is as lawful in this as in a tragedy, and mean people as in a comedy." Fletcher's social mingling included not just common people and kings but also gods, and his plot combinations fused pastoral elements with spectacular dei ex machina.

Tragicomedy, however, did not outlast the reign of the Stuarts: no new tragicomedies were written after 1700, and over the course of first half of the eighteenth century, they stopped being produced in their original forms. Thomas Southerne's 1696 adaptation of Behn's *Oroonoko* for the stage, a tragicomedy with a tragic ending, retained the second part of her narrative, though he made Imoinda white and replaced the romance of the first part with a comic plot of his own invention featuring the Welldon sisters' search for husbands in the colonies, which thereby respected the unity of place. His comic plot was eliminated in 1759, its vulgarity having been found to be incompatible with the tragedy. Yet, while tragicomedy flourished, it provided a dynamic template for new generic combinations, with significant implications for the eighteenth-century novel. If there is a sense in which tragicomedy died and was reborn in the novel, this generation involved the transmission not only of the generic elements, comedy and tragedy, that it reconfigured but also of traces of its performance DNA; both were transmuted into narrative form in Behn.

After the Restoration, neoclassical drama theory imported from France assumed even greater importance than it had for Sidney, though it did not interfere with the popularity of tragicomedy. "Improved" Shakespeare, for example, featured the elaboration of existing female roles and the creation of new ones in response to the new law requiring female roles to be played by actresses, as well as the incorporation of more music, dance, and spectacle. When Cordelia was preserved from death so that she could marry Edgar in Nahum Tate's *King Lear* (1681), and in the operatic *Macbeth* (1663) and *The Tempest* (1674), the tragicomic elements of Shakespeare were made explicit and enhanced, even though, at the same time, the attempt was being made, in Dryden's *All for Love* (1677) and *Troilus and Cressida* (1679), to bring his plays into greater conformity with the neoclassical rules. Shakespeare's Polonius had captured the generativity of generic combination in his famous catalogue: "tragedy, comedy, history, pastoral, pastoral-comical, historical-pastoral, tragical-historical, tragical-comical-historical-pastoral."[17] This depiction of classification failing to keep pace with proliferation is a joke at Polonius's expense, but tragicomedy produced not only monstrosities. Tragicomedy treated comedy and tragedy as modular components available to be energetically disassembled and recombined, as can best be appreciated in its strict split-plot form.

In Dryden's *Marriage a la Mode* (1671), one of the purest examples of the genre, the high plot, which deals with usurpation and the restoration of legitimate succession, turns on the fate of pastoralized royal lovers who speak in rhymed heroic verse, whereas the lower plot addresses the problem of sustaining sexual desire in marriage in prose. Clear generic markers map perfectly onto the social geography of the court and the town, which are thereby united into a harmonious whole, but this balance proved unstable and vulnerable almost instantaneously to disintegration. Dryden's quasi-tragic plot was tipped over into the ludicrous in Buckingham's satire *The Rehearsal* (staged 1671, published 1672), which took aim both at Almanzor, the outsized hero of Dryden's two-part heroic play *The Conquest of Granada* (1670–1671, published 1672) and at Leonidas, the heir to the throne in *Marriage a la Mode*.[18] Performed regularly for the rest of the century, both *Marriage a la Mode* and *The Rehearsal* were successful, but the last performance of the former in its entirety was given in 1700, the year of Dryden's death. In 1707, Colley Cibber dropped the high plot and combined the lower plot with the comic elements of another of Dryden's tragicomedies, *Secret Love* (1667), under the title *The Comic Lovers; or, Marriage a la Mode*. Tragicomedy incubated other performance forms as well, including rhymed heroic drama, court masque, and possibly also, given its spectacular and musical orientations, pantomime and ballet, but the contributions it made to prose fiction on the basis of the breakup of its constituent parts are most evident in Behn.[19]

The first parts of *Oroonoko* and *The Fair Jilt* are divergent enough from their second parts to prevent them from functioning simply as vehicles for the main characters' backstory. Though chronological and sequential, the first parts' stories of the main characters' pasts are incompletely explanatory; they function neither allegorically nor by means of a clear subordination of subplot to a main plot. Instead they are related in a more freestanding way, for which tragicomedy makes it possible to account.

The two narratives of *Oroonoko* are distinct generically: the first part consists of the romance of the titular Prince Oroonoko and his beloved Imoinda in Coramantien; the second part, of the tragedy of their reunion as slaves in Surinam. Rachel Carnell has suggested that Behn, who wrote only one tragic play in her dramatic career, channeled her interests in tragedy into narrative form in *Oroonoko*.[20] Though the second part is indeed tragic, Carnell, like many of the novel's other commentators, does not pay much attention the first part. The less familiar *The Fair Jilt* tells the story of Miranda, the female fop in fashion whose "love of quality" drives her beyond the bounds of morality. In the first part, she attempts to seduce Prince Henrick / Friar Francisco in the monastery and, when that fails, falsely accuses him of rape; in the second, having married Prince Tarquin, the imposter "last prince of Rome," she talks him into trying to kill her sister to procure her fortune. The couple is permitted to live happily ever after in his native Holland, a reward for her having given up her foppishness and succumbed to the transformative powers of love. Yet the sheer narrative weight given to Miranda's bad behavior and the cursoriness with which this ending is produced make her development difficult to perceive.

The romance part of *Oroonoko* diverges from the tragic part in tone and tex-
ture as well as geography. The narrative offers concrete details only about Surinam; Coramantien remains a generic exotic location drawn from romance or
heroic drama, where the lovers, before they are separated, sigh a thousand sighs
and pledge their vows with a thousand assurances. Though the entire narrative is
framed by Behn's first-person speaker, she recedes from view after introducing the
history of the royal slave with descriptions of the natural beauties of Surinam and
the commercial transactions of the slave trade. She resurfaces occasionally in the
first part to remind readers of the oral nature of the story, before becoming a fuller
participant in the story's second part.[21] That the first part comes from Oroonoko's own mouth emerges casually. As Behn's narrator remarks in the first few paragraphs of the story: "What I could not be witness of, I received out of the mouth
of the chief actor in this history, the hero himself." Oral transmission bolsters the
text's status as a "true history," as it is subtitled, rather than as "the adventures of
a feigned hero," but this aspect, critical to the novelistic elements of *Oroonoko*, cannot smooth over the disjunctions of the two narrative lines.[22] The Coramantien
narrative is only capable of being integrated retrospectively, and it cannot be integrated completely through the experience of the "I" speaker because she is not the
main character of either part. If Behn here can be understood to contribute to the
evolution of narrative techniques for delivering backstory, her innovations flow
from the modularity of the narrative parts provided by tragicomedy. Tragicomedy offered a structural compromise formation through which romance narration
could become novelistic independent of probability.

The loose architecture of relations between the parts of tragicomedy accommodated the romance and tragic parts of *Oroonoko*, permitting Behn to experiment with the specific capacities of prose fiction to represent exotic settings and
generate the brutality of tragic immediacy not possible on the stage. Though Southerne's play remained popular onstage, at its tragic climax, Oroonoko kills first
Imoinda and then himself with a sword; at the end of Behn's narrative, not only
has Oroonoko been whipped and hot pepper applied to his wounds, but he has
cut off some of his own features in emulation of the stoic heroism of the Indian
captains before being disemboweled, then sewn back together, and finally drawn
and quartered by the British colonizers. The hyperviolence of this treatment has
elicited allegorical interpretation from critics starting with Laura Brown, suggesting another aspect of Behn's lack of interest in realism.[23]

In *The Fair Jilt*, Miranda acquires a susceptibility to the transformative powers of love on the basis of two experiences that barely intersect: the two men she
has manipulated, Friar Francisco and Prince Tarquin, end up in the same prison,
which links them in a scenic fashion. Though Miranda's retraction of her false

accusation leads to Francisco's release, it does not prevent Tarquin from being sentenced to death. Her penitential gesture may clear the way for the married couple's reward—she is described as "the now-repenting beauty"[24]—but they are only permitted to enjoy their "happily ever after" because of a spectacular failure that matches the failed seduction of the priest: Tarquin's botched execution.

Not only are the two episodes linked scenically, but they also echo each other rhythmically with each one culminating in a spectacular scene whose dramatic trajectory is abruptly redirected. Miranda is first inflamed by sexual desire and then infuriated by her failure in the confessional, and her seduction attempt parodies the bedroom scenes for which Behn was famous. Tarquin bravely faces the executioner, but when the headsman fails to do his office properly, Tarquin sustains only a minor injury in his shoulder. Just as the erotic scene turns into one of revenge, the somber scene turns into one of celebration. To everyone's amazement, the crowd carries Tarquin's live body to safety. The botched execution parodies tragedy and also averts it. The self-parody of the first theatrical scene combines with the parody of the second one to produce a prose tragicomedy whose commitment to realistic representation is difficult to ascertain and perhaps beside the point.

In both the comic exaggeration of the seduction and the journalistic rendition of the averted tragedy, Behn pays scrupulous attention to body placement, gesture, and lines of visibility. In a study of the ways things enter eighteenth-century prose, including the novel, Cynthia Wall points out that Behn's descriptive style (like Eliza Haywood's) relied on stage directions, but this underestimates the significance of the stage.[25] As Wall's own example of Tarquin's failed assassination of Miranda's sister Alcidiana outside the playhouse suggests, the theater served as a location; it also provided a frame of reference for Behn's fiction in other ways as well. Anne Widemayer has helpfully disclosed in the spatial configuration of key scenes in *Oroonoko* Behn's use of stage space when characters hidden on the scenic stage observe the action on the forestage.[26] Our understanding of the early novel's debts to and divergences from staged performance, however, also require the terms of drama's genres to capture the social consequences.

According to Carnell, Behn applied the categories of tragedy to female experience in *The Fair Jilt* and other prose narratives because the stage was inhospitable to tragic heroines, but here she overlooks the advent of she-tragedy. In portraying Behn's turn to prose as a refutation of the stage, Carnell both underestimates its impact and brushes aside its traces. She argues that Behn presented "not quite virtuous" protagonists like Miranda for political purposes: to replace the conventions of Tory Restoration drama with a Tory novelistic realism that validated domestic experience.[27] But the precedent for the attenuation of tragic outcome, even when deserved, existed in tragicomedy that ended happily. In bringing together tragic or near-tragic representations of royalty or aristocrats with stories of more ordinary people, moreover, tragicomedy forged a compromise ripe for exploration in narrative, though Behn's featured well-born heroines.

Tragicomedy had a significant influence on the structure of Behn's short narratives. The hybrid genre functioned more generally as a vehicle for transmitting the valences of tragedy and comedy to the eighteenth century with different, though related, consequences for drama and prose fiction, suggesting that tragicomedy opened the door through which the novel entered the literary arena. The consequences of its influence will best be captured when the novel is considered in terms of its relation to the genres of drama and the medium of performance; these will remain invisible when the novel is either segregated from or opposed to the stage.

GENRE 2: THE GENRE SYSTEM

Renaissance literary theory had granted to writers of "new comedy," Menander and Terence, the right to set fictional stories about private people in the contemporary scene on precisely the ground that such stories could not be proved false. Though William Nelson observed that the privilege did not extend to genres other than comedy, the flourishing of tragicomedy in the seventeenth century expanded comedy's range, making it relevant to understanding some of the developments in prose fiction that could grant even ordinary characters tragic stories.[28] For Joseph Addison, who in *Cato* (1713) had produced one of the most regular neoclassical tragedies in English, tragedy raised questions about the moral exemplarity of heroic behavior shown onstage and about poetic justice, whose mechanical applicability he deplored as producing excessively predictable results. Although he described tragicomedy as monstrous in *Spectator* 40 (16 April 1711), the tragedies he singled out in contrast paradoxically illustrated the hold it continued to exert: his list of tragedies to be admired included Southerne's *Oroonoko* and Tate's tragicomic *King Lear*.[29] Comedy, meanwhile, raised concerns about the decorum of laughter, which Addison associated with ordinary terrestrial rather than celestial life. The same objects that cause "mirth" in mankind may "cause Pity or Displeasure in higher Natures": for Addison, laughter was not possible before the Fall of Man.[30] Comedy's beneficial affects, its capacity to unbend the mind and protect against the Spleen, needed to be weighed against its socially leveling capacities.

This concern can also be found in the 1734 *Vade Mecum*, which Samuel Richardson published as a guide to apprentices. There comic theater posed a double threat: no longer tethered to morality, its mimetic capacity to influence viewers by example could move dangerously across social lines. When modern plays dramatized "Persons in upper Life," they appealed to the experience of high life, whereas the men of business often portrayed in them would appear not as models but as dupes or fools; when comedies and tragedies took the lower and middling classes as their subject, they tended to disregard "Poetical Justice," celebrating instead "odious and detestable Characters while punishing honest ones."[31] Richardson warned young apprentices that comedy would supply a lesson only in crime. These anxieties about the immorality of the stage have led some critics to treat Richardson as antitheatrical, but what emerges with greater force is his observation of the absence of moral diversions aimed at lower and middling audiences.[32] Richardson spotted a gap in the market: the failures of comedy in particular here clear the ground for *Pamela* (1740) insofar as it both represented the moral behavior of a lowly servant girl and aimed to use reading her words to inspire morality in lower and middling readers.

Tragicomedy's mediation of the social valences of comedy and tragedy was one of the factors in the use of either in the legitimation of prose fiction up through the middle of the eighteenth century. Both William Congreve and Henry Fielding used drama theory in the prefaces to *Incognita* (1692) and *Joseph Andrews* (1742), respectively, and Richardson described *Clarissa* (1748) as a modern tragedy.[33] The persistent application of dramatic terms in discussions of the novel demonstrates the effort to assimilate it into the old canon of Poetry. Samuel Johnson did not include novelists in *Lives of the Poets* (1779–1781), though he did include playwrights; novelists only got their own collective biographical treatment in Sir Walter Scott's *The Lives of the Novelists* (1821–1824). The narrative of the novel's rise that dates its crystallization to circa 1740 can obscure just how long it took for it to be accommodated in the domain of literature: the term "novel" was only regularized once Poetry came to be displaced in the early years of the nineteenth century.[34]

As the Russian Formalists understood, there is no more significant symptom of literary historical change than changes in the genre system, which they described as semiautonomous and evolving: semiautonomous because any genre is defined in relation both to other genres and to previous manifestations; and evolving because belonging to a genre involves both adoption of and resistance to conventions.[35] Yury Tynyanov observed that "in the theory of literature, definitions are not the foundation but merely the after-effect which is, moreover, constantly being altered by the literary fact."[36] The failure to define in advance the characteristics of any genre will not impede the tracking of systemic generic change, in which imitation and succession can also function as displacement. Parody, moreover, occupies a special place as both symptom and engine of such change. If Behn's displacement of tragicomedy from drama to novel helped to initiate the evolution of the genre system from Poetry to Literature, Wordsworth's registration of the joint contributions of the upstart genres, the novel and melodrama, in the preface to *Lyrical Ballads* can signal its completion, even if he yoked together "frantic novels" and "stupid and sickly German tragedies" only to exclude them.[37]

Wordsworth helped to render obsolete the one-to-one collation of rhetorical, social, and literary spheres that had been imagined by Thomas Hobbes more than a century before. Although, like Hobbes in the "Answer to Davenant," Wordsworth refused to confine poetry to verse, he rejected the earlier notion of genre that had informed Hobbes's map of poetry's "regions": denizens of court, city, or country could be distinguished by different rhetorical—and therefore generic—registers.[38] As Wordsworth's interest in the language of ordinary men suggests, social status retained significance, but its role in the valuation of poetry changed as generic distinctions came to rest on the uses to which the genres were put, now more fully distinguished from the places with which they were associated. Condemning sensationalism both onstage and in novels, Wordsworth foregrounded the different capacities of poems, plays, and novels to induce reflection and elevated a suprageneric category of serious Literature, confusingly called "poetry," on the basis of its autonomy from popular taste. The distinction between serious and popular was critical to the social valences of Literature, as John Guillory has argued in *Cultural Capital*, but that distinction assumed its function as the genres came to be understood as inflected by media, a process that got worked out, at least in part, through the relations between drama and the novel.[39]

Whereas Wordsworth lumped together melodrama and the Gothic novel in order to dismiss them both because of their popularity, others writing in the increasingly international ambit of Gothic, Sturm und Drang, and melodrama, opposed drama and the novel to each other. In Johann Wolfgang von Goethe's *Wilhelm Meister* (1795–1796), for example, Wilhelm debates with Serlo and the rest of his troupe the relative merits of drama and the novel to determine which is superior.[40] In "To the Artist" (1807), Elizabeth Inchbald contrasted the novel to the drama in explicitly political terms: "The novelist is a free agent," she proclaimed. "He lives in a land of liberty, whilst the Dramatic Writer exists but under a despotic government."[41] These considerations of the relative merits of drama and the novel staged a competition over privilege in an aesthetic hierarchy that grounded the contrast between them in their media differences.

Over the course of the eighteenth century, the relationship of novel and drama shifted from one of conjunction, novel-and-drama, to one of disjunction, novel-or-drama. The emergence of the verb form "to dramatize" in 1780–1783 suggests that earlier adaptations were not understood to involve crossing firm lines between contrastive, even opposing, categories but instead, perhaps, as translating aesthetic codes from one format to another that shared common ground. The new configuration, novel-or-drama, can support the construal of the relationship as a competition over "market share," though, as Ros Ballaster has pointed out, the rivalry might more fruitfully be understood as rhetorical rather than actual: then, as now, sequels, spin-offs, and adaptations for other platforms enhanced profits rather than diminishing them.[42] Otherwise-valuable analyses of the relationship between the novel and the stage by Emily Anderson, Lisa Freeman, Nora Nachumi, and others have tended to assume that they were opposed from the start.[43] Here, however, the critics import backward the construal of the relationship between print and performance as an opposition, an idea that only emerged as such at the very end of the eighteenth century, as I will argue in the next section. Novels and plays, particularly melodrama, shared the problem of popularity, which highlighted the similarities—indeed, the collaboration—between them. Like the novel, melodrama also failed to fit the ancient categories of tragic or comic. As multimedia spectacle that maximized affective impact with politics that were difficult to determine, melodrama also helped to intensify attention to media. Exceedingly popular and exceedingly spectacular, melodrama challenged the novel as *the* measure of popularity.

As late as 1822, in the first number of the *Noctes Ambrosianae*, the innovative precursor to *Blackwoods* magazine that featured a roving cast of characters who drop by Ambrose's tavern to discuss politics, literature, and the making of a magazine with Christopher North, the editorial persona of John Wilson Croker, the status of drama in the organization of the genres is what is at stake in his dialogue with a writer named O'Doherty. O'Doherty wants to finish his tragedy, but the Editor does not "think [the drama] at present a good field for the extension of genius." Although to this point, drama had upheld the standards of taste, it has now come to be debased by sensationalism; there is a paucity of new drama even worthy of the name. In response to these editorial pronouncements, O'Doherty produces an awkward classification of popular drama as "a novel without narrative parts."[44] Here the old eighteenth-century instability of the term "novel" persists, but now it dominates drama in the sense that drama is defined in relationship to the novel rather than the reverse. Shared by drama and the novel, popularity names one of the conditions for the generic redefinition of both drama and novel in terms of media.

The speakers explore performance as "the chief difference" between plays and novels and conclude that the novel appeals to the imagination and the drama appeals to the senses, one of the chief means of subordinating drama to the novel.

Then they produce an encomium to Byron and Goethe as the best *dramatists* of the time. The hybrid and multiform writing of these men of the theater can be included in the category of drama even though it aimed at performance only ambiguously at best.[45] Byron and Goethe prop up the dignity of drama, which can be retained on the condition of its segregation from popular performance in the wake of a new emphasis on the distinction between print and performance that the invention of the term "closet drama," first applied to Byron by William Gifford in a contemporaneous review of *Sardanapalus* for the *Quarterly Review*, also reflected.[46]

The *Noctes* speakers thus used "drama" the way Wordsworth used "poetry": to measure the heights of literary achievement. For Wordsworth, Shakespeare, in his capacity as the exceptional poetic genius, proved the rule that popular drama, which he did not conceive Shakespeare to be writing, did not belong in the category of serious literature. Wordsworth's application of the term "poetry" as a superlative is a hangover from the shift from Poetry to Literature, even as poetry's domain was generically narrowed. If Wordsworth's opposition of novels and melodrama to poetry brought the first two together because of their popularity, the opposition of print to performance pushed novels and plays further apart by giving the media difference between them greater prominence than it hitherto had enjoyed.

MEDIA 1: PRINT AND PERFORMANCE

Although plays were largely read rather than seen in performance during the Interregnum, when the theaters were closed, there is no evidence to suggest that reading and seeing plays performed were understood as competing rather than mutually enhancing activities once the theaters reopened in 1660.[47] Curiously, differences that must have been observed were not remarked on in print until the end of the eighteenth century. Theater historian Michael Booth began his classic essay "Theater History and the Literary Critic," in which he warned critics interested in drama that they would ignore performance and its histories at their peril, with a citation of Charles Lamb. In his 1811 essay "On Shakespeare's Tragedies," "Lamb seems to have been the first to face the dichotomy between the response to performance and the response to text."[48] This is not entirely accurate: in Elizabeth Inchbald's "Remarks" on the collection of 125 plays included "as acted" in *The British Theatre* (1806–1808), she regularly noted the differences between the experiences of reading plays and seeing them performed.[49] These treatments, more or less contemporaneous, suggest that the opposition between performance and print has a history.

To understand how the contrast between reading plays and seeing them performed morphed into this media opposition will involve but not be reducible to the histories of print and performance: who read what and who attended which performances are also relevant. The following sketch is not exhaustive but symptomatic: after an overview of the history of printing plays in the long eighteenth century, I follow Shakespeare, the figure for a national literary culture who was the occasion of Booth's polemic. As the reception of Shakespeare suggests, there was a long and uneven history of the entanglement of reading drama and attending its performance.

For much of the eighteenth century, plays were printed to coincide with their performance, a practice suggesting that seeing a performance enhanced rather than diminished the desire to read plays, and vice versa. As Richard Steele had noted in the preface to *The Conscious Lovers* (1722), "the greatest Effect of a Play in reading is to excite the Reader to go see it."[50] The delays between theatrical performance and play publication that had been the norm in the 1690s decreased in the eighteenth century, with publication, a process with which dramatists increasingly were involved, coming to be almost simultaneous with performance by the 1730s, though publication preceded performance in the case of opera.[51] Although ultimately the printing of Addison's *Cato* coincided with its performance in April 1713, Jacob Tonson, as Tom Keymer has noted, paid Addison more than one hundred pounds for the right to print it in advance.[52]

The mutual enhancement of reading plays and seeing them performed also informed practices of adaptation that went in both directions: novels were adapted for the stage and plays' plots and characters taken up in novels. Intermediary hybrid forms also existed: for example, the freestanding episode of the three men who establish a tent community outside London in Daniel Defoe's *Journal of the Plague Year* (1722) is rendered as a minidrama; on the other hand, George Colman the Elder's *Polly Honeycombe* (1760) was subtitled a "Dramatick Novel" but was a play nevertheless.[53] Tracking Shakespeare's sources in novels and histories in *Shakespeare Illustrated* (1753), Charlotte Lennox suggested the transformative capacity of reading to turn plays into narrative form.[54]

The history of printing plays that had been performed, however, changed substantially during the first few decades of the nineteenth century. Although anthologies of drama "as it was performed," such as Longman's or Bell's, were highly successful publishing ventures, this trend reversed not long thereafter, and by 1820, the publication of performed drama was reduced significantly.[55] Among the disincentives to the publication of performed plays was the likelihood of piracy, with financial advantage flowing neither to the dramatists nor to the playhouses in which their work had originally been staged. Richard Brinsley Sheridan's *School for Scandal* (1777) did not appear in an authorized edition during his lifetime because withholding it from print permitted him to maximize profit from and otherwise control the performances of his own work at Drury Lane, which he managed and owned.[56]

In the Parliamentary hearings leading up to the passage of the Dramatic Copyright Act (Bulwer-Lytton's Act) in 1832, the actor William Charles Macready was asked if he believed "the general diffusion of literature to have been among the causes of the decline of the drama." He replied, "I do, particularly to the novels and romances which have been written, by which a person can procure the same excitement and amusement at his fireside for the small price he pays to the circulating library."[57] Plays had been second only to novels in the newly established circulating libraries of the 1740s, in which "Novels and Plays" were classed together. By the beginning of the nineteenth century, however, "Poetry and Drama" came to be grouped separately from "Fiction etc." The British Library and the Bodleian officially adopted both as separate subclassifications of literature in 1911, following the scheme recommended by the International Congress for Librarians held in Brussels in 1910 and retained to this day.[58]

For Daniel Barrett, the diminished publication of performed plays for a reading audience that consumed increasing numbers of novels resulted in "drama and literature [coming to be] almost completely divorced."[59] Julie Stone Peters disagrees, demonstrating that play publication got reoriented through a distinction between literary playwrights and theater hacks, a point that the dialogue from the *Noctes Ambrosianae* confirms. Although Peters would call into question the alienation of drama from literature, her analysis of the compatibilities of print and performance yields a genealogy of the division between literary drama and popular theater that nevertheless supports a modified version of Barrett's point: popular theater was divorced from literature, a category that nonetheless retained Shakespeare and some other "classic" playwrights. The library reclassification from "Novels and Plays" to "Poetry and Drama" illustrates the same shift that occurred from novel-and-drama in the neoclassical organization of Poetry to novel-or-drama in the suprageneric organization of Literature under the joint pressures of popular forms and an expanded market for print. "Poetry and Drama," on the one hand, and "Fiction," on the other, continue to organize both libraries and brick-and-mortar bookstores in our time, which, perhaps, materializes the almost exclusive association of fiction with the novel. In some ways, it would seem that "Poetry and Drama" have been consigned to the old world of Poetry, while the novel has come to constitute the world of fiction, a source, perhaps, for Gallagher's fictionality that provides another view of the trade-off: the dropping out of the picture of literature's other genres and their joint histories.

Print history reveals that reading plays and seeing them performed were hardly mutually exclusive activities. For literary history, however, the question remains: How did the relationship between them modulate into a media opposition between print and performance? In this development, the imaginative engagement elicited by melodrama and the novel, and the means by which they elicited it, were as significant as their popularity. It is easy to grasp quite quickly melodrama's contribution to the construal of the differences between print and performance as a media opposition. Reading a melodrama is not the best way to appreciate it as multimedia spectacle. The difficulties in imagining the visual and aural dimensions as they would have been realized in performance would have contributed to a felt difference between reading and seeing the play. Thomas Holcroft's translation of Guilbert de Pixérécourt's *Çoelina, ou l'enfant du mystère* (1801), often credited with being the first English melodrama, includes such stage directions as "Music to express discontent and alarm," "Music, to express chattering contention," "Music to express pain and disorder."[60] Such music would have played simultaneously with the action, thus providing the earliest version of a soundtrack, an experience that is naturalized for us via film in the form of piano accompaniment to the silents but that the silents themselves had borrowed, along with acting styles, from stage melodrama. Reading such stage directions highlights the absent auditory component that would have accompanied viewing. Although incidental sounds like thunderclaps had been indicated in the stage directions since the seventeenth century, continuous musical accompaniment to the action and persistent stage directions would have heightened awareness of media differences.

If reading the increasingly spectacular contemporary plays of the 1790s pulled away from the experience of seeing them performed, so did the experience of a "classic" playwright like Shakespeare, especially considering the discrepancies between printed Shakespeare, with its history of editing and emendation, and performed Shakespeare, which routinely featured "improvements" contributed by others' hands. William St. Clair has proposed that ordinary readers would not have been able to afford to read Shakespeare until intellectual copyright restrictions were lifted in 1774 because the plays would only have been available in the expensive folio editions published by the Tonsons.[61] Don-John Dugas and Robert Hume agree that, at least until the 1730s, most people would have encountered Shakespeare only in performance, thus disposing of the question of the discrepancy between read and performed Shakespeare.[62] But Jan Fergus has challenged St. Clair on the availability of Shakespeare at midcentury, demonstrating the availability of quartos in the circulating libraries.[63] Taking a different tack and focusing on the earlier half of the period, Maximillian Novak surveys the ample critical response to Shakespeare between Dryden and Pope and asserts that the extent to which Shakespeare was read has been underestimated by St. Clair and Dugas and Hume. Extrapolating from the inclusion of Shakespeare's first folio in impoverished Lewis Theobald's extensive book collection, Novak observes that there is no data on the availability or price of secondhand books in the period.[64] Fergus's and Novak's research exposes that the history of print does not coincide with the history of reading.

Rather than examining the contributions that the long history of adaptations and editions of Shakespeare may have made to the media opposition between print and performance, St. Clair and Dugas and Hume import it into their analyses. Michael Dobson, by contrast, has suggested that there was no strong differentiation between print and performance up until the age of Kemble. The 1756 edition of *Hamlet*, "As is now acted by His Majesty's Servants," for example, included the lines that remained unspoken in the production.[65] In the reverse of our use of quotation marks for what is said, unsaid lines were set off in single quotation marks, a typographical practice found in many printed plays that this edition explains: "This play being too long to be acted upon the Stage, such Lines as are left out in the Acting, are marked thus '.'"[66] This print practice differentiated between print and performance without insisting that one form or the other was authoritative; rather, it suggests that reading Shakespeare involved both.

The preface to a collated edition of *Hamlet* (1770) provides another example. There Charles Jennings provided a "Sketch" summarizing each act, thereby giving a handy reference to jog readers' memories in case they lost sight of the whole play while attending to editorial matters in an edition that produced the lines and their variants side by side. The sketch retained stage directions and actors' gestures, even supplementing those provided in the "original." The player king and queen "enter very lovingly embracing," for instance, and in act 4, scene 7, Ophelia enters, "fantastically drest with straws and flowers."[67] These descriptions are designed to bring to mind performances, or to get readers to imagine scenes in their own minds, as a necessary accompaniment to the production of Shakespeare in print. Both print and performance were required in the production of an authoritative Shakespeare.

Read and performed Shakespeare in the second half of the eighteenth century also reflected novel-reading, as the reception of *King Lear* makes clear. In the postscript to the first edition of *Clarissa*, in which Richardson used Addison on poetic justice to support his choice to let his heroine die, he added a footnote about Nahum Tate's revised ending to Shakespeare's play, exhorting Garrick from his ideal perch as both actor and theater manager to restore the play's original ending: "If it were *ever* to be tried, *now* seems to be the time."[68] Richardson expected his readers to attend performances of Shakespeare; this appeal to Garrick proposes that perhaps now that they have read *Clarissa*, they will be able to tolerate the death of Cordelia.

Richardson understood that his readers were playgoers; but like Garrick in this appeal, men of the theater could also sometimes be glimpsed as novel readers. Increased dissatisfaction with adaptations of Shakespeare expressed in the press after 1753 perhaps indicated a growing sense of the difference between printed and performed Shakespeare.[69] Colman the Elder responded in 1768 with a production of *King Lear* that restored some of Shakespeare's language, although it neither brought back the Fool whom Tate had eliminated nor altered Tate's comic ending. Comparing the relative strengths and weaknesses of Tate and Colman in *The Dramatic Censor* (1771), Francis Gentleman concluded, "The tragedy, in its original state, exhibits a Beautiful collection of poetical flowers, choaked up with a profusion of weeds," but not before speculating that the play would have been better if it had begun after the daughters' marriages.[70] Proposing to reorient the division of the kingdom to reflect Lear as a father who approves or disapproves his children's marriages rather than as a king intent on manipulating questions of succession, Gentleman here supplies the play with a novelistic, because domestic, motivation for the action.

In *Mansfield Park*, Jane Austen demonstrated another intermediary experience of Shakespeare: reading him aloud. Despite Fanny Price's distaste for and reluctance to participate in the amateur theatrical production of *Lovers' Vows*, she cannot help but be moved by Henry Crawford's reading aloud of a scene from *Henry VIII*. Henry's reading, moreover, is equally admired by Mrs. Bertram, Fanny, and Edmund, who agree, "It was truly dramatic." Though Austen's novel has often been taken to express an underlying antitheatricality, further clarification of Fanny's response to Crawford establishes that his earlier performance had been objectionable for his use of the role of Anhalt to seduce Maria Bertram: "His acting had first taught Fanny what pleasure a play might give and his reading brought all his acting before her again; nay, perhaps with greater enjoyment, for it came unexpectedly, and with no such drawback as she had been used to suffer in seeing him on the stage with Miss Bertram."[71]

In response to Edmund's commendation of his uncommon eloquence, Crawford explains, "I do not think I have had a volume of Shakespeare in my hand before, since I was fifteen.—I once saw Henry the 8th acted.—Or I have heard of it from someone who did—I am not certain which. But Shakespeare one gets acquainted with without knowing how. It is part of an Englishman's constitution." This universal, national, or at least upper- and middle-class English access to Shakespeare comes by means of print, performance, and ubiquitous citation: as Edmund responds, "one is familiar with Shakespeare in a degree from one's earliest years.

His celebrated passages are quoted by everybody; they are in half the books we open, and we all talk Shakespeare, use his similes, and describe with his descriptions."[72]

With Crawford only reading Shakespeare when he had to in school, his reading seems a bit desultory, but Austen recuperates it even while condemning his acting to demonstrate his attractions. She differentiates between print and performance and thereby grants the media difference the incipient capacity to organize the genres of the new canon of literature. In having Crawford's reading aloud from Shakespeare praised and his acting in a melodrama condemned, she also recapitulates the discrimination of serious from popular literature, thus demonstrating the negative contributions that popular novels and plays made to the new category of serious literature from which they came to be excluded.

MEDIA 2: PERFORMANCE, MIMESIS, AND THE LIMITS OF NOVELISTIC REALISM

As Patricia Michaelson and Abigail Williams have each observed, the extract from Shakespeare that Henry Crawford reads aloud was included in the elocutionary handbook *The Speaker*, by William Enfield (1774). As these scholars show, not only were novels by Frances Burney and Jane Austen read aloud, but they seem also to have been written with that purpose in mind.[73] In chapters 4 and 5 on Burney and Austen, respectively, I examine their novels as they reflect the conventions of the drama that their authors read, wrote, and read aloud and their experiences of professional and amateur theatrical performance, a cross-genre and mixed-media milieu that improves our knowledge of them at the levels of form and technique. Here, the comparison of the ways the category of media was used to address literature in the elocutionary movement and our own time shows its tendency to overshadow the category of genre, which, once observed, can be corrected. A more general exploration of how to think the categories of media and genre together that builds on the significance of the medium of performance for a media-sensitive account of the novel as a genre also corrects the overprivileging of realism in media-blind accounts. This discussion thus lays the conceptual grounds for the chapters that follow.

Performance was important as a medium for reading in general, and not just reading literature, at least up through the end of the eighteenth century. Samuel Johnson's "common reader," an abstraction that "erected a defense against the frightening possibility that England was becoming a 'nation of authors' in which 'every man must be content to read his book to himself,'" responded to the expansion of print culture at the same time as it registered the difference between individual silent reading and sociable reading aloud.[74] The general applicability of performance to reading in the elocutionary movement brings out its specific significance for the novel.

With the publication of *Lectures on Elocution* in 1762, Thomas Sheridan had founded the elocution movement, which codified ways of making print immediately available by remediating it as performance. Sheridan divided *Lectures on the Art of Reading* (1775) into two parts, one for prose and one for poetry, with no mention of drama or the novel, but in *Chironomia* (1806), his follower Gilbert Austin devoted a chapter to the intersection of performance and reading across the genres of print from financial reports to epic poetry, including both drama and the novel. Austin measured reading aloud on a scale from "Intelligible" to "Correct," "Impressive," "Rhetorical," "Dramatic," and "Epic," thus incorporating the literary genres as superlatives. Singling out for praise the rare reader of drama who modulated each character's voice and thus spared his hearers the disruption that "breaks the interest of a scene" caused by the need to identify them all by name, Austin here could have described Henry Crawford's "truly dramatic" reading. To the more common, merely correct, reader, Austin recommended that this identification be provided "in a dry sort of under voice." Although he disdained novels for their dangerous sedative quality, Austin provided instructions for "Novels, or modern fictitious biography that are so frequently the subject of private reading," especially among the young: mere narrative parts should be read rapidly, interesting scenes should be read impressively, and "many of those [scenes] which are constructed like those in a regular drama require to be read in a similar manner."[75]

It is significant that the medium-specific orientation toward performance was not, and could not have been, medium exclusive: it exempted neither Sheridan nor Austin from the protocols of print. Sheridan developed pronunciation guides in his phonetically respelled *A General Dictionary of the English Language* (1780), and Austin's *Chironomia* developed a system of notation for gesture. Equally notable is that their investment in the medium of performance came at the expense of genre, or at least, it licensed a lack of attention to the literary specificity of the genre categories. Austin's use of the genre terms as superlative measures of praise echoes or anticipates the superlative applications of "poetry" by Wordsworth and "drama" by the *Noctes* writers and Jane Austen's characters. His treatment of the novel as "modern fictitious biography," like the *Noctes* character O'Doherty's definition of popular drama as a "novel without narrative parts," reflected the sustained instability of the term "novel" that coincided with a changing genre system.

A similar overshadowing of genre by media can be found in John Guillory's history of the media concept, the most significant intervention in its uptake for literary criticism. Key moments in his "history of an *absent* concept—the concept of a medium of communication"—include the recognition that communications can fail in John Locke's understanding of words as vehicles for transferring meanings from one person's mind to another's, which "partially detaches the concept of medium from the older concept of [an] art" of communication. Later the medium of poetry is thickened as it comes to be freed from the strictures of clarity first articulated in John Stuart Mill's famous definition that "eloquence is heard, poetry is overheard" and then in Stephane Mallarmé's notion that "you can't make a poem with ideas, . . . you make it with words."[76] For Guillory, Mallarmé returns to Locke's words with the difference that now poetry can revel in its own linguistic materiality because it is supported by a distinction between literary language as art and nonliterary language as a medium of communication. Guillory thus lays the grounds for the emergence of the specific understanding of media as the (frequently technological) vehicle by which meaning is conveyed not in the recent digital revolution but rather in the longer-term historical transformations undergone by the category of rhetoric.

Guillory takes poetry as a synecdoche for literature but gives no account of this selection. Drama, moreover, is entirely absent from his analysis, as is the elocutionary movement and so, too, any sense of either rhetoric's or literature's implication with the medium of performance. Yet it is impossible to ignore the performance context in Mill's definition of poetry as overheard: the relevance of drama as a genre and theater as an experience of performance persisted in the dramatic monologues of Tennyson and Browning that put readers in the position to overhear.

Guillory's silence on the matter of genre and concomitant demotion of drama are perfectly congruent with twentieth-century histories of eighteenth-century aesthetics that have treated metaphorically the interest in theatricality expressed by David Hume, Adam Smith, Denis Diderot, and others, even though the actual theater provided the dynamics of the experiences they sought to describe and plays furnished a significant number of their examples.[77] The significance of the theater to and the implication of the medium of performance in the emergence of aesthetic theory indicate a different account of mimesis than the one usually given by the history of the novel, in which the novel has been overexpanded as a genre, on the one hand, and too narrowly confined to the aesthetics of realism, on the other.

The classical tradition spawned two treatments of mimesis: an Aristotelian division into three of imitative making—poetry, drama, and narrative—and a Platonic opposition of imitation, most often associated with drama though equally applicable to all artistic representation, to diegesis, that is, narrative. McKeon argues in his synoptic treatment of novel theory that ideas of realism derive from the latter opposition, thereby laying bare the convergence of the opposition of drama to the novel with the conflation of the novel and the aesthetics of realism.[78] McKeon sticks here to the Platonic line; he crosses over into Aristotelian territory when he makes claims for the novel as a genre, but as the novel becomes a super-genre, the category of genre is disabled. By contrast, the history of the novel's relation to the theater foregrounds the continued coexistence of Platonic and Aristotelian understandings of mimesis across the eighteenth century, in which concerns about the moral impact of both novels and plays, expressed in the desideratum of poetic justice, informed the delineation of the genres' strengths and limits. Although Guillory tracks the media concept back to Aristotle, our own media moment might suggest instead the alignment of the Platonic distinction of mimesis/diegesis with problems of mediation and media and the Aristotelian triad epic/drama/lyric with problems of genre. This configuration would acknowledge that it may not be possible in the history of literature to pry genre and media apart. It is also hard to see what is to be gained from their segregation. Although thinking them together poses some problems for the dominant narratives of the novel's emergence, it also enables some solutions.

Thinking genre and media together extends accounts of the novel length-wise: the generic identity of the novel could only cohere once the displacement of the category of genre from its earlier centrality, where it had reigned supreme in the organization of Poetry, was complete. It also expands accounts of the novel in width, broadening the scope to accommodate its mediation by other genres, including drama. The collation of genre with media, made explicit by the formulation of print and performance as an opposition, marked the completion of the displacement of Poetry and enabled the category of genre to be overshadowed by the category of media, but thinking those categories together productively complicates accounts that identify the novel's aesthetic achievements as ones that it, and only it, can achieve. These have been presented by Ian Watt, Michael McKeon, Nancy Armstrong, Catherine Gallagher, and others, under the rubrics of formal realism, domesticity, or fictionality itself, but the novel never was exclusively realist; some of its most profound effects, moreover, are those that are also produced by other art forms.

McKeon's account of the realism of the novel uses György Lukács's "double reflection," that is to say, a reflection of the world and a reflection of the process by which that reflection is accomplished, to investigate the ways the novel recapitulates its formal procedures at the level of content. On this basis, he argues that the novel's self-reflexivity helps to make it the privileged genre through which realism and domesticity are coarticulated.[79] In this association of realism with domesticity, McKeon follows Erich Auerbach, for whom the signal achievement of realism as practiced by the nineteenth-century French novelists Balzac, Stendhal, and Flaubert was to overcome the classical rule of distinct levels of style that relegated the ordinary to comic or grotesque representation and reserved tragedy for aristocrats. Auerbach thus recognized Aristotelian and neoclassical drama theory and registered the shift from Poetry to Literature, though his great work, *Mimesis*, has licensed the disregard of both in most subsequent period-based scholarship on the novel. These aspects of generic codification remained significant to novels up through the elevation of the novel as an art, a phenomenon that dates to the later nineteenth century, as shown by the Victorianist scholar Nicholas Dames and the Americanist Mark McGurl.[80]

In Auerbach, moreover, realism was conditioned by that which it could not contain or recapitulate, that which operated at its margins. He thus kept the realist tradition in check and registered that the history of the novel includes many novels that were not realist. Recently Elaine Freedgood has proposed that the privilege granted to the nineteenth-century realist novels stems from the replacement of the idea of the novel as dramatic, best exemplified by Henry James's scenic method, by a notion of novelistic form embraced by post-1960s Anglo-American critics' encounter with structuralist narratology that is constituted by "near zero degree diegesis and focalization, a non-interfering paratextual apparatus, denotation as reality effect, a referential scaffold not at odds with fictionality, and omniscient narration."[81] As Freedgood shrewdly observes, this is more of a critical fantasy than an accurate depiction of the Victorian novel, whose lack of formal coherence was once widely recognized, as Dames also points out. Freedgood's genealogy of criticism of the nineteenth-century novel suggests that the novel did not achieve full autonomy from the drama for much longer than histories of the novel would lead us to believe, a view that the privilege granted to novelistic realism has helped to obscure.[82]

Freedgood also observes that narrative theory's treatment of diegesis as world-making derives from Gérard Genette's uptake of film theory, which, in Jean-Louis Baudry's classic discussion of the apparatus, adheres explicitly to the Platonic dyad.[83] In the domain of narrative theory, media once again overshadows genre. Unfortunately, with narratology's commitments to narrative as a universal and transhistorical mode, it has little to say about medium specificity, notwithstanding its interests in cross-media translation.[84] Exceptionally, Monika Fludernik has recognized some of the ways the early novel was "greatly aided by drama," a process especially visible in the hands of Aphra Behn.[85] Her account of Behn's legacy to Fielding, Oliver Goldsmith, Wilkie Collins, and George Eliot includes the transposition of dramatic scenes into episodes and the development of "the consciousness scene," in which free indirect discourse was used to establish characters' subjectivities.[86] But her reflections on what narratology has to do, first to establish "that drama is a bona fide narrative genre" and then to "integrate narratological accounts of drama within a general model of narratological levels and instances (narrator, narratee, etc.)," indicates why her work has proven the rule: narratology, when applied across media, is not only incapable of registering the differences media make; it is designed not to do so.[87] In order to think about medium specificity in literature, and perhaps in film and television studies as well, for that matter, it will be necessary to think about media together with genre.

Thinking media and genre together in the history of the novel obliges us to recognize that novelistic realism was mediated by the genres of literature, including drama, and by its media, performance as well as print. The media concept, as the foregoing treatment of performance as a medium for literature proposes, is variable in location, as Guillory's analysis of the instrumentalization of communication affirms. To be found at various scales that require different measures, from the vast in categories such as "print," "performance," "music," "film," or "the digital" to the minute in "font," the minuscule in "font size," or the niche in "card stock," "paper weight," or "ink formulae," any given literary object will exhibit many media characteristics simultaneously. Inquiry into how one medium brushes up against or affects the others will be enhanced by an account of the object's status, use, or market orientation. For this reason, the media concept cannot be used alone in literary analysis: it will require motivation toward literary representation or other matters of concern in literary interpretation, on the one hand, and stabilization or, at least, the organization of its variable scales, on the other. Print on its own, for example, as many of the media characteristics just enumerated suggest, can tell us nothing about the literariness of books. Applications of the media concept to literary analysis require the integration of the category of genre. Examples of this integration are offered in the following chapters of this history of the novel's relation to the stage.

Although longer and wider than some other histories of the novel, this one, perhaps paradoxically, is more unified, at least at the level of genre. It can include those narratives that have been consigned to an alternative genealogy of the Romantic novel because they include nonrealist Gothic or supernatural elements or depend too heavily on structures of overdetermination or fate rather than development, a feature sometimes seen as a hangover from romance.[88] At the intersection of genre and media, and on the cusp of the displacement of Poetry by Literature and the inflection of categories of genre by media, melodrama makes a particularly rich contribution to this history of the novel.

Shaped by Gothic novels among others, melodrama's emergence onstage at the end of the eighteenth century heightened awareness of media per se. Popular across the media of print, performance, and, later, screens as well, melodrama paradoxically became a mode in which medium-specific techniques of representation came to be prized. Yet melodrama's significance for narrative in novels has not been appreciated largely because of the low cultural value generally assigned to it, its conventionality, and its feminizing emotional intensities. This disdain, however, also expresses a hangover of the modernist dismissal of the accoutrements of Victorian narrative and its dramatized narrator, as can be seen in D. A. Miller, for example, who kicked Fielding's, Thackeray's, and George Eliot's voluble narrators out of a new Parnassus of Style presided over by the divine Jane Austen.[89] In the opening interrogative of *Persuasion*'s last chapter, "Who can be in doubt of what followed?," by contrast, Garrett Stewart detects a "faint whiff of interlocution" from which he extrapolates a suppressed readerly apostrophe. Austen's famous narrative economy and psychological realism depend heavily on the conventions of the stage, as I illustrate in chapter 5. For Stewart, who is after another continuity in the long history of the novel, that of the readerly address, the hallmark of modernism was its disdain for talkative Victorian narrators, with their theatrical air.[90] He thus exposes one of the dynamics in play when Miller followed the lead of Virginia Woolf, for whom cozy Victorian fiction, with its narrators' addresses to readers, kowtowed to the tyranny of the ordinary middlebrow reader.[91]

In a book about realism as both a mode of representation and a signifier of a historical period, Fredric Jameson has acknowledged the persistence—even the necessity—of melodrama, realism's shadowy other. It is shadowy, in Jameson's account, because he only gestures toward its conventional treatment of evil in looming villainy, on the one hand, and its association with theatricality in the genealogy that Michael Fried has given of painting and conceptual art, on the other. Jameson understands that for Fried, as well as for others, "the association of melodrama with theatricality raises the more general issue of rhetoric in modern times and its repudiation, not only in modernism as such but also in the course of the development of the realist novel."[92] Though Jameson identifies the importance of melodrama, he discusses it in passing, but this history of the novel corroborates Jameson's recognition by identifying the consequences of melodrama's emergence on the novel and on the genre system that it, together with the novel, ushered in, after which the two went their increasingly separate ways. If Behn's uptake of tragicomedy inaugurated a mode of collaboration between the novel and the stage that melodrama brought to a conclusion, of sorts, for most of the intervening period, it occurred under another generic rubric: the comedy of manners. Chapter 2 tracks the interaction of genre and media in the migration of the comedy of manners from the stage to the novel by following its hallmark plot: the reform of the rake.

THE REFORM OF THE RAKE FROM ROCHESTER

TO INCHBALD

> Reformation cannot be *sudden* work.
> —Samuel Richardson, *Clarissa* (Letter 116)

> The good end happily, the bad unhappily. That is what Fiction means.
> —Oscar Wilde, *The Importance of Being Earnest*

WHEN GILBERT BURNET PUBLISHED *Some Passages of the Life and Death of Rochester* in 1680 describing the deathbed repentance of the notorious rake John Wilmot, he contributed a crucial and long-lived narrative to English culture, one that fascinated eighteenth-century dramatists, novelists, and poets and evidently their audiences as well: the reform of the rake.[1] Not that many stories of the rake's reform predate Rochester's and then not by much: Molière's *Dom Juan* was only published in 1682 in a severely limited edition, its controversial subject matter having forced its withdrawal from the stage after fifteen performances in 1660; he had adapted Tirso de Molina's *El burlador de Sevilla y convidado de piedro*, which was first published in 1630.[2] Whereas Continental versions of the story explored supernatural and religious elements—the stone statue that comes to dinner and the carting of the libertine off to hell, familiar from Mozart's *Don Giovanni*—English examples highlighted the Protestant rake's reform, perhaps in more secular terms, in relation to marriage. The rake's reform contributed a crucial element to the Restoration stage as well as to the eighteenth-century novel, and his story drew a host of moral and aesthetic issues in its wake.

Controversies arising from the problematic credibility of the rake's reform and the morality of its demonstration stalked the story from its inception. The same issues of reform, credibility, and morality that shaped Burnet's account of Rochester's death and its reception also informed debates over how best to represent the rake's reform in plays by Colley Cibber and Sir John Vanbrugh and in novels by Samuel Richardson and Henry Fielding. Although the moral inspiration apparently provided by the rake's reform in either narrative representation or performance remains impossible to measure, its capacity to inspire controversy is irrefutable in both dramatic and narrative responses to and rewritings of the story. The shared goals across the media of pamphlet, play, and novel and their burnishing of each other's techniques can best be captured by tracking the comedy of manners as a genre.

The contributions that the *Pamela* controversy made to the novel are well known, and the earlier controversies not unfamiliar, but the recapitulation of the earlier debates by the later one is not usually discussed. This perspective offers a number of advantages to the theatrical history of the novel. When Richardson took up the plot of the rake's reform, he did not abandon the set of problems explored first in Burnet's pamphlet and then in some of the plays associated with the Collier controversy. On the contrary, the entanglement of eliciting both credibility and moral emulation remained in Richardson's adaptation of the story to the form of epistolary narration. Following the rake's reform across the media of print and performance from the pamphlet to the plays to the novel thereby makes it possible to disengage the joint preoccupation with credible representation and moral exemplarity from the aesthetics of realism in the history of the novel. The radical nature of Richardson's achievement was partly to usher the comedy of manners from the stage to the novel, where it reached its apotheosis in Jane Austen. Recognizing the importance of realism without allowing it to overwhelm the story of the comedy of manners' migration across media clears the way for the examination in subsequent chapters of the differences between Richardson's and his female heirs' treatments of marriage, along with the disclosure of the formal narrative features they borrowed from the stage to convey their positions.

The successive controversies display a consistent preoccupation despite their different mediations of the story of the rake's reform: What were the best ways to represent convincing reform and convey its moral force? Tracking some of the narrative and dramatic innovations used to do so keeps in the foreground the issue that was fundamental in the period: the moral force of aesthetic form. The chapter concludes with a discussion of *Wives as They Were, Maids as They Are* (1797), the last original play by Elizabeth Inchbald and one in which the reform of the rake, Bronzely, provokes the reform of all the other men of the play, and her first novel, *A Simple Story* (1791), which, in the character of Miss Milner, features a female rake. Inchbald's hybrid writing problematizes the familiar narrative of generic progress in which novels take up and sophisticate the representational project begun on the stage. By displaying the mutual influences of the novel and the drama, Inchbald can bring the arc mapped by the transformation of the comedy of manners up to the end of the eighteenth century.

THE RAKE AND HIS REFORM

A glamorous figure, the rake has attracted a significant amount of critical analysis, though not all that much attention has been paid to the representations of his reform.[3] This element of his story, however, posed a challenge in print, onstage, and in novels for the ways it brought together, however ambiguously, the problem of pleasure and the problem of belief: how to represent the rake's dangerous sexuality and his heartfelt reform and control their capacities to seduce and inspire—whether to better behavior or incredulous laughter. According to Elaine McGirr, the rake went from hero to villain to marginal between 1660 and the end of the eighteenth century, a path through which she charts an increasingly rigid codification of the gender binary that developed in the wake of the two-sex system described by Thomas Laqueur: as the heroic rake who is too much with women is villainized, his effeminacy, which in the one-sex model might threaten to turn him into a woman, is transformed in the two-sex model into a threatening hypermasculinity.[4] McGirr observes the rake's appearance in prose tracts and poetry as well as in plays and novels but portrays his containment in the development of a straightforward generic progression from the stage to the novel, where he is first moralized and then dismissed.

McGirr's example of this marginalization is the readily detectable and quickly defused sexual danger posed to the heroine by the noble rake, Lord Merton, in the last volume of Frances Burney's *Evelina* (1774). But in a more central plot of that novel, Evelina has difficulty first distinguishing the seductive motives of Sir Clement Willoughby from the conjugally oriented attentions of Lord Orville and then effectively distancing herself from the former's improper advances, for which she ultimately requires Orville's aid. Jane Austen kept this unreformed rake in view when she named Marianne Dashwood's caddish lover Willoughby in *Sense and Sensibility* (1811). The dangers posed to women by aristocratic seducers like Austen's Willoughby, who may or may not develop an interest in marriage, remained a popular literary plot for longer than McGirr's account permits.[5] Although the rake's progress from the stage to the novel cannot be narrated in terms of his containment, the theatrical concept of the rake as a stock character makes it possible to narrate the influence of the theater on the novel and the contributions it made to narrative technique and to literary aesthetics more generally.

So too does the idea of the repertory. In *The Rakish Stage*, Robert Hume used performance records to reveal the persistent popularity of Restoration comedy up through 1760.[6] He established that its initial audience was more socially diverse than had been imagined and attacked an overinvestment in a courtly audience's enjoyment of the representation of recognizable figures like Rochester, even though some of these identifications remain acceptable to other scholars.[7] He charted the plays' responses to social and political change, developing a typology of stage rakes that distinguished among debauched figures who were already married, young sowers of wild oats who went on at the end of the play to be married, and adulterous husbands who kept only a mistress or two. He thereby laid the grounds for the multiplication of subgeneric distinctions that provided some traction on the plays' values and still organize the drama anthologies of the period. Like McGirr, Hume conveyed the rake's lively energies and much of the significance of his long-standing popularity. However, the challenge posed by his reform requires putting some of the analytic tools of theater history, stock character and repertory, to work outside the theater and replacing the generic splintering by a wider concept of genre that can be applied across plays and other forms of literature. The capacity of the story of the rake's reform to generate representational innovation across the media of print and performance can best be captured through a consideration of the genre of the comedy of manners.

To locate in Burnet's account of Rochester's deathbed conversion a source for some depictions of the rake's reform onstage and in novels involves acknowledging two major differences. The rake posed two threats: to morality and to marriage. Those plays and novels that tackled his reform either aimed to resolve both at once in a convergence that hinged on its credibility or called the relevance of credibility to morality into question. Burnet's account of Rochester's reform, by contrast, raised questions of credibility independent of marriage. This difference lays open to view the way the aesthetics of realism developed out of interpenetrating problems of credibility and morality as one among other possible aesthetic responses, on the one hand, and wedges open the identification of the realist novel and domestic fiction, on the other, making it possible to address separately questions about the novel's form and its different investments in marriage. A new view of the relations among the comedy of manners, female bildungsroman, and domestic fiction can emerge as a consequence.

Second, Burnet was ostensibly reporting the truth, and his pamphlet is usually treated as nonfiction. In fact, the authenticity of Rochester's conversion remained controversial for biographers and historians concerned with whether it actually had happened: this was a live issue for Graham Greene, who was sympathetic in his 1934 biography to the possibility of an authentic conversion, and for Christopher Hill, who found it necessary in 1980 not only to record the controversy but also to weigh in on the side of skepticism.[8] With this aspect ultimately undecidable, Burnet's account suggests that fiction may be the domain best suited to capture intensely affecting, private, and unverifiable subjective experience. As a narrative of intense personal transformation, its rhetorical resemblance to other fiction of the period makes it amenable to literary critical description. Perhaps these similarities also helped to motivate Rochester's frequent entry into literary texts.

The authenticity of Burnet's account was called into question practically from the moment of publication. The conclusion to Nathaniel Lee's 1681 play *The Princess of Cleves*, for example, raised doubts about the capacity of deathbed repentance to demonstrate moral character: as is said of Count Rosidore, Rochester's stand-in, "He well repents that will not sin, yet can; / But death bed sorrow rarely shows the man."[9] Burnet himself had anticipated such skepticism, fending it off from within the document itself by using some of the conventions for how to tell the truth in narrative that critics associate with the history of the novel.[10] The title page announcing, "Written by his [i.e., Rochester's] own Direction on his Death-Bed," draws on Rochester's authority as an aristocrat and Burnet's as an Anglican Divine even as it conforms to the documentary claims that frequently underwrote the generic assertion, "true because in print."[11] Burnet lets readers know that other Divines also witnessed the conversion and reproduces verbatim Rochester's letter of June 25, 1680, inviting him to pray that God will accept his deathbed repentance (134).

Burnet not only asserted the authenticity of Rochester's reform but also sought to demonstrate it, recording Rochester's account of how he came to be "persuaded of the truth of Christianity and of the power of inward Grace" (140) as follows: "He said to me That as he heard it [Isaiah 53] read, he felt an inward force upon him, which did so enlighten his Mind, and convince him, that he could resist it no longer: For the words had an authority which did shoot like Raies or Beams in his Mind" (141). Burnet himself called this account "strange" (140), but it delivers what might be the least easily refuted part of the document: the subjective experience of reform, behind which lies the Christian conversion narrative, in which it is crucial that transformation is experienced and known but not by way of reason.[12]

Burnet's invocation of Rochester's strange mental "raies or beams" raises questions about the capacity for even realist fiction to be fully adequate to authenticity, no matter how insistently it may signal it. This incompletion plagued both the plays and the novels that dealt with the rake's reform after Rochester's death; moreover, it was one of the motors driving the distinction of realism as an aesthetic end in and of itself from the moral inculcation of virtue with which it was conjoined in the dominant texts of eighteenth-century literature—including some novels such as Richardson's. Subjective experience could come to be elaborated in psychological terms, although, as in the narrative of Rochester's conversion, it could also take external and even supernatural form.

Burnet exploited the individual experience of conversion for the impact he hoped it would have on readers, yet his account inspired, or failed to inspire, as much, if not more, because of Rochester's exemplarity as because of its credibility. Indeed, Rochester's status as an aristocrat and as England's first print-culture poet-celebrity highlights the social landscape in which the aspirational dynamics of imitation took place in plays and novels. Although Rochester did not seek publication for most of his poems, he seems not to have cared when they made their way into print miscellanies within a few years of their composition.[13] He may not have aimed beyond a courtly audience toward a wider public, but his name and the widely circulated stories associated with it, especially after his death, made legible in print a number of issues, including libertinism, the diminishing status of aristocratic authority, and the value of moral reform.[14] In the long aftermath, rakes in novels including Richardson's Mr. B. and Lovelace, Charlotte Brontë's Rochester, and even Thomas Hardy's Alex D'Urberville retained their elevated social status and their threatening power, perhaps a reflection of the bourgeois novel's moralizing tendencies.

Rakes in other media, however, experienced steep social decline. Tom Fashion, the younger brother of Lord Foppington in Vanbrugh's *The Relapse* (1696), slides into poverty; Tom, Bevil's servant in Richard Steele's *The Conscious Lovers* (1722), adopts rakish manners to go along with the cast-off clothes of his master; Macheath of John Gay's *Beggar's Opera* (1728) goes to jail even if he ultimately eludes the hangman.[15] The middle-class Tom Rakewell of William Hogarth's *A Rake's Progress* (1735) inappropriately imitates the extravagance of an aristocrat.[16] In *Tatler* 27 (June 9–11, 1709), Steele worried about the spread of rakish behavior across status lines.[17] Erin Mackie has analyzed the association of the rake, as a figure in literature and in life, with the gentleman highwayman and the pirate to demonstrate their joint contributions to genteel masculinity.[18] Kristina Straub has analyzed the proliferation of sexy footmen in plays and at the theater.[19] Male servant seducers can be found in plays, including David Garrick's *The Lying Valet* (1741) but the only ones I have been able to find in novels before D. H. Lawrence's *Lady Chatterley's Lover* (1928) are Lafleur, the valet in Laurence Sterne's *A Sentimental Journey*, who is French, and Joseph Andrews, who is not really a seducer, having had that role foisted upon him by the amorous Lady Booby.[20]

Yet the devolution of the rake onstage was not itself a straightforward matter. Mackie's superb analysis demonstrates the complex relationship between sexual privilege and cultural nostalgia already present in Rochester's fame. She contextualizes the heterosexualization and criminalization of the rake in changing conceptions of patriarchy, politics, status, and empire. Compounding these social and ideological factors, however, were the rhythms of the repertory itself: the plays in which the rake was demoted were performed simultaneously and alongside the plays in which he was not, at least until around 1760, when some of the more sexually explicit ones, like George Etherege's *The Man of Mode; or, Sir Fopling Flutter* (1676) and Cibber's *Love's Last Shift* (1696), were dropped, and others, like William Wycherley's *The Country Wife* (1675) and Vanbrugh's *The Relapse*, were altered to make them more acceptable.[21]

Daniel Gustafson has recently shown that until 1745, Restoration rake plays including *The Man of Mode*, Aphra Behn's *The Rover* (1677), Thomas Shadwell's *The Libertine* (1676), and *The Country Wife*, were revived an average of two or three times a year.[22] He uses the resources of the repertory to call into question the narrative of the decline of the rake, put forward in theater histories that have attended only to new plays, and to contextualize the debate between Steele and John Dennis over the social, political, and moral significance of Dorimant, the rake of *The Man of Mode*.[23] Were "Dorimant and men of his ilk fine gentlemen or social sovereigns?" For Gustafson, the debate illustrates the ways the rake's personal sovereignty could "help the autonomous liberal subject navigate new structures of governmentality attached to civil society and commercial theatres," structures ushered in by the Hanoverians.[24] Christopher Tilmouth casts the debate, and the continued relevance of the rake to which it attests, in economic terms, disclosing the strands of libertine egoism preserved in both Dennis's enthusiasm for the morally reforming capacities of the stage and the Christian heroism proposed by Steele as these were retooled for economic conquest by Bernard Mandeville.[25] Both critics register the sustained popularity of the rake; their differences suggest that his capacity to signal, if not always to harmonize, competing ideologies contributed to his appeal.

Dennis's preoccupation in *A Defence of Sir Fopling Flutter* (1722) with the rake's gentility, in particular, makes it worth wondering about the extent to which the coexistence onstage of variously socially positioned rakes freed novels to address other aspects of his story, especially the credibility of his reform, a matter perhaps made more urgent by the coexistence onstage of rakes who reformed alongside those who did not.[26] Whereas depictions of the realist novel as a bourgeois or domestic form have observed the perpetual association of a sexualized villainy with social power and prestige, they have not identified the fixed depiction of the rake as an aristocrat in novels as a debt to the stage.[27] A hypothetical division of labor could be posited between drama and the novel that assigns problems of representing social status to plays and problems representing credible interior transformation to novels, but confirmation can follow only from a fuller consideration of the generic collaboration between them.

It is also worth noting that the *Man of Mode* ends with Dorimant poised to go off to the country to woo Harriot, the wealthy Lady Woodville's daughter, though he has undergone no overt signs of moral improvement. This conclusion points only ambiguously to some possible future reform through marriage. No such ambiguity plagued the rakes in *Love's Last Shift* (1696) and *The Relapse* (1696): already married, they either reformed or relapsed. In these plays, the capacity of marriage to confer or contain moral improvement was itself incomplete, but the embodiment of moral virtue in women onstage had consequences for the novel's treatment of the convergence of the rake's reform and his marriage.

Loveless, the married rake of Cibber's *Love's Last Shift*, was reformed to virtue by Amanda, his wife. Vanbrugh depicted him ten years later as having relapsed, thereby calling into question the longevity, and therefore also the credibility, of Cibber's representation of reform. At stake in this debate was the moral force of dramatic examples of virtue, a matter that should be considered in relation to the Collier controversy over the reform of the stage even if the plays predated by two years Collier's publication of *A Short View of the Immorality and Profaneness of the English Stage* (1698). Collier made explicit the moral and aesthetic assumptions that Burnet had used in his narrative of Rochester's deathbed conversion: that the convincing demonstration of reform would inspire reform and, conversely, that representations of vice unpunished would promote vicious behavior. These assumptions animated both the playwrights in 1696 and the novelists in 1740 alike.

Burnet's interest in inspiring moral reform was not limited to his exploitation of Rochester's deathbed conversion. The de facto head of the Orange propaganda machine on the eve of the 1688 invasion, Burnet advocated the reform of manners and morals that served, as Tony Claydon persuasively argues, to legitimate William's reign.[28] Although as a nonjuror, Collier was utterly hostile to the legitimacy of the Glorious Revolution, he nevertheless extended to stage manners the program that had originated at William and Mary's court and had filtered out to the rest of the country in the establishment of the Societies for the Reformation of Manners around 1690.[29] As clergymen, both Collier and Burnet actively promoted the reform of licentious behavior such as excessive drinking, carousing, and sexual indulgence, for which Rochester, and his counterpart stage rakes, were taken as convenient emblems.[30] Hume has called into question the use of the Collier controversy to explain the rise of sentimental plays, and others, writing in his wake, have characterized Collier's significance to theater history in other ways.[31] Most recently, Lisa Freeman has affiliated Collier's antitheatricality with other moral panics, both earlier and later, over the changing constitution of "the body public."[32] Collier clearly articulated the theory of aesthetic response underwriting the program of reform, whose application reached beyond satire and was understood to do so by his contemporaries, both playwrights and novelists alike.

For Collier, not only did characters' immorality express authorial immorality; but the very representation onstage of characters whose immorality was not properly punished promoted immorality. Smutty language, lewd applications of scripture, abuse of the clergy, making the top characters libertines, and giving them success in their debauchery: these were the means by which the English stage encouraged vicious behavior.[33] Unless vicious characters were punished and smutty language and immoral behavior expurgated from the stage, plays would not only condone but would also promote the very same bad behavior in their viewers: this monkey-see, monkey-do theory of response to aesthetic en- or discouragement imputes a mimetic force to the aesthetic object. Collier imagined the impact of plays independent of their credibility; they inspired imitation on his account because they attracted emulation regardless of their verisimilitude, realness, or realism. Notwithstanding the literalism of the one-to-one correspondence he drew between onstage examples and offstage imitation, in his concern with response regardless of credibility, he was no outlier. He highlighted the joint implication of the problem of authenticity or authentication, which addressed the question of whether rakish reform really happened, and the problem of realistic or convincing representation, which addressed the question of how reform was presented. Indeed, the extent to which these ultimately came to be successfully pried apart remains a difficult matter to determine, with crucial consequences for aesthetic theory in general and the history of the novel in particular, especially with regard to the hypothetical division of labor between plays' depictions of characters in terms of their social status and novels' depictions of them in terms of their interiorities.

Not only did Steele and Dennis return to the debate over the moral effects of the unreformed rake onstage more than fifteen years after Collier's attack, but the idea persisted all the way to the end of the century that literature had the capacity to promote the behavior it illustrated in readers as well as playgoers. The *Critical Review* warned that *Dangerous Connections*, the English translation of Pierre Choderlos de Laclos's *Les liasons dangereuses*, published in 1784, two years after the French original, was itself "dangerous in a great degree, nor is the poetical justice a sufficient antidote"; and the *Monthly Review* declared, "The pretence of 'instruction' is an insult on the understanding of the Public."[34] Indeed, this idea periodically resurfaces in our own time, even if the focus tends to be screen rather than print media: concerns that watching violence on television, for example, or playing violent videogames produces violent behavior prompt much media coverage as well as studies undertaken in psychology, sociology, and media studies. The relations between the aesthetic and moral force of literary representation and their connections to the kinds of belief they elicit, however, are not matters most fruitfully taken up in the lab that tests cognitive responses to literature, whose confirmation bias about the nature of literature should invite skepticism. Neither the history of the novel alone nor that of antitheatrical discourse can tell us as much as the history of technique, on the one hand, and the history of aesthetic theory, on the other, about the ongoing exchanges between narrative and drama across the media of print, performance, and their cinematic, televisual, or digital mediations.

Yet the history of the novel, and in particular its development of realism, according to Michael McKeon, permitted aesthetics to be separated out from politics, morality, and religion. The aesthetic here maps onto a secularization narrative to which two prior contributions are essential. One grows out of the Collier controversy, which enabled the recognition of the author's property rights. According to McKeon, the literary author could emerge as owner of his or her intellectual property out of the distinction of the author from his or her characters and of satire from libel.[35] More specifically, the separation of the author from his or her characters laid the ground for the determination of degrees and kinds of authorial ethical responsibility in the distinction of satire from libel.[36] The second is the replacement of drama by the novel. At the heart of the aesthetic, according to McKeon, lies a disarticulation of realism from reality enabled by the generic shift. "Drama, not narrative, was the battlefield on which the necessity of representing actuality in literature was challenged and defeated," he has proposed, going on to speculate, "It's as though the theory and practice of the novel first learned the idea of the aesthetic from drama, and then replaced drama as its generic home."[37]

McKeon here describes developments fundamental to the emergence of the literary author and critical to the program of the realist novel. But the account overlooks a number of things. First, realism is only one mode of expression that fiction can take: realism and the aesthetic are not coextensive terms. Second, the replacement of drama by the novel did not happen in the eighteenth century, neither in criticism nor in aesthetic theory nor in authors', readers', and audience members' aesthetic experiences. Third, the detachability of the aesthetic, as the perennial resurgence of moral panics attests, proved reversible. When, in *The Importance of Being Earnest,* Oscar Wilde's Miss Prism tells her ward Cecily that in the novel she has written, "the good ended happily, the bad unhappily. That is what Fiction means," her ridiculous sententiousness ironizes but does not render completely dismissible the perennial desire for poetic justice, which remains persistent in vernacular criticism despite the equally long-standing disdain for its production of mechanical results.[38]

The strange "raies and beams" shooting into Rochester's head, the ostensible vehicles for and outward signs of the rake's reform, mark the limit for restricting the aesthetic to the production of realism. These emanations are one solution to the problem of how to render the experience of reform convincing; the stage and the novels offered others, some more credible than others. Both thus aided in the separation of techniques of virtual realistic representation from questions of actuality, as McKeon argues, and perhaps more centrally, from questions of morality, though, as successive controversies over representing the rake's reform attest, these detachments emerged in neither a linear nor a progressive fashion, nor were they permanently achieved. A messier account that looks at the ongoing relationship between plays and novels provides a richer inventory of representational technique and the contradictions that motivated the development of both.

Plays presented reform as a climactic, often sudden, punctual moment, a coup de théâtre that frequently stressed the limits of dramatic representation, though these could be transcended through performance. Novels, meanwhile, temporally elaborated reform as a matter of development to be delivered as a matter of narrative process. Offering neither performance history nor reader response, the following account of the successive controversies emphasizes instead the ongoing dialogue between the ways reform was scripted in drama and narrated in novels. Rather than seeing them only as alternatives to each other, I demonstrate that questions of aesthetic expression and response in both formats had a provocative logic of their own independent of realism.

REFORMING THE RAKE IN PLAYS

Cibber's *Love's Last Shift* (1696) shared Burnet's and Collier's belief that the stage could function as a vehicle of reform by virtue of what was presented on it. Cibber's rake, Loveless, newly returned to London after ten years of extramarital Continental adventures, is reformed by his wife at the play's climax. Amanda, having disguised herself as a whore to seduce her husband, unveils her true identity and successfully appeals to his sexual satisfaction as well as his pity to reclaim him in a celebration of the sexual pleasures of marriage, now revealed also to include forgiveness.

The play has long been seen as a compromise formation that exploited a desire for titillation even as it trotted out a moral in the end, a view captured by the frequently applied but never attributed "four acts of bawdy, one of reform."

Challenging the identification of Cibber's reform drama as sentimental, however, McGirr has observed the significance he gave to married women's sexuality as the prompt and guarantee of male reform.[39] She thus goes a long way toward redeeming a feminist Cibber from more than a century of neglect. Valuably, she situates the rake's reform in an ensemble of reform in which the fop plays a critical part, a view that holds true for Cibber's other plays, as well as for a significant number of stage comedies about the rake's reform.

Yet by treating Cibber's plays as satirical rather than sentimental, McGirr relies on a strict opposition between satire's appeal to reason and sentiment's appeal to the passions without recognizing the proximity of the two categories that Matthew Kinservik has demonstrated.[40] Furthermore, whereas McGirr argues that Cibber's celebrity depended on his immediacy in performance, notably in his direct appeals to the audience in many asides, prologues, and epilogues, Julia Fawcett has proposed that Cibber's immediacy was an effect produced not so much by self-exposure as by an "over-exposure," a performance in which his "real" self could be held back or evacuated.[41] Cibber's immediacy effects, whether they were mediated by performance or print, flowed from the correspondence he assumed between what was shown onstage and the responses it would have inspired in audiences. Such a correspondence between representation and response can be found in Cibber's writing as well. The *Apology for the Life of Colley Cibber* (1740) established parallels between the amusements Cibber provided at the theaters and the linguistic and textual devices he used to describe them, especially prominent among which were digressions for the purposes of readerly diversion and announced as such. Of this echo effect, Darryl Domingo insightfully observes that Cibber's style is "so similar [to what it describes that] it becomes at times reciprocal."[42] Cibber thus staged on the boards and on the page the connections between morality and aesthetics that Collier made explicit. The formulation of both, in which these connections were depicted as immediate, or not requiring mediation, was contentious.

In *The Relapse*, Vanbrugh was more skeptical than Cibber about the exemplarity of what was presented on the stage. He remained committed to the stage as a vehicle for morality, though he did not agree about the ways it could be transmitted most effectively. As his title signals, Vanbrugh's play called into question the permanence of Loveless's rehabilitation. But his simultaneous critique of and dependency on Cibber can also be seen in his enlargement of the fop Sir Novelty Fashion, a role Cibber wrote for himself in *Love's Last Shift*. Vanbrugh not only gave the fop more prominence in the action but also elevated him to the peerage as Lord Foppington, a role again taken by Cibber. In Vanbrugh's play, as in Cibber's, the fop's extravagance functioned to make the rake look more rather than less socially acceptable. Foppington thus provides an illustration in Susan Staves's "A Few Kind Words for the Fop," where she argues that the figure was an avatar of genteel manners who softened the rake's outsized phallic masculinity.⁴³ But the relation between the fop and the rake was also one way Vanbrugh dramatized his complex relation to Cibber, the whole matter of reform, and how it should be represented.

In the town plot, Foppington cannot manage his own mistress and attempts to make an assignation with Amanda, who boxes his ears, and when he draws his sword in response, he receives a wound from Loveless, the seriousness of which he drastically overestimates; in the country plot, he is duped out of his wife by his younger brother and dunked in the horse pond, which ruins the clothes he has been shown to be so meticulous about. The expensive marriage celebration with which the play ends, a masque featuring a cynical dialogue between Hymen and Cupid, serves to celebrate the younger brother's marriage, with Foppington footing the bill. The fop's excessive and incorrigible investments in style make the rake look more reformable, but Vanbrugh's critique turns on the exposure of this illusion: his rake remained unreformed. The elaboration of the equally unreformed fop was a backhanded gift to Cibber, who got the role of a lifetime in Foppington. By taking marriage as the arena in which reform succeeded or failed, Cibber and Vanbrugh together paved the way for Richardson's fusion of the credibility of reform and the reward of virtue by marriage in *Pamela* and Fielding's critique in *Shamela* and *Joseph Andrews*.

Vanbrugh's skeptical revision of Cibber's play begins with Loveless, having left Amanda in the country to come to London on business, returning to the scene of temptation—the theater. There he has a relapse while watching a play about someone just like himself. Loveless reports to Amanda, "Know then I happened in the play to find my very character, only with the addition of a Relapse, which struck me so, I put a sudden stop to a most harmless entertainment, which till then diverted me between the acts. 'Twas to admire the workmanship of Nature in the face of a young lady that sate some distance from me: she was so exquisitely handsome."⁴⁴ Seeing a play about a relapse, Loveless claims, has chastised him out of his own relapse by forcefully reorienting his attention from what is going on in the theater to what is going on onstage. Despite this testimony to the stage's power to reform, however, Loveless is not reformed. He goes on to have an adulterous affair with the very woman whose beauty he admires from across the room: Berinthia. Loveless's relapse is not prevented by the relapse he sees onstage; ironically, he both imitates the behavior of his character onstage and fails to be improved by this imitation. In this tongue-in-cheek mise-en-abyme, *The Relapse* exposes the failure of the theater to reform its audience.

Collier had singled out Vanbrugh's play as "a Heap of Irregularities," but the failure of Vanbrugh's Loveless to be reformed asserted, against Collier's and

Cibber's one-to-one correspondence between what is shown onstage and what happens in the audience, that one cannot be moved by what does not inspire belief.[45] Like Collier, Vanbrugh was most interested in the play's impact on its audience, though he had a more refined understanding of the mechanisms for eliciting credibility that derived from his recognition of their capacity to fail. The Cibber-Vanbrugh dialogue, in making explicit the limits of staging credible reform, thus contributed to the distinction of a theory of aesthetic response that was most invested in the force or impact of what is represented on behavior, that is, one that judges aesthetics in terms of morality, from a theory of aesthetic form that was most interested in the techniques for eliciting belief regardless of behavior. One example would be the distinction of realism as an aesthetic end in and of itself, though realism would not be the only kind of aesthetic goal that could be so distinguished.[46]

Vanbrugh's Loveless may be a more credible rake for not being reformed, but when his play refers to its own theatricality, audience immersion is interrupted, and the illusion is momentarily destroyed. This self-referentiality mounts a critique of the credibility of the dramatic representation of reform and hence of its exemplary capacities. Revealing Loveless's failure to reform and breaking the theatrical frame at the same time, however, allows questions of morality to resurface, which they continue to do periodically even, and possibly especially, in highly sophisticated realist texts of our own day. This simultaneity brings out the inadequacy of realism to stand for the relations between force and form; it also exposes the error of seeing their extrication as permanently achieved, either by the sophistication of realist techniques in Vanbrugh or in novels or by the theorization of fictionality itself, views put forward by McKeon and Gallagher, respectively; instead it draws attention back to representations of the rake's reform.[47]

Cibber's *The Careless Husband* (1704), his most successful play and another Foppington vehicle, could be understood as a response to Vanbrugh's critique of his capacity to stage believable reform.[48] Identifying the play as a satiric comedy, Cibber thereby signaled his interest in working not only by means of negative example but also by providing a sympathetic model. Kinservik's characterization of the Collier controversy as centrally concerned with the status of satire leads him to explode the opposition of satirical to sentimental drama in the period; the success of both, significantly, is measured by their impact on the audience.[49]

The play features the conversion to virtue of the aptly named Sir Charles Easy in what came to be known as the "steinkirk" scene. Lady Easy, having discovered her husband, with his wig off, and her maid, Edging, in a postcoital snooze, places her steinkirk, a fashionable scarf named after the neckwear worn in a battle the English lost to the French in 1692, over his head to protect him from catching

Figure 2.1. Colley Cibber's *The Careless Husband* (act 5, scene 3) (The British Library Board, source 1084 l.i p. 1)

cold. He awakens, and when he realizes that his wife now knows about but will not reprimand him for his adultery and that she still cares, he repents his libertine ways and reforms (see figure 2.1).

Elizabeth Kowaleski-Wallace, in her analysis of the play, has traced the material history of the steinkirk to argue for the affiliation of Lady Easy with consumer culture; for McGirr, the fact that Lady Easy does not replace the covering for her cleavage attests to the role that married women's sexuality plays in reclaiming rakish husbands to virtue.[50] This reform, however, is also supported by a different kind of stage business.

Having shown Sir Charles asleep, Cibber provides a literalized scene of reform in which the rake physically wakes up to virtue. The sleeping figure, as David Roberts has pointed out, would seem to offer a limit case for theatrical representation.[51] What kind of acting does it take to perform sleep? Is it possible to give a bad performance? Representing unconsciousness, the "sleeping" actor obtains the lowest threshold of performance; he acts in the most minimal fashion and does so ostentatiously. Cibber's embodiment of a less-than-conscious morality is exactly what Pope, following Fielding, who each prized more classical forms of self-knowledge, had excoriated in him.[52] But waking up to virtue also offers a version of seeing the light in Burnet's account of Rochester. Like Rochester's rays, Sir Charles Easy's awakening externalizes and naturalizes an internal process of reform, thus making it accessible to representation. In both the narrative of Rochester's reform and Cibber's play, morality is underwritten by the credibility of the representation, even if neither can be guaranteed.

If the play's fictional status gave it the capacity to deflect the question of credibility, the uncertain authenticity of rakish reform continued to generate skeptical alternatives as if no such deflection had occurred. Though not usually discussed in this context, the *Pamela/Shamela* debate revisited this same territory marked out by the plays associated with the Collier controversy, with both Richardson and Fielding applying to prose fiction the criteria originally generated by and aimed at the stage.[53] If the comparison of reform of the rake plays and novels exposes a generic division of labor between the drama and the novel, it is not one in which theories of aesthetic and moral response are coordinated in plays and elaborated along separate lines in novels, as accounts of novelistic realism would lead us to expect. Instead, *Pamela* and *Shamela* extended into the novel the positions occupied by Cibber and Vanbrugh. Richardson and Fielding's shared goal of writing morally improving and convincing narratives of reform should not be overshadowed by their joint contributions to the distinction of moral force from aesthetic form.

The stage provided a crucial intermediary step in the process of identifying the morality of reform with the credibility of its representation, here seen to be independent of the aesthetics of novelistic realism. The problem that Fielding and Richardson clearly had in mind was the moral impact of the representation of the reform of the rake, and their readers would have recognized this problem from its stage treatments. Fielding pretended to assume that Cibber wrote *Pamela*, as his parody of Cibber's *Apology* in the preface to *Shamela* asserts.[54] Cibber, moreover, recognized the connection between the drama of reform and *Clarissa*: in a characteristic mix of appreciating others and self-promotion, he identified the dramatic roots of *Clarissa* and claimed to have contributed to the characterization of Lovelace in a letter he published about the novel in the *Gentleman's Magazine* (1748) in the persona of "Sir Charles Easy."[55]

Cibber, I am proposing, served as a transformational object for those authors who produced innovative representations of reform in either novels or plays: Vanbrugh, Richardson, Fielding, and later, Burney. The term "transformational object" comes from psychoanalytic theorist Christopher Bollas, of the Independent Group, and it names an object that enables personal growth, including creative or artistic development. Though Bollas describes how engagement with this kind of object works for individuals, nothing in his account precludes its application to groups.[56] In chapter 4, I return to Cibber to track the ways he enabled the novelistic projects of Fielding and Burney, marked by their inclusion of performances of his play *The Provoked Husband* in *Tom Jones* and *The Wanderer*, respectively. The rest of this chapter pursues the treatment of marriage as the measure of the rake's reform in comedies of manners, first in the novels of Richardson and Fielding and then in the hybrid writing of Elizabeth Inchbald. The arena with the highest stakes for sexuality, male as well as female, marriage, even if it could not guarantee male virtue, could nevertheless contain it—or at least readmit those men who strayed. Plays had developed the spectrum of possible types and manners for both sexes even as they articulated the place of wives as the embodiments and arbiters of virtue. Going back to the 1660s, some rakes had settled down to marriage on the stage, and when rakish reform and marriage converged in *Pamela*, Richardson brought these key elements together along with the aesthetics of response developed for the stage.[57] That combination proved critical to his locating at the heart of novel what the critics Nancy Armstrong and Michael McKeon have called "domestic ideology."[58]

READING (AND) THE REFORM OF THE RAKE

Richardson was suspicious of the sudden reform Cibber had staged, though he was sympathetic to the practice of representing reform in order to inspire it. Curiously, he put this critique in Lovelace's mouth when he credited Clarissa with the capacity to reform him, but warned, "Reformation cannot be a *sudden* work."[59] Richardson here seems to claim for the epistolary novel the capacity to demonstrate the steps that, unlike staged representation, may convincingly render gradual mental and emotional processes of transformation. But the speech, which Lovelace utters to Clarissa in a bid to spend more time with her, is reported by her in Letter 116 to Anna Howe, where it occasions her admiration for his self-knowledge. The double-voicedness of the insight thus cannot help but register the dark threat of extending any credibility to Lovelace. Even as Richardson sought to align novelistic realism with moral demonstration, his own editorializing in the second and subsequent editions of *Clarissa* prevents us from taking this as finally or fully achieved, as the persistent re-enactment of the *Pamela* controversy among critics who champion Richardson over Fielding or vice versa until even quite recently suggests.[60] Reading Richardson's novel in the context of the successive controversies over the rake's reform suggests that it is not possible completely to pry apart realism as an aesthetic goal from questions of authenticity and morality. McKeon's depiction of the dialectical relationship between Richardson and Fielding that produced novelistic realism is powerful, but it underestimates the degree to which problems of authenticity and morality continued to be bound up in both Richardson's "naïve empiricism" and Fielding's "extreme skepticism" and overestimates the degree to which the distinction of the aesthetic from other issues was achieved by the novel alone.

In *Pamela*, not only is Mr. B.'s reform predicated on his reading of Pamela's letters and journals, but his reading the same material as the novel's readers read (though at a different pace) is also meant to model "right" reading, that is, the kind of reading that leads to reform. It is worth reserving judgment on the question of whether the transposition of the problem from the stage to the novel is a tacit assertion that the novel is capable of representing the reform that cannot be staged. In any case, the moral claims of Richardson's novel have less to do with its realism than with the delivery of reform by means of reading.

In *Shamela*, Fielding's skeptical critique foregrounds the material status of letters to call into question their capacity to deliver reform: as printed matter, they are subject to falsification, decay, and loss and are thus incapable of guaranteeing right reading. The transparency of letters in Richardson and their status as theatrical props in Fielding thus return to the terms of the earlier stage debate, in which Cibber had presented Loveless's moral reform as exemplary for the spectators of *Love's Last Shift* and Vanbrugh had critiqued it in *The Relapse* by calling into question not only its permanence but also its availability to be imitated credibly. For Richardson, as for Cibber before him, the exemplary content of the story of reform inspired imitation because of the transparency of the medium in which it was delivered; for Fielding, as for Vanbrugh, by contrast, the medium of reform is thickened by self-reference to the medium itself.

Mr. B. reads what we read and is converted to virtue and thus prepared to marry Pamela. Pamela's existence is entirely bound up with her letters, as William Warner and Tassie Gwilliam each observed when they zeroed in on her sewing the cache of letters into her dress.[61] James Grantham Turner has analyzed the intermedial uptake of Richardson's embodiment of the reading experience in *Pamela* without placing sufficient emphasis on his coordination of the content and the experience of reading the letters.[62] In Richardson's representation of reform and his desire to produce it in his readers, he offered the equivalent to Sir Charles Easy's awakening to virtue when he literalized the experience of reading. For Fielding, however, readers bring their own mind-set to the experience of reading independent of the content of what is read: reading can reveal, but it cannot convert.

Fielding exploited the fact that Richardson could not guarantee the experience of reading as reform modeled by Mr. B., using Shamela's letters instead to expose her hypocrisy by describing the discrepancies between her stated and actual intentions and actions. This can best be seen not in the letters in which Fielding parodies Richardson's writing to the moment but in the letters in which Shamela summarizes and evaluates events. In her first letter to her mother after her marriage, Shamela writes,

> Madam,
> In my last I left off at our sitting down to Supper on our Wedding Night,* where I behaved with as much bashfulness as the purest Virgin in the World could have done. The most difficult task was for me to blush; however by holding my breath, and squeezing my Cheeks together with my Handkerchief, I did pretty well.[63]

The asterisk signals a note at the bottom of the page that reads, "This was the Letter which is lost." Fielding here uses the resources of print that Pope and Swift had skillfully exploited to cast doubt on the authority of Richardson's first-person epistolary narrative. He also borrows resources from the stage, such as Shamela's technique for self-induced blushing. Fielding invites us to think of her letters as written from a position "off-stage" or "back-stage," behind her husband's back.[64] Shamela continues, "Well, at last I went to Bed, and my Husband soon leap'd in after me; where I shall only assure you, I acted my part in such a manner, that no Bridegroom was ever better satisfied with his Bride's Virginity. And to confess the Truth, I might have been well enough satisfied too, if I had never been acquainted with Parson Williams."[65] By providing her mother with assurances rather than technical sexual details, Shamela voices an ostensible modesty that parodies the inadvertent titillation that Pamela provides; yet—and this is Fielding's one-two punch—Shamela immediately proceeds "to confess the Truth" that her modesty is entirely false. The satisfaction described is not about truth but instead about sexual pleasure or lack thereof.

Shamela may perform virtue in the fictional world of the novel that Fielding treated metaphorically as a stage, but her "vartue," easily imaginable in performance, is also an effect of reading and, partly, of print. "Vartue" both imitates the sound of her speech and is a visual sign of her illiteracy, a print-based joke that depends on reading. In *Shamela*, Fielding assembled an arsenal of theatrical and print devices; their amalgamation theatricalizes the novel, a project he pursued in his subsequent novels, as I discuss in chapter 3.[66] This kind of theatricalization has a long afterlife: its traces can be found not only in narrators' direct addresses to readers (or even to characters) but also in the presence of letters in dialect in Tobias Smollett's *The Expedition of Humphry Clinker* (1771), Thomas Holcroft's *Anna St. Ives* (1792), and Frances Burney's *Camilla* (1796).

It is worth considering the possibility that in *Shamela*, Fielding was inspired to critique the transparency of Pamela's letters as the vehicle of Mr. B.'s reform not only by Vanbrugh's similarly skeptical critique of the inspiring behavior Cibber's Loveless transparently transmitted to the play's audiences when he reformed but also by Lord Foppington. Unusually, Vanbrugh had scripted into *The Relapse* the character's distinctive comic pronunciation, inspired, perhaps, by Cibber's performance of the role in his own play. In Vanbrugh, this verbal tic reaches ridiculous proportions when Foppington's brother, Young Fashion, reads aloud a letter in his accent, as if he had written it that way: "'Tis possible I may be in Tawne as soon as this letter . . ."[67] The joke about Foppington's writing may be only secondary to Young Fashion's caricature of his brother's speech, but the absurdity of writing with an accent is emphasized when the play is read. Behind Shamela's "vartue" lies not only Cibber's performance of Foppington but also Fielding's reading of Vanbrugh's play.

Meanwhile, Eliza Haywood's *Anti-Pamela* (1741), which makes the same critique of Richardson as did Fielding, that underneath Pamela's appearance of virtue lay a duplicitous whore, also clarifies the moral status of epistolary fiction. Like *Shamela*, the backbone of *Anti-Pamela* consists of letters from Syrena Tricksy to her mother describing her adventures, but these letters are framed by a narrator who intermittently provides readers with key pieces of information. Haywood's mixed narrative mode shares Fielding's critique at the same time as it embraces Richardson's notion that reading inspires reform. Haywood seems to have exhausted the capacity of letters to represent Syrena's hypocrisy before she reached the end of her interest in Syrena's degeneration. Though letters remain a vehicle for both Syrena's seductions and her exposure, with the occasion of their publication making up part of the novel's plot, Haywood augmented them by a third-person narrator whose breathless delivery of a variety of seduction scenarios would have struck her many readers as familiar from the wildly successful *Love in Excess*. In the novel's second half, this narrator often turns to address readers directly with moralizing comments on Syrena's behavior. When Syrena fails in the end to snag a rich husband or, indeed, any husband at all and is banished from polite society, Haywood's transformation of Richardson's subtitle "Virtue Rewarded" to "Feign'd Innocence detected" is complete. Tom Keymer and Peter Sabor point out the change in audience from Richardson, who aimed to cultivate "the principles of Virtue and Religion in the Minds of the Youth of Both Sexes," to Haywood, who published "as a necessary Caution to all young Gentlemen."[68] Haywood used the narrative-epistolary combination to produce a more accurate morality tale out of Richardson's materials by asserting the abundance of Syrenas and the rarity of Pamelas. She thus shared with Fielding the critique of Richardson's morals on the grounds of probability. Like Richardson, however, she accepted exemplary reading as a vehicle of reform; unlike him, she located her faith in the moralizing capacity of fiction through the force of negative rather than positive example. Pamela's virtue and Syrena's vice are both transparently accessible through their letters, and both can reform, or so their authors believed, the first by providing a role model and the second by providing a counterexample that, with the aid of a narrator, also functions as exposé.

Although Fielding was equally interested in the moral improvement of his audience, he did not think improvement or reform could be achieved this way. Shamela's letters reveal her nature but not because they are transparent vehicles of (either her or his) authorial control; rather, her self-expression occurs in a context that periodically calls its own access to truth into question. It is not just that Shamela really is a whore; Fielding would also have us question the access of letters, or any representation, to the truth of her nature. This is what William Empson dubbed Fielding's "double irony" and McKeon his "extreme skepticism."[69] McKeon's formulations teach us that Richardson's empiricism and Fielding's skepticism are expressed but not exhausted by the differences between a first- and third-person narrator, which is confirmed by the example of Haywood's mix of epistolary and omniscient narration.

Though Fielding was skeptical of the novel's ability to inculcate morality by the kind of reading modeled by Richardson in Mr. B., he nevertheless retained intact Richardson's transfer of aesthetic theory from the theater to the novel. Fielding's assertion that Pamela is a sham amplifies Vanbrugh's skepticism about the possibilities for representing the rewards of either virtue or reform. For Vanbrugh, as for Fielding, virtue is its own reward, as Worthy recognizes in the last act of *The Relapse*, when Amanda resists his seductions. That this has its own erotic logic can be seen in the ambiguity of Worthy's last speech, in which he simultaneously renounces his sexual interest in her and defers to another time his attempt to seduce her.

After having declared, "There's Divinity about her," which has transformed "the wild flame of Love, the Vile, the gross desires of Flesh and Blood" into an adoration that suspends physical desire, at least temporarily, Worthy breaks into rhymed verse:

Cou'd Women but our secret Councils scan,
Cou'd they but reach the deep reserves of Man,

> They'd wear it on, that that of Love might last,
> For when they throw off one, we soon the other Cast.
> Their Sympathy is such ———
> The Fate of one, the other scarce can fly;
> They live together, and together dye.[70]

Alone on the stage, Worthy addresses the men in the audience, by means of which he enjoins the women to follow Amanda's example: by wearing the robes of virtue, they will prolong love. Like the line that breaks off, however, Worthy's reform cannot be sustained: after the dash, his speech devolves into double entendre. Extending the metaphor of casting off the clothing of virtue, his final words cannot avoid conjuring a scene of naked sexual bliss. They recall the earlier scene in which Loveless carries Berinthia offstage to bed over her quiet protestation of virtue as she whispers, "very softly," as the stage directions tell us, "Help! I am ravished."[71] Loveless's lie to Amanda about how the theater prevented his relapse provides another example of the same dynamic. Reform is not demonstrable for either Fielding or Vanbrugh, since its very display is perverse—even more perverse than adultery.

Indeed, Fielding can harness the pleasures of aesthetic response to morally improving ends, as the end of *Joseph Andrews* shows. In an homage to the stage tradition of scenes in bed that, at the same time, reveals the limitations of what can be shown onstage, Fielding both veils and unveils Joseph and Fanny naked in their nuptial bed. After their wedding ceremony, Fanny undresses. "How, Reader," proclaims Fielding's narrator, "shall I give thee an adequate Idea of this lovely young Creature!" Words will not suffice, and the narrator invites readers to picture Fanny herself. "Joseph, no sooner heard she was in Bed, than he fled with the utmost Eagerness to her. A Minute carried him into her Arms, where we shall leave this happy Couple to enjoy the private Rewards of their Constancy."[72] Fielding ostentatiously avoids describing what he might consider to be a Richardsonian scene of prurience by turning us away from Fanny and Joseph's privacy. The narrator's interruptions of readers' attention by means of the direct address, or by turning our heads away from the scene, direct us toward the natural perfections of the naked couple that cannot or will not be described. Like Vanbrugh's Loveless's moment of self-referentiality or Worthy's arrested line, Fielding's narrator's direct address points to domestic problems or erotic pleasures (the unreformable rake or the sexual intercourse of Fanny and Joseph) by exposing their limited access to description. The private or domestic at the moment of moral crisis or reward is located at the threshold of realism; it can only be indicated by pointing.

Fielding's skepticism was not directed toward reading as a source of moral improvement but toward its capacity to be modeled so that it produced moral improvement in readers. Instead of avatars, he provided readers with regular interruption by means of narratorial intrusions, inset narratives, and every other device he could think of to make readers aware that they were reading. He thus presented self-conscious, as opposed to immersive, reading as a moral good in and of itself, a form of active mental self-interrogation as a prerequisite to moral action.[73] These interruptive techniques served both of Fielding's goals at once: to deliver the skeptical critique at the same time as they directed the reading experience.

Neither Richardson nor Fielding exhausted his interest in the reform of the rake (or lack thereof) with *Pamela*, *Shamela*, and *Joseph Andrews*; indeed, in *Clarissa* and *Tom Jones*, both revisited the plot and its problems. Though Fielding's novels are too episodic ultimately to be contained by the category of the comedy of manners, in addition to the reform of the rake plot, they also display other ways of adapting theatrical elements to narrative form that I describe in chapter 3. The convergence of the reform of the rake plot with marriage in *Pamela* supports its identification as a comedy of manners, especially considering Richardson's influence on Frances Burney and Jane Austen, though ultimately, it too has significant features that distinguish it. Curiously, these divergences crystallize when *Pamela* and *Clarissa* are compared to their dramatic adaptation by others, which I also discuss more fully in chapter 3. Naturally these adaptations for the stage strip their sources of epistolary form; they also highlight two other features independent of formal realism.

First, Goldoni's disclosure of Pamela's aristocratic birth contrasts and thereby serves to emphasize Richardson's commitment to bringing together high and low, as Lynn Festa has pointed out.[74] Richardson may not depict a range of behavior styles and social levels in *Pamela*, as do the stage comedies of manners, to assemble an inventory of true wit or politeness, but his conjoining of high and low can be as readily associated with the wishfulness of romance as with novelistic realism. Second, marriage is not on the horizon in *Pamela*, given in advance to determine the shape of events; instead it emerges as a solution to a plot interested in other problems—at least initially. Entirely expected in the comedy of manners, the surprise of the marriage solution in *Pamela* not only expresses Pamela's naivety, perhaps in order to ward off critiques like Fielding's, but also, more importantly, is a symptom of the novel's innovative harmonizing of older expectations, including that the rake will reform, with newer possibilities for narrating the reward of virtue, as promised by the novel's subtitle. Readers' complaints about the novel's inability properly to capture the rhythms of genteel speech, on the one hand, and objections to Pamela's supposed aspirations as a social-climbing schemer, on the other, attest to Richardson's radical reorientation of the stage comedy of manners that accompanies the features for which his novel is usually celebrated: the exploitation of the materiality of print in the first-person voice of a lowly servant girl.[75] Appreciating the radical characteristics of Richardson's novel independent of their affiliation with its formal realism also brings out a key difference between Richardson and some of his female heirs as the comedy of manners completes its migration to the novel.

In many critical analyses of Richardson's achievement, he resembles Keats's eagle-eyed Cortez surveying the Pacific, the space the novel will come to occupy, yet domestic fiction written by the women who took up his mantle, including Frances Burney, Elizabeth Inchbald, and Jane Austen, fits more comfortably than his own does under the rubric of the comedy of manners. In part, this is because their novels were invested in social panoramas, vast ones like Burney's or tiny ones like Austen's; in part, it is because they did not sustain marriage as a surprise, though they retained it as the resolution—and perhaps they could not because marriage was so intimately bound up with female destiny in the period. Later chapters are devoted to Burney's and Austen's theatrical narrative strategies as they contribute to the development of female bildungsroman; in the remainder of this chapter, however, I look at Inchbald's handling of the rake's reform onstage and in her novel *A Simple Story* (1791) in order to track her inheritance of the plot from the tradition of stage comedy as it came to be filtered through Richardson.

THE REFORM OF THE RAKE AT THE END OF THE CENTURY

Between 1745 and 1767, *Love's Last Shift*, *The Relapse*, and *The Careless Husband* were performed regularly on the London stage. The first all but disappeared from the repertory between 1768 and 1800; Richard Brinsley Sheridan's hugely popular *A Trip to Scarborough* (1777) dropped the Amanda-Loveless plot from *The Relapse* and reoriented the action around Foppington's country courtship. *The Careless Husband*, however, continued to be staged intermittently, and of the three plays mentioned, only it was included in the twenty-five-volume collection of plays "as acted" that Inchbald edited for Longmans: *The British Theatre* (1806–1809). Yet the reform of the rake plot featured regularly in her own comedies *I'll Tell You What* (1785), *Every One Has His Fault* (1793), and *The Wedding Day* (1794). She most fully exploited its conventionality for comic effect when she had Bronzely, the rake of her last original play, *Wives as They Were, Maids as They Are* (1797), say, "I always make love to every woman in the house [because] they all expect it."[76] That play concludes with two weddings and four reforms. Not only does the rake of the play reform; so do the other men: Lord Priory, the patriarchal husband of the woman Bronzely has attempted to seduce; Mr. Dorrillon, the father of the lead maid; and Sir George Evelyn, her fiancé.

The multiplication of reform in *Wives as They Were* has proven troubling to critics. Paula Backscheider, Misty Anderson, and Daniel O'Quinn have not agreed on how to read the play's ending. Backscheider sees the patriarchs as having been sufficiently chastised by the outcome of the rake's reform to make the marriages with which the play ends more palatable; for Anderson, by contrast, the play turns on the joke "that there is no joke that can moderate the power of husbands and fathers."[77] O'Quinn proposes an intermediary solution, suggesting that Inchbald's recommendation of a modified patriarchal marriage stems from her treatment of virtuous women as the site of ethical value in their capacity not only to reform but also to harmonize ancient and modern mores.[78] As this critical discussion suggests, the exemplary moral force of the rake's reform has here taken on the political coloration of Inchbald's Jacobin feminism.

But the abundant flow of male reform prompted by that of the rake also reflects the influence of *A Simple Story*, Inchbald's first novel, in which she had explored two plot novelties: the possibility of a female rake in Miss Milner and the extension of the story of reform to a nonrakish man in Dorriforth/Elmwood, the husband/father. An appreciation of the theatricality of *A Simple Story* helps to clarify the novelistic aspects of her play. Indeed, the hybridity of Inchbald's treatment of the reform of the rake plot in both her novel and her play requires careful consideration if we are to understand the status that questions of moral exemplarity and its representation onstage or in novels continued to have in the new configuration of the relation between reading (novels or plays) and seeing performances at the end of the century. Inchbald constructs complex experiences of temporality that address the ongoing significance of the past in the present in both the play and the novel; these reflect the convergent concerns of the genres even as they also register the divergent media capacities of reading and performance.

Terry Castle has observed Inchbald's self-consciousness about the rake's conventionality in Miss Milner's reflection, upon being questioned about her coquettish behavior by Miss Woodley, that loving a rake has become simply too cliché.[79]

What, love a rake, a man of professed gallantry? impossible.—To me a rake is as odious, as a common prostitute is to a man of the nicest feelings—Where can be the pride of inspiring a passion, fifty others can equally inspire? or the transport of bestowing favours, where the appetite is already cloyed by fruition of the self-same enjoyments? [P]ut in

> competition the languid love of a debauchée, with the vivid affection of a
> sober man, and judge which has the dominion? Oh! In my calendar of
> love, a solemn lord chief justice, or a devout archbishop ranks before a
> licentious king.[80]

The rake's ubiquity across the theatrical repertory and in novels, here casually associated with the prototypically licentious monarch, Charles II, underwrites the
rakish Miss Milner's setting her sights instead on her guardian, Dorriforth, a Catholic priest. He undergoes a double transformation, first into her husband and
then from too severe into loving father to their child, Matilda.

A hiatus of seventeen years separates Dorriforth's two reforms, each of which
is treated in its own volume. Critics have ascribed the abrupt shift between the
two parts to Inchbald's composition of the novel at two distinct periods in her
life.[81] The conjunction of her biography with the greater appeal of the racy first
half of the novel over its moralizing second half, with its fairy-tale plot echoes and
repetitions, has made it easy to overlook the novel's coherence, which lies in the
hybrid nature of her writing. The short first chapter of the novel's second half lists
the key changes of the intervening years; the next chapter begins with the same
intensive and close focus on characters' emotional interactions offered in the first
half of the novel. Although the capacity to handle an elaborated temporality in
minute detail would seem to suit the novel better than the stage for the representation of development, especially after Richardson, Inchbald opted instead for a
narrative equivalent of an act drop, the lowering of the curtain between acts that
had come into theatrical practice in the middle of the eighteenth century. Moreover, the compressed replay of the plot of a man reformed by love of a woman is
reinforced by Matilda's extreme physical resemblance to her mother.[82]

The novel's ending offers another view of the hybridity of Inchbald's writing:
Matilda's marriage to Rushbrook, the man whom her father had named heir to the
estate, can only be realized by readers' surmise. "Whether the heart of Matilda,
such as it has been described, could sentence him to misery, readers are left to
surmise—and if he supposes that it did not, he has every reason to suppose their
wedded life was a life of happiness."[83] This appeal to readers explores the representational capacity of the novel to go beyond the conventional ending of stage comedy
in marriage. Readers are engaged to surmise and imaginatively project Matilda
sentencing Rushbrook to misery by refusing his offer before accepting, presumably
with vicarious joy and relief, precisely that conventional marriage ending.

A Simple Story actually ends two sentences later by recommending a proper
education for women as well as men. Inchbald's invitation to readers to project
beyond the book's end operates, on the one hand, like an epilogue to a play inso

far as the narrator appears after the end of the action to wrap things up. Yet the narrator's address is also novelistic insofar as it adapts Fielding's technique of directly addressing readers even as it also makes explicit a Richardsonian program of reading as an engine of (female) pedagogy.[84] The kind of education provided by reading permits an imagining of Matilda as both daughter and wife; she is thereby contrasted to her poorly trained mother. Education by reading retrospectively contains and neutralizes the incestuous overtones the novel had explored first in Miss Milner's seduction of Dorriforth, her guardian, into her husband and then in Dorriforth/Elmwood's aversion to the sight of his daughter, who looks too much like his wife.

Inchbald had used a tableau for the climactic scene that inaugurated Dorriforth/Elmwood's transformation from obdurate into loving father. Horrified that he has seen her, Matilda faints into his arms.

> When he found her in his arms, he still held her there—gazed on her attentively—and once pressed her to his bosom.
>
> He was going to leave her on the spot where she fell, when her eyes opened and she uttered, "Save me."—Her voice unmanned him—His long-restrained tears now burst forth—and seeing her relapsing into the swoon again, he cried out eagerly to recall her—Her name did not however come to his recollection—nor any name but this—"Miss Milner—Dear Miss Milner."[85]

Others have observed that this tableau reflects Inchbald's experiences of the stage first as an actress and then a playwright; along with the act drop and the epilogue, the novel adapts stage techniques to narrate moments of emotional intensity.[86] Yet the novelistic aspects of *Wives as They Were* have not been described before. The scene of Bronzely's reform at the hands of Lady Priory, the patriarchal wife, which prompts the rest of the men's reform, provides the best dramatic example of Inchbald's hybrid style.

Bronzely has brought Lady Priory to his home in order to try her virtue—with her husband's permission. At first he presents himself as providing her with the opportunity to revenge herself on her ungrateful husband. When she rejects this as a bad bargain since she will only be trading in one tyrannical man for another, he attempts to rouse her terror. Upon hearing that she "is in a lonely house where [he is] the sole master and all the servants slaves to [his] will," she, as the stage directions indicate, "calmly takes out her knitting, draws a chair and sits down to knit a pair of stockings."[87] Lady Priory's unflappability not only reverses the expectations of an audience that had consumed plays and novels about rakes, including Gothics in which the woman is always terrified, but also shocks Bronzely: he is

Figure 2.2. Pierre-Etienne Lesueur, *Les Tricoteuses Jacobines* (The Jacobin Knitters, 1793)

oddly cowed, both awed and embarrassed by her calm, sustained, productive activity. His response to her knitting registers its complexity as an emblem of female power in which the novelistic domesticity of a Pamela or a Clarissa cannot be separated from the threatening specter of the revolutionary *tricoteuses*, the women who were only allowed to attend the executions during the Terror if they also engaged in domestic duties (see figure 2.2).[88]

Here Inchbald reverses the temporal valences placed on the old-fashioned wife and the fashionable seducer. Unlike two of Lesueur's knitters, who gaze avidly at the execution by guillotine, however, Inchbald wife perhaps resembles more closely the third one who looks calmly out at the viewer. Inchbald thus proposes to synthesize Jacobin feminism with a kindlier female domesticity in the figure of the knitting wife, whose usual bodily posture (head inclined, hands busy), though not depicted in this print, can readily also be associated with reading. The excessive male reform that the wife prompts, in Inchbald's coup de théâtre, thereby relegates the rake to the past of the ancien régime and the Restoration stage.

In Inchbald's remarks on Cibber's *The Careless Husband* in *The British Theatre*, she had proposed that the play had more of an impact in the reading than in the staging: its gestures and occurrences are "of that delicate, as well as probable kind, [that make] their effect not sufficiently powerful in the representation— whereas in the reading, they come to the heart with infinitely more force, for want of that extravagance, which public exhibition requires."[89] This oblique reference to the delicate scene of Sir Charles Easy's reform, with its dependence on gestures like the wife's covering of the husband's head so that he can awaken to virtue, conveys Inchbald's awareness that the audience for plays, as well as for drama anthologies, consisted of not just any readers but novel readers. Her remarks signal the extent to which Collier had triumphed: with the licentiousness of the "rakish stage" consigned to the past and unreformed rakes no longer represented on the stage, even reformed rakes were best understood by reading. But she also translated Cibber's play into novelistic terms for theatrical purposes, as can be seen in the gestural language she used to stage reform: in the wife's silent knitting, Inchbald provided an emblem whose emotional power was amplified for an audience of readers of Richardson.

Denis Diderot had wished for a name other than "novel" for "the works of Richardson, which raise the spirit [and] touch the heart," even going so far as to call *Pamela*, *Clarissa*, and *Grandison* three great dramas in his *Eloge de Richardson* (1762).[90] Diderot thus registered that Richardson had captured the aesthetic and moral force of the theater for the novel. Like Diderot, Inchbald was interested in translating back onto the stage Richardson's achievement in the genre of private reading that moves the heart. Like Diderot, she used the stage to critique the ancien régime, reaching out to the novel for the means to distance her plays from the aristocratic and patriarchal norms embedded in the theater's conventions to reinvent drama for a bourgeois novel-reading audience. She availed herself of the plot innovations that the novel supplied for the stage, translating the narration of development that could take Richardson volumes into dramatic moments of sustained or suspended action that speak to the heart. The hybridity of her work yielded new techniques for representing temporality and necessity in both the drama and the novel. Inchbald's oeuvre thereby calls into question the narrative of generic progression in which drama cedes its place to the novel.

The strange title of the play, *Wives as They Were, Maid as They Are*, with its suggestion that women can occupy different temporalities and thus harmonize, as O'Quinn has suggested, otherwise irreconcilable values, points to the resolution that Inchbald found in the serial representation of maidenhood and wifedom in both the novel and the play. Reversing the usual sequence from maidenhood to wifedom, the play's title highlights that in the unfolding of time, the past may be succeeded by the present just as "were" gives way to "are," but newer values will not always supersede older ones. Capturing the logic of the repertory itself, the title projects not the replacement of maids by wives but rather their coexistence: coquettish maids who gamble may nevertheless make dutiful wives and may even, the play seems to suggest, become the better wives for their youthful exploration of limits. The abundance of male reform in the play's conclusion thus embraces the promise of this compromise even as its contagion also underlines male reform as stage magic, indeed, wish-fulfillment.

For Christina Lupton, the future that Inchbald is able to project in *A Simple Story* derives from the contrast she draws between the mother and the daughter as readers, which amplifies the novel's strange temporality. For Lupton, Inchbald's novel reflects the promise it holds out as a book to be read in the world.[91] But just as Inchbald pushes readers to imagine beyond the ending of *A Simple Story*, so she does in *Wives as They Were*. In her remarks on her own play, Inchbald drew attention to the resemblance between Miss Dorrillon, the play's main maid, and Miss Milner, though she also highlighted their differences. Though, like Miss Milner, Miss Dorrillon is witty, flirty, and seductive, she is granted a happy marriage with the prospects of some financial independence, whereas Miss Milner, having committed adultery after marrying Dorriforth/Elmwood, must die. When Mr. Dorrillon, in disguise as the nabob Mr. Mandred, goes to visit his daughter in debtors' prison, he first offers her one thousand pounds if she will give up gambling or go to live in the country. But he drops these conditions, pays her debts, and reveals himself to her, having come to recognize her essential good nature when she wishes that money could be made available to her father, whom she believes to be impoverished and still in India. Inchbald does not mention it, but in reforming her father, Miss Dorrillon is also like Matilda, though her happiness exceeds Matilda's as well. In contrast to Matilda, however, who must marry Rushbrook, the cousin who has taken her place as her father's heir, when Miss Dorrillon accepts the "milder government" of marriage to Sir George Evelyn, audiences wondering what happened to the one thousand pounds could assume that in marrying with her father's approval, she would receive a generous settlement and not be as utterly dependent a wife as Miss Milner, Matilda, or Lady Priory. Inchbald's play would have been read as well as seen in performance, and the looping temporality that Lupton associates with reading the novel would also have been produced by the play consumed either way. The kind of future Inchbald projects may thus be more the by-product of literature than of the experience of reading print that Lupton supposes.

With the play's female embodiment of virtue, *Wives as They Were* indicates the state of the comedy of manners onstage at the end of the century, but *A Simple Story* cannot be said to do so for the novel. Better examples would be Burney's *Evelina* (1778), whose epistolary narration cannot obscure its theatricality and whose fusion of manners and morals is elaborated in her later novels across increasingly wide social panoramas, and any of Jane Austen's major novels (as I discuss in chapters 4 and 5). Yet Inchbald's hybrid techniques for representing temporality and necessity survived not only in her second novel, *Nature and Art* (1796), but also in Godwin's *Caleb Williams* (1794). The tree that represents domestic fiction as it grew into female bildungsroman had roots in the stage comedy of manners, but the contributions of Inchbald's theatricality branched off in melodrama (as I discuss in chapter 5).[92]

More than 150 years after Rochester's death, Charlotte Brontë made the rake's reform central to the conclusion of her 1847 novel *Jane Eyre*. "Reader, I married him": Jane marries Rochester, the aristocratic rake, because presumably he has reformed and not merely been reduced by his crippling experience in the fire. The credibility of his reform, avouched in marriage though open to question at least in my students' minds, is presented in Jane's direct address to readers, which fuses the first-person female narrator that the history of the novel associates with Richardson with the technique of narrative interruption by an omniscient narrator that it associates with Fielding.[93] With this narrative innovation, Brontë can represent the culminating point in this history of the comedy of manners. Recapitulating the problem of the rake's reform, its credibility and morality now depend wholly on Jane, who here interrupts to remind readers of the novel they hold in their hands.

I N "ELOGE DE RICHARDSON" (In praise of Richardson, 1761), Denis Diderot described the great novelist's achievement in terms of the theater:

> O Richardson! On prend malgré qu'on en ait, un rôle dans ses ouvrages, on se mêle a la conversation, on approuve, on blame, on admire, on s'irrite, ou s'indigne. Combien de fois ne me suis-je pas surprise, comme il est arrivé des enfants qu'on avait menés au spectacle pour le premier fois. . . . J'étais devenu spectateur d'un multitude d'incidents.[1]
> [O Richardson! Whether we wish to or not, we participate in your works, we intervene in conversations, we approve, blame, admire, feel irritation or indignation. Many a time I have caught myself, as it happens to children taken to the theater for the first time. . . . I had become the spectator of a multitude of incidents.]

Many critics since Diderot have appreciated the drama of Richardson's novels. Its presence was so overwhelming that it led Mark Kinkead-Weekes, one of its most insightful analysts, to reverse the usual contrast between Richardson and Fielding: "The paradox then is that it is Richardson and not Fielding who is the dramatist."[2] The opposition of Richardson to Fielding at the heart of the history of the English novel, however, has distorted the perception of the ways that theater shaped the conditions of possibility for both novelists.

In Diderot's comparing himself to a child at the theater for the first time or describing his involvement with Richardson's book as that of a participant, a witnessing spectator more than a neutral observer, he proposed that Richardson's novels produced an ideal theater in which one became so involved that one forgot where one was. Fielding repudiated this sort of immersion, seeking instead to keep readers conscious of their imaginative engagement by an assemblage of narrative techniques designed to interrupt it, techniques that were theatrical not only because they were inspired by his experiences in the actual theater as a playwright and stage manager but also because they aimed to remind us that to read fiction was to enter a mental theater and that both to enjoy and benefit from it fully was to retain an awareness of that imaginary location. Though the narrative achievements of both can be understood in terms of the theater, the opposition of Richardson to Fielding and the equation of the history of the novel with the history of realism in the dominant accounts of the novel since Ian Watt have often conspired to make Richardson look downright antitheatrical.[3]

But Tom Keymer has discerned in the worry about going to the theater expressed in the early *Vade Mecum*, Richardson's handbook for apprentices, a civic orientation aimed at increasing their productivity rather than an attack on the theater per se.[4] And as Ros Ballaster has pointed out, Pamela may worry about theatrical mimesis in the novel's second part, but her letters to Lady Davers also report on London theatrical culture, thus revealing it to be one of the "twin 'sources' for the novel."[5] Pages of *Clarissa* and *Sir Charles Grandison* consist of dialogue laid out in play-like fashion, with stage directions but no name tags.[6] Dramatic adaptations of *Pamela* and *Clarissa* in England and on the Continent attest to the fact that many of Richardson's eighteenth-century readers understood him in relation to the theater. Just as the rivalry between the two novelists has led critics to overestimate Richardson's antitheatricality, so it also has induced them to overlook the function of letters in Fielding.

Letters belong in the arsenal of interruptive narrative techniques that Fielding used in *Joseph Andrews*, *Tom Jones*, and *Amelia*, where they can take their place among the more familiar devices: addresses of the narrator to readers, inset narratives, and the suppression of key details that reverse the moment-by-moment unfolding of the plot associated with Richardson's writing "to the moment." Though Fielding's use of letters in novels is anti-Richardsonian, its roots in his previous theatrical practice can bring out the theatrical aspects of Richardson's own epistolarity. Albert J. Rivero has argued rightly that Fielding's plays should not be seen as interesting only as prelude to his accomplishments in the novels.[7] Disclosing the consistent function of letters across Fielding's plays and novels does not subordinate his theatrical to his novelistic achievement but rather illustrates the continuities across them, inviting a recasting of his narrative techniques not in terms of realism but in terms of theatrical influence.

Fielding's letters, alongside dramatic adaptations of Richardson's novels, also prompt a re-evaluation of Richardson's narration. To see the dramatic aspects of both novelists provides a way to mitigate the force of their opposition, a significant factor in the decline of Fielding's critical fortunes, according to Robert D.

Hume.[8] Michael McKeon has depicted Richardson and Fielding as having contributed dialectically to the crystallization of the English novel as a genre.[9] In McKeon's account, Fielding is conservative and Richardson progressive for many reasons, paramount among which is their novels' different interests in the ordinary. Richardson's investment of virtue in the maidservant Pamela, for which she is rewarded and elevated, is of critical importance to the ideological contrast, since the reward of Fielding's characters tends to involve coincidence and other forms of wish-fulfillment deriving from romance in which they are restored to the good fortunes they deserve based on birth. But Fielding's interest in the ordinary is expressed in setting, rather than character, in both the novels and the plays, which McKeon ignores. From the range of inns that Joseph Andrews and Tom Jones visit to Parson Trulliber's pigsty to the prison in *Amelia*, characters from across the social spectrum interact in a range of ordinary, if not low, locations, both rural and urban. Many plays are set in Grub Street, as well as in various underworlds below the ordinary, both literal and mythological, such as the brothel of *The Covent Garden Tragedy* and the Hades of *Eurydice*. McKeon is right to characterize the relationship between Richardson and Fielding as dialectical, but by describing the results of their collaboration in immanent literary rather than ideological terms, we can restore to view some of Fielding's overlooked contributions. Disclosing the significance of the theater at the heart of the history of the novel supplies an account of narrative features overshadowed by a fixation on realism that has granted oversized importance to the interpretive category of character and produced misleading accounts of the modes of identification and embodiment it supposedly elicits.

LETTERS IN FIELDING'S PLAYS

Considering Fielding's initial response to *Pamela*, it should not be surprising to discover his hostility toward letter-writing in general. "For my own part, I solemnly declare, I can never give Man nor Woman with whom I have no Business (which the Satisfaction of Lust may well be called) a more certain token of a violent Affection, than by writing to them, an Exercise which, notwithstanding, I have in my time printed a few Pages, I so much detest, that I believe it is not in the Power of three Persons to expose my epistolary Correspondence."[10] Of the seventy extant letters in Fielding's correspondence, the fewest among eighteenth-century biographical subjects, Martin Battestin observes with frustration, "most of them [are] short, perfunctory and dull."[11] Moreover, they have been ignored by all but his biographer. By contrast, a full scholarly edition of Richardson's voluminous correspondence is projected to appear in twelve volumes and has received editorial, biographical, and critical attention.[12] Yet, ironically, Fielding's use of letters plays a crucial role in both his plays and his novels.

Alan Stewart has pointed out that letters were the most common stage property in the Renaissance and a stock plot device for bringing news from abroad or elsewhere into the action. He has suggested that letters might also have functioned as a sort of crib sheet for actors in need of a prompt.[13] These functions persisted on the Restoration stage, where letters also acquired a further use: letters of assignation, especially those that women inappropriately write to men, regularly fall into the hands of husbands or fathers to provide convenient engines of plot in comedies. Insofar as they can be forged, misdirected, and intercepted, they further intrigues, yet insofar as they can be produced as documents that verify the true intentions and identities of their writers, they also provide resolution. Fielding was not the first to observe the double capacity of letters, but he fully exploited it as a paradox.

Letters appear in many of Fielding's plays, including *Love in Several Masques* (1728), *The Temple Beau* (1730), *Rape upon Rape*, later called *The Coffee House Politician* (1730), and *The Old Debauchees* (1732), in which Jourdain, one of the titular debauchees, confesses among his sins having sent himself a love letter like Petulant does in Congreve's *Way of the World* (1700), though he has done so not to enhance his own reputation as a lover but to ruin that of the woman.[14] Letters sometimes appear in scenes of composition. In *Love in Several Masques*, Lady Trap tricks the ingénue Helena into writing a letter to Meritol, thus setting up an assignation she later attends disguised as the younger woman (act 2, scene 9; act 3, scene 13).[15] Fielding here telescopes a number of scenes from William Wycherley's *Country Wife* (1675): one, in which Pinchwife, having discovered Margery writing to Horner, dictates a letter of rejection into which she nevertheless manages to smuggle her own declaration of love (act 4, scenes 3–4); and another, in which Margery persuades him that another letter to Horner is one she has written on Alithea's behalf, and he, accordingly, helps to set up an assignation between Alithea and Horner that Margery will attend disguised as her sister-in-law (act 5, scene 1). Wycherley's play is on Helena's mind, as Tiffany Potter has pointed out, when she tells her uncle that she knows how dangerous a china shop can be.[16]

More often than letters' composition, plays treat their receptions, which frequently involves their being read aloud. Fielding's *The Universal Gallant* (1735), like Sir George Etherege's *Man of Mode; or, Sir Fopling Flutter* (1676), opens with Mr. Mondish, a latter-day Dorimant, reading aloud a letter from a mistress about the end of their affair. Fielding also uses letters incidentally in *The Author's Farce* (1730) and *A Wedding Day* (1743). Though handwritten rather than printed, letters belong among the other material artifacts of the literary public sphere, the vehicle for much of the satire of the self-referential plays, including *The Author's Farce*, *The Tragedy of Tragedies* (1731), *Pasquin* (1736), and *The Historical Register and Eurydice Hiss'd* (1737).

Among the other conventions of the Restoration stage Fielding inherited and retooled for the 1730s, Potter has emphasized his development of a kinder, gentler version of late seventeenth-century libertinism that finds fullest expression in the "natural sexuality" of *Tom Jones*.[17] But alongside philosophy, politics, and gender ideology, it is crucial also to bear in mind Fielding's characteristic substitution of the Lovelesses and Lovemores of the plays of the 1690s by Lovegirlos.[18] He exploded conventions by exaggerating them to the point of silliness, as the flourish of the extra syllable "o" conveys. Some of the same wild inventiveness of the irregular plays can be found in his experiments with narrative form in the novels.

The generic polyvalence that Fielding associated with the novel in the preface to *Joseph Andrews* when he identified it as a "comic Epic-poem in Prose" is inspired by its accommodation of the ridiculous, which he took pains to establish as his province especially insofar as it could be distinguished from the burlesque. His discussion of the burlesque, however, remains unstable. The inclusion of burlesque diction is acceptable, though its sentiments must be excluded; he evokes Shaftesbury's dismissal of "mere burlesque" for its lack of classical precedent but then claims, "But perhaps I have less Abhorrence than he professes for it: and that not because I have had some little Success on the Stage this way; but rather as it contributes more to exquisite Mirth and Laughter than any other; and these are probably more wholesome Physic for the Mind . . . [than] a Tragedy or a grave lecture."[19] Fielding here denies that his success onstage is an influence on his interest in the burlesque in prose fiction, but this denial is rhetorical: a litotes, it serves to draw attention to the continuities between them.

According to Judith Frank, Fielding imported the social dynamics from his burlesque plays into his novels. However, in her investigation of the preface to *Joseph Andrews* as a canon-forming gesture, she portrayed its elevation of the novel as requiring the containment of its representations of the poor, which involved displacing "the 'Burlesque' from the voices of his lower-class characters to the voice of the gentleman author [in] an attempt to ward off the possibility that the poor might imitate their betters."[20] But the burlesque was not restricted to the poor voicing the privileges of the gentry; it could also involve relocating social prestige and privilege to low and even underworldly domains, as Fielding did when he set heroic action on Grub Street or in brothels or among puppets or ghosts. Roger Lund appreciates the extension of the burlesque beyond the theater to embrace mock-heroic poetry and prose, though he nevertheless agrees with Frank that "if *Joseph Andrews* marks the rise of the novel, it also reveals the decline of burlesque."[21]

Before it declined, however, burlesque, like tragicomedy a significant genre in the seventeenth century, had exerted pressure on the neoclassical categories of genre notwithstanding its dependence on classical norms. Among the precedents for the freedoms Fielding took with strict generic classification onstage and in the preface to *Joseph Andrews* is John Gay's *The What D'Ye Call It* (1715), which Gay had identified as "tragi-comi-pastoral farce."[22] In the preface, Fielding may have used classicism to elevate *Joseph Andrews*, but the ambivalence of the contrast he drew between the novel and his own theatrical productions suggests the aesthetic continuities between them. His treatment of letters onstage makes these continuities visible, for it provides a template for some of the interruptive techniques of his novels.

Though not wildly successful in performance, *The Letter-Writers; or, A New Way to Keep a Wife at Home* (1731) is worth examining as Fielding's most extensive dramatic treatment of letters.[23] The play also exhibits characteristic topicality, generic inventiveness, and burlesque tendencies: in it, Fielding injected a new use of anonymous letters, to extort money, into the familiar plot of older husbands trying to keep their younger wives.[24] During the last three months of 1730, a rash of incidents had followed on the heels of newspaper accounts of the case of George Packer, a Bristol-based shipbuilder who received letters threatening to set fire to his house and murder his sisters if he did not deposit money in a marked hole in Swan Lane. As Thomas Lockwood remarks in his introduction to the play, "By the end of November, almost every London paper was printing (or in most cases reprinting) stories of incendiary extortion attempts, attacks and countermeasures, often also reproducing the letters."[25] In an update of Aphra Behn's *The Lucky Chance; or, The Alderman's Bargain* (1686), whose Sir Cautious Fullbank and Sir Feeble Fainwould band together to protect their assets, among which they include their women, Fielding's mercantile men, Mr. Softly and Mr. Wisdom, send each other's wives anonymous threatening letters in a futile attempt to induce them to stay at home. Their wives, meanwhile, send signed *billets doux* to Rakel, the lover they share without knowing it. The plot twists of this play exploit letters' equal capacity for intimacy and anonymity, exposing the ways these can be flip sides of the same coin and providing an example of how they functioned together in the bourgeois public sphere.

The three-act farce develops the contrast between Mrs. Wisdom, who is intimidated by the threatening letter into entertaining her lover at home, which she gets away with when her husband arrives unexpectedly because she can hide him in the closet, and Mrs. Softly, who goes out on the town despite the threat and gets caught at home in a tryst with Rakel because she has no closet. Though this difference may help to explain why one woman is more willing to stay at home than the other, the disclosure of marital infidelity in each case turns out practically to be immaterial. Rakel is accused of having stolen papers from Mr. and Mrs. Wisdom's closet. He is taken into custody when he is found under a table, where Mrs. Wisdom has been obliged to hide him after her husband takes away her key to their closet.[26]

The escalating absurdities culminate in the table being overturned to expose Rakel, who is then apprehended. The action is resolved when first Rakel and then the wives are informed that the anonymous threatening letters have been sent by the husbands, and Rakel produces the signed letters the wives have written to him to force a compromise. He has the final word:

> Pray ladies, let me give you this Advice: If you ever should write a Love-Letter, never sign your Name to it—And, Gentlemen, that you may prevent it—Think not by any Force or sinister Stratagem to imprison your Wives. The Laws of England are too generous to permit the one, and the Ladies are generally too cunning to be outwitted by the other.—But let this be your Maxim:
> Those Wives for Pleasures very seldom roam,
> Whose Husbands bring substantial Pleasures home.[27]

This play shares with Fielding's others a characteristic push into absurdity designed to expose power dynamics and social conventions. In *The Letter-Writers*, the contents of letters need to be announced if they are to serve their purposes onstage, no matter what their purpose; this publicity dovetails with Fielding's aim to expose the dangers of taking any kind of correspondence at face value. Asserting the equivalence between seeming opposites, intimate love letters and anonymous threats, Fielding finds through repetition and farce one of the means he uses to interrupt narrative immersion at several key moments in the novels: the materialization of letters that treats them more as objects than as vehicles of communication.

LETTERS IN DRAMATIC ADAPTATIONS OF RICHARDSON

That letters, especially published familiar letters, were ambiguous, neither clearly transparent transcriptions of the sincere heart nor clearly social performances codified by formality and convention, was made especially clear in the 1730s with the publication of Pope's letters, as Tom Keymer masterfully brings out to contextualize Richardson's adoption of epistolary narration for the novel.[28] Ian Watt claimed that a large part of Richardson's strength lay in his identification of epistolarity with the novel as a genre, which thus realized to its maximum potential the literary importance of print; he also contended that "the intimate or private effect of the letter form would be lost" on the stage or through oral narration.[29] Yet letters, as we have seen, were frequently used onstage to produce the impression and conse-quences of intimacy, a use Fielding pushed into parody in *The Letter-Writers* along with the private space associated with their composition, the closet. Richardson had incorporated the dramatic function of closets into some of the climactic scenes of *Pamela*, the stage function of which was retained in the dramatic adaptations of the novel even if they also marginalized the novel's letters.

One might perhaps be forgiven for expecting letters to have a bigger or dif-ferent role in the "*Pamela* media event," as William Warner has wittily called it, but the dramatic adaptations instead reduce letters to what amounts to Pamela's leitmotif.[30] Our first views of Pamela in Henry Giffard's *Pamela, a Comedy*, the anonymous *Pamela; or, Virtue Triumphant* that Keymer and Peter Sabor tentatively ascribe to Dance, and Goldoni's *Pamela* feature Pamela at a writing table either just having completed or in the process of writing a letter to her parents. In none of these plays, however, does she read that letter or any letters at all; instead she muses aloud about the occasion of its composition. The theater in this way pro-vides backstory to the letter-writing of the novel.

Letters retain their use in the intrigue plot of Giffard's adaptation. The inten-tions of Belvile, the play's version of Mr. B., to propose a sham marriage are brought to Pamela's attention when Mrs. Jewkes confuses two letters from him, sending the one intended for her on to Pamela by mistake. Keymer and Sabor iden-tify the high point of the young Garrick's performance as Jack Smatter, Lady Davers's foppish nephew, in the only scene of letter-reading among the dramatic adaptations of the novel, which occurs in the play's final act. This letter, of Gar-rick's own composition, is from Colebrand (whom the play transforms from Swiss to Frenchman) to Mrs. Jewkes, whom he has tricked into marriage. "The letter allowed full scope to [Garrick's] virtuoso skills: the impecunious product of Lichfield grammar school playing a wealthy, aristocratic fop, who in turn is imi-tating a course, scheming, Frenchman, speaking broken English and denouncing Mrs. Jewkes as 'a damn'd heretique old Vitch . . . more proper for Monsieur de Devil, dan for Your tres humble Serviteur, at a Distance.'"[31] Letters are not here the agent of reform but of comic *éclaircissement*. Belvile's change of heart occurs not because he has read Pamela's writing but because Parson Williams and John Arnold have hidden themselves separately in Pamela's room, from which vantage they witness her attempted rape. Williams interrupts first, "enter[ing] from behind," according to the stage directions, "and interpos[ing]" himself between Pamela and Belvile.[32] Belvile assumes that Williams is his rival and has been secreted away with Pamela's knowledge. Then Arnold emerges from the closet to clarify that overhearing Belvile's instructions to Mrs. Jewkes has prompted him to engage Williams in a joint defense of Pamela's virtue. Belvile's recovery to virtue is expressed in his apology to Williams and his making amends to Pamela "by making her eternally [his] own."[33] The play thus adapts the story to suit its medium: whereas in the novel, reading in private leads Mr. B. to reform, onstage, witnessing does; just as reading is the mode by which novels are absorbed, so witnessing (or spectating) is the mode for taking in plays.

The anonymous *Pamela; or, Virtue Triumphant*, which stays closer to the novel, includes some theatrically problematic scenes, including one of Pamela clambering over the garden wall with stage directions describing bricks falling down on her, leading Sabor to propose that the play could afford to follow Richardson more closely because it seems not to have been intended for performance.[34] The possibility of a dramatic adaptation of *Pamela* that was not intended for the stage is itself testament to the range and impact of the *Pamela* media event as well as to the readiness to hand of theatrical forms. These adaptations found their own ways to generate the effects of intimacy that print letters had produced but that Watt worried would be lost. They illustrate the interpenetration of novels and plays even as they do so in medium-specific terms. This relationship is not best grasped in analyses that oppose the novel and the stage, for they will not be able to capture the shaping effects each had on the other even as the development of different medium specificities contributed to their growing distinctness from each other and formed the grounds upon which they came to be opposed. The status of letters in dramatic adaptations of Richardson gives a glimpse of a moment in this history.

In *The Afterlife of Character*, David A. Brewer treats the continuations and adaptations of *Pamela* among similar treatments of other literary characters.[35] He is alert to characters' cross-media mobility, but his main interest lies in the consequences for the idea of proprietary authorship. As a result, he backgrounds the means that are used to move characters across media. He quotes Lady Mary Wortley Montagu, who, in a letter to her daughter, wrote that she was "sorry not to see more of P. Pickle's performances," but he abbreviates her sentiment to a desire to see more *tout court*.[36] In the equivalence he posits between visualization and dramatization, he builds on James Grantham Turner's treatment of the intermedial adaptations of *Pamela*, in which Turner rightly rejected Peter Brooks's argument in *The Melodramatic Imagination* that the novel as a genre repudiated the theater: Turner proposed instead that "the successful novel approaches the condition of painting and the theater; that its most significant moments can be identified as scenes."[37]

Ironically, however, Turner's understanding of fictional referentiality as a problem of embodiment becomes the means through which an opposition between novelistic and dramatic representation is smuggled back in. When Turner suggested that the paintings by Joseph Highmore and Philip Mercier that illustrated the novel, like the plays that adapted it, were attempts to give a body to the nobody of the novel to provide literal opportunities for seeing what the novel supplies only to the mind's eye, he described their use of "dramatic immediacy [to] operate directly to arouse the spectator, male or female," and thereby ignored those readers of Richardson, like Fielding, Haywood, and the other anti-Pamelists, who had found the novel to be pornographic in the first place because it already had elicited the kind of seeing that led to arousal.[38] Turner here adopted Catherine Gallagher's theory of the novel as "nobody's story," to which Brewer provides an important modification: he sees the main attraction of fictional characters to lie in the perpetual feedback loop they offer between material embodiment and immaterial virtuality, at least to those readers who pick up their pens.[39]

In accumulating evidence of a literary commons that can pressure "from below" an overly unified concept of authorship, however, Brewer downplays the significance of the theater, a curious choice since the concept of proprietary authorship that he would call into question is problematized most obviously in performance, a venture involving more people than the playwright. The choice flows from his primary commitment to the critical paradigms of the material history of the book, which backgrounds or ignores differences of genre, as well as media other than those associated with writing and printing. This produces a significant omission: notwithstanding his attention to adaptations of Richardson, as well as to George Colman the Elder's farce *Polly Honeycombe: A Dramatic Novel* (1761), of which he has produced an edition, Brewer does not recognize the ways it adapts *Clarissa*.[40]

Perhaps the degree to which it may strike contemporary readers as counterintuitive that there was a dramatic, let alone farcical, adaptation of Richardson's masterpiece can measure the difficulty in going back around the dominant paradigm of the realist novel to appreciate the theatrical culture out of which it emerged. Yet there were a number of dramatic adaptations of *Clarissa* in France and two in England, according to Lois Bueler, who, along with *Polly Honeycombe*, identifies Robert Porrett's *Clarissa; or, The Fatal Seduction, a Tragedy in Prose* (1788), which was printed by the author but never staged.[41] Whereas Colman's farce cannot be seen as a point-for-point adaptation of Richardson's novel, its intermedial scenes of reading repay consideration. Brewer brings out the close relationships between performance and print in Colman's farce, but as its subtitle, *A Dramatic Novel*, suggests, it also presents the hybrid consequences of the proximity of the novel to the stage in the play's satirical treatment of novel-reading.[42]

Clarissa is certainly evoked in Colman's play: on Polly's being forced by her parents to entertain Mr. Ledger as a suitor, rather than Mr. Scribble, the man with whom she plans to elope, she says in an aside, "What a monster of a man!—What will the frightful creature say to me?—I am now, for all the world, just in the situation of poor Clarissa."[43] She mentions Clarissa again alongside other characters of Richardson's novel to draw out the parallels between her situation and theirs, though she also names other novels' heroines at other points in the play, including Sophia Western. The heroine enters reading a novel in the play's opening scene, and she reads almost continuously throughout. Upon receiving a three- or four-page letter from Scribble, she reads, the stage directions inform us, making a few interjections about his style while her nurse talks.[44] Colman's treatment of reading exaggerates the differences between the private, silent acts of imaginative engagement and the social interactions of dialogue or communication to demonstrate that reading entails both. Novel-reading licenses Polly Honeycombe to pursue her own desires, but she does not first read alone silently and then externalize into action her individuality; instead, as she becomes a socially legible version of what she has read silently, aloud, and with multiple interjections, her self-determination is realized as a derivative performance.

These scenes of performed reading in Colman's farce, like the one in Giffard's *Pamela*, bring out that reading and acting do not oppose each other because the former involves imaginative disembodiment and the latter requires embodiment. Not only do these plays each offer instances of embodied reading, they also stage performances of reading aloud and, in doing so, support Brewer's emphasis on sociable reading. His insight, that fictional characters offered their readers a perpetual feedback loop between embodied materiality and virtual immateriality that drove then, as it does now, to a sociable and interactive production of fan fiction, modifies the presumption that reading is always and only solitary. He thus corrects Gallagher's proposition of fiction as a no-body problem, Deidre Lynch's treatment of the novel as the (only) site for the achievement of character's full potential, and, perhaps more surprisingly, Lisa Freeman's insistence that drama is as significant to the category of character as are novels.[45] Yet Brewer too remains overly invested in the opposition of novels and plays: his joint commitment to print and to the category of character orients him toward problems of content rather than media; consequently, he does not go far enough to reverse the opposition of drama and novels.[46]

The scenes of reading in both Giffard and Coleman are scenes of sociable reading aloud, but they also suggest that reading and acting, instead of being opposed, might be better understood to offer differently mediated versions of ways of paying attention to or absorbing literature.[47] Although drama, by definition, is embodied performance and the stage presents us with real bodies in contrast to the imaginary bodies presented by prose fiction, stepping back from the category of character to the category of attention makes visible that the mode of reading Richardson proposed in *Pamela*, in which immersion in the drama of the story leads readers to subordinate their situations to imaginatively enter into that which was represented, can be generalized across the page and the stage: it is one in which readers or audience members imaginatively share bodies with characters through identification with them (an identification Colman parodied as imitation). But this is not the only mode of attention-paying in novels or other kinds of literature. The interruptive mode that Fielding proposed also applies across novels and plays.

The scholarly treatment of the problem of fictionality as it permits the imaginative engagement of readers (Gallagher) and gives rise to the mechanisms for vicarious identification with characters (Lynch) or resistances to it (Freeman) has assumed that the processes of suspension of disbelief and imaginary identification can be historicized and that the mechanics of vicarious identification work basically through character. The historicist aim is admirable, but the investment in the category of character ends up unnecessarily privileging one genre of literature over another or one genre of novels (realist ones) over others. The variability of genres of fiction and modes of identification is best captured instead through other features of style and technique, available to both novelists and dramatists alike, through which the rhythms and directionalities of attention can be mapped, even if individual investments cannot be generalized with certainty. Furthermore, both readers and playgoers can identify with things other than character. The theatrical history of the novel supplements the current catalogue of style and technique with elements that could ground a future history of the imaginative identification that fiction elicits, whether by means of reading or performance. Though Richardsonian reading may make the architecture of the theater disappear, as it did for Diderot, such reading is not antitheatrical, as Richardson's narrative adoption of dramatic conventions and the dramatic adaptations of his novels illustrate.[48]

The status of letters in *Shamela* and *Joseph Andrews* owes much to Richardson, but Fielding also extended in his novels the functions he had given to letters in his plays. Fielding did not let viewers or readers forget the fictional status of what was presented, frequently accomplishing these reminders by appeals to viewers' or readers' embodiment that often emphasized the limits it placed on their perceptions and understanding. Jill Campbell has shrewdly observed that in the novels, Fielding crafted a prose style designed to make readers aware of their embodiment, thereby problematizing the idea that reading offers a disembodied experience and performance an embodied one.[49] The status of letters (and reading) across Fielding's plays and novels reveals a consistent aesthetic program: if Richardson staged letters in his novels, Fielding theatricalized them, thereby proposing that the experience of fiction, read or viewed, entailed a self-consciousness about it for which he developed techniques that entered into the toolkit of later novelists.

LETTERS IN FIELDING'S NOVELS

Perhaps it is not surprising that most of the handful of letters in *Joseph Andrews* hew closely to its parody of *Pamela*. The first two are from Joseph to his sister, Pamela, acknowledging her report of her lady's death and informing her of Lady Booby's having fallen in love with him. Later in book 1, when Joseph is a virtual prisoner at the Inn, Fielding continues the parody when Joseph's demands for writing materials are refused. Subsequent letters reflect Fielding's departure from the plot of *Pamela*, though the occurrence of a few in inset tales, nevertheless, furthers his critique of immersive reading epitomized by the epistolary mode.

A lady on the stagecoach with Parson Adams tells "The History of Leonora, the Unfortunate Jilt." In a ludicrous satire on epistolary fiction, she recites Leonora's entire correspondence from memory. Another letter reproduced in the inset tale of Mr. Wilson conveys the winning lottery ticket that eases his financial strain and allows him to complete his reform from rake to gentleman farmer. In the first instance, Fielding continues to take potshots at the verisimilitude of the epistolary mode; in the second, he prioritizes the letter as a prop rather than as a medium of communication, thus extending the critique of the reform of Mr. B. by means of reading Pamela's writing that he had put forward initially in *Shamela*.

The interpolated tales of *Joseph Andrews* play the time of reading against the time of telling to position readers so that they are maximally self-consciousness of their own act of reading. Both the "History of Leonora" and Mr. Wilson's tale extend over a number of the novel's chapters to highlight the disjunction between the discrete printed segments that readers read and the integrated listening experience of the characters. Jeffrey Williams has proposed that the curiosity of the characters that listen to these inset and orally delivered tales is coded as an irrepressible desire for novelistic forms, but significantly, though these characters become immersed in the tales they are told, readers' attention is interrupted.[50]

In *Tom Jones*, letters occur alongside another of Fielding's characteristic narrative techniques: the omission of crucial details. A. D. McKillop long ago observed that Fielding "uses with special frequency in the later books the statement that he is omitting something for one reason or another."[51] One of the things Fielding consistently omitted is direct representation of changes of mind or heart, that is, the kind of transformation best illustrated by the narratives or dramatizations of the rake's reform that we examined in chapter 1. Although Tom is too innocent to be considered a rake, the elaborate plot of the novel is nevertheless invested in his reform, which is as important to its resolution as the revelation of his birth and his restoration to Mr. Allworthy's favor and fortune. In a classic essay on the novel's plot, R. S. Crane pointed out that all three conditions must be met in order for Sophia to agree to marry Tom, once her father has approved the match.[52] Although Sophia is aware of Tom's sexual encounters, first with Molly Seagrim and then with Mrs. Waters, his promiscuity does not seem to interfere with her love for him.[53] Rather, it is his proposal of marriage to Lady Bellaston that presents an obstacle as insurmountable as her father's disapproval. It is only after Tom finds out, in a letter Sophia writes to him, that she has read his letter to Lady Bellaston that his process of reform can be said to begin.

Not only do Tom's feelings of regret get rather minimal treatment, but the narrator refuses to give access to them. About Tom's response to Sophia's letter declaring she knows of his marriage proposal, which Tom reads in jail, where he is being held on charges for murder pending the results of his duel with Mr. Fitzpatrick, Fielding's narrator says, "Of the present Situation of Mr. Jones's Mind, and of the Pangs with which he was now tormented, we cannot give the Reader a better Idea, than by saying, his Misery was such, that even Thwackum would almost have pitied him. But bad as it is, we shall at present leave him in it, as his good Genius (if he really had any) seems to have done. And here we put an End to the sixteenth book of our history."[54] Instead of Tom's mental state, we next get a description of his interaction with Mrs. Waters, in which he refuses further sexual intercourse. After she informs him that Mr. Fitzpatrick is not in any mortal danger, the narrator declines to represent the rest of their conversation, in which Mrs. Waters uttered many things "some of which it would do her no great Honour, in the Opinion of some Readers, to remember; nor are we quite certain but that the Answers made by Jones would be treated with Ridicule by others" (vol. 2: 912). Mrs. Waters then leaves the jail "not altogether so pleased with the penitential Behavior of a Man whom she had at her first Interview conceived a very different Opinion" (vol. 2: 912). The chapter closes with Tom, once again tormented by the thought that Sophia "had disclosed his Letter to her Aunt, and had taken a fixed Resolution to abandon him" (vol. 2: 912). Tom's refusal to engage in any further dalliance with Mrs. Waters, however coyly it may be evoked, speaks louder than the descriptions of his penitence.

The most significant example of the refusal of Fielding's narrator to show characters' changes of mind occurs in the description of Mr. Allworthy's dawning recognition that he has misjudged Tom. To Nightingale and Mrs. Miller's glowing reports of Tom's generosity, Mr. Allworthy responds by signaling that he hopes to be able to change his mind in the future, though at the moment, he cannot bring himself to do so. Yet recollecting his old fondness for Tom brings tears to his eyes. Here the narrator interrupts and stops the flow of events.

> As the Answer which Mrs. Miller made may lead us into fresh Matters, we will here stop to account for the visible Alteration in Mr. Allworthy's mind, and the Abatement of his Anger to Jones. Revolutions of this Kind, it is true, do frequently occur in Histories and dramatic Writers, for no other Reason than because the History or Play draws to a Conclusion and are justified by Authority of Authors; yet though we insist upon as much Authority as any Author whatever, we shall use this Power very sparingly, and never but when we are driven to it by Necessity, which we do not at present foresee will happen in this Work. (vol. 2: 924)

In place of a portrait of Mr. Allworthy and his mental state, the next chapter produces verbatim the object that had initiated the alteration: Square's letter. The narrator renounces the kind of representation that would depict Mr. Allworthy with tears in his eyes and expatiate on his reflections, as well as its justification by the authority of other kinds of authors. As in the scene of the penitent Tom in jail, however, the refusal to go into detail about internal mental changes signals that a change of heart is already under way, even if the transformation lies beyond the bounds of description. The artifact that prompts Allworthy's change of mind, like Sophia's letter to Tom and his subsequent rejection of Mrs. Waters's advances, constitutes evidence for what might otherwise be taken as unverifiable assertions of internal change, assertions made on the authority of authors. But the authority of these letters rests on their delivery in print in books. The evidence they offer is unstable: not only is it subject to interpretation, but it also has no status outside the text and can therefore shore up the narrator's authority as easily as undermine it. Furthermore, the reverse order in which readers first receive the announcement of Mr. Allworthy's change and only afterward are shown its cause, disrupts, and not for the first time, the expectation that narrative will unfold sequentially, moment by moment.

In *Amelia*, there are a number of scenes crucial to the plot that feature letters that produce essential transformations independent of their contents. Terry Castle has identified the Haymarket masquerade as central to the novel, using it to make sense of the vacillations between satire and sentiment that have made *Amelia* appear less than fully coherent to many critics, but the action that dominates this episode is the reading of Dr. Harrison's letter decrying adultery.[55] Colonel James, the addressee of Dr. Harrison's letter, inadvertently drops it, and Colonel Bath picks it up, leading Captain Booth mistakenly to believe that it is Bath who intends to seduce Amelia. Even before these consequences unfold, three young Bucks intercept it and proceed to read it aloud, making fun of it as they go along. This scene offers Fielding the opportunity to provide a virtuoso display of a variety of idioms, as Dr. Harrison's sober sententia and argument from scripture are repeatedly reinterpreted and interrupted by the Orator and his fellows, who ultimately propose to subscribe to Handel to have the "ditty" set to music.[56] This scene's theatricality is reminiscent of Garrick's reading of Colebrand's letter in Giffard's *Pamela* as well as others of reading onstage.

The letter is crucial to the resolution of the novel's plot, moreover, because when Booth realizes that Harrison meant it for Colonel James, he recognizes that Amelia's unexplained reluctance to socialize with James stems from her desire to preserve both her virtue and Booth's life by preventing him from challenging James to a duel. Overwhelmed by her goodness, Booth then confesses his own adulterous relationship with Miss Mathews. The letter thus becomes an inadvertent agent of reform in this novel, though not for its having been read properly.

The strange status of this letter is underscored when Amelia, upon having heard and accepted Booth's apology, reveals that she had already known about their affair, having received a letter from Miss Mathews without mentioning it, a letter that we, like Booth, have been led by Miss Mathews to believe she destroyed. Castle takes the narrator to task here for what she characterizes as anomalous misdirection. She reads this transformation of the narrator from trustworthy to unreliable as a consequence of the masquerade that has prompted everyone to become different from themselves.[57] However, like the letters in *Tom Jones* that prompt reform or changes of heart, these two letters provide the occasion for the Booths to recognize and reaffirm each other's status as ideal mate.

Fielding here uses letters to further the plot but not because of their contents; not only is access refused in this last example, but so is information about the letter's mode of transmission. *Amelia* does contain some other letters that are read and understood by their recipients; their contents are transcribed so that they are accessible to readers as well, but when this happens, the narrator emphasizes this transparency. For example, when Amelia receives a letter from Colonel James in book 10, chapter 8, Fielding risks redundancy, having the narrator report, "a Porter brought the following Letter, which she immediately opened and read," followed by a transcription.[58] Fielding thus insists that letters are occasions. Furthermore, no matter how minor, letters as occasions trump letters as vehicles of information; they are always props first and only secondly a medium of communication whose transparent access to their contents is thus compromised.

The occurrence of letters in inset narratives in *Joseph Andrews*, alongside narrative omissions in *Tom Jones* and at critical plot points in *Amelia*, suggests that they belong among Fielding's more familiar characteristic narrative techniques. The inclusion of letters in this loose assemblage of devices, moreover, reveals at the core of his narrative method a commitment to guiding readers without modeling reading in characters by pointing "offstage" and beyond the page.

The letters in *Amelia* constitute one of the ways Fielding found to maintain a narrative perspective that is quite close to that of the characters' without being identical to it, that is to say, without being in the first person: he makes readers into spectators of the action who retain, unlike Diderot upon reading Richardson, a capacity to observe independent of character. Critics have struggled to situate his last novel in the oeuvre, seeing in it Richardsonian aspects that derive not only from its sentimental plot but also from its provision of readers with only as much information as its characters have, deprived of the larger perspective of a magisterial narrator or author-figure that dominated *Tom Jones*. By including many correspondents in *Clarissa*, Richardson had characters' perspectives correct, contradict, or modify one another. Fielding's interest in training readers to decode experiential processes is similar, but he sought in a third-person narration closer to the action than that of *Tom Jones* to promote affective involvement with characters by controlling the flow of information rather than by modeling reading directly in the narrative.[59] For both novelists, rereading became a significant way to control reading that also gauges each one's attitude toward it.

In *Pamela*, Richardson staged rereading in Mr. B.'s reading Pamela's writing; *Clarissa* both dramatized rereading prompted by the hermeneutic desires of the characters and enlisted rereading in the second and subsequent editions, where it was controlled by the textual apparatus of cross-referencing. By contrast, Fielding forced readers to reread, a direct demand filtered through the mediation of neither a character nor an editor. Perhaps because it is more didactic, we can see this most clearly in book 4, chapter 10, of *Joseph Andrews*, in which Fielding interrupts the action with a characteristic intervening scene consisting of an inset moral tale that provides not only a scene of telling but also a scene of reading.

Visiting Parson Adams's household, Lady Booby inquires if his eight-year-old son, Dick, can read, and Adams enjoins him to display his talents at the close of chapter 9. Chapter 10 opens, "'Leonard and Paul were two Friends.'—'Pronounce it Lennard, Child,' cry'd the Parson.—'Pray, Mr. Adams,' says Lady Booby, 'let your Son read without Interruption.' Dick then proceeded. 'Lennard and Paul were two Friends, who . . .'"[60] Although we first read "Leonard" at the same time as Dick reads it aloud, the sounds do not coincide with what Dick says and Lady Booby and

Parson Adams hear. However, we do not immediately grasp the discrepancy, only coming to recognize that Dick has mispronounced "Leonard" when Adams corrects him. Reading the phonetically correct though misspelled "Lennard" ironically offers rapid confirmation of Dick's earlier misreading, an irony deepened by the textual absence of Dick's mispronounced utterance: Leo-nard. Reading this passage aloud would entail reading it twice, since one would be obliged to go back to produce Dick's mispronunciation correctly. This is not Adams's only correction of his son's mispronunciation; neither is it Lady Booby's only plea to let him continue. As in the other examples from this novel, *Tom Jones*, and *Amelia*, Fielding here forces a rereading that insists on the divergence of readers' experience from that of the characters.

Like with Shamela's "vartue," Fielding works the visual resources of print in tandem with the evocation of a fictional performance or utterance, exploiting the differences between them to bring the limits of fictional referentiality into visibility and thereby to ensure that readers' immersion is not complete. As Jill Campbell has observed, "Fielding's prose makes us feel, sentence-to-sentence as well as chapter-to-chapter and book-to-book, our embodiment as readers."[61] Supplementing his syntactic resources by other means, including this scene of reading, to insist on readers' embodiment, Fielding questions the ways some kinds of fiction get readers or audience members to subordinate their bodies to those of the characters who are represented. By highlighting the purposes to which this identification can be put, and by controlling readers' rereading, he would expose the many ways authors exert their own authority. By obliging readers to become aware of these pressures, he also provides ways to resist them.

Fielding's refusals across the novels to describe internal changes, his reliance on letters as props, and his dramatizations of reading play with the limits of what can be represented in novels, and they do so in more or less explicit relation to the theater, where reading, if it is to communicate meaningfully, must be performed. Working at the level of syntax, Campbell persuasively connects Fielding's extensive use of medial punctuation to his experiences as a playwright and theater manager.[62] In a reading of *Tom Jones*, Angus Fletcher and Michael Benveniste see the gaps, absences, and coincidences of plot that elicit the narrator's digressions as a reflection of his status as a character among other characters rather than as some string-pulling providential figure who exists on a plane removed from, and above, the action, thus echoing the point about Fielding's dramatized narrator made long ago by Wayne Booth.[63] Replacing Crane's insistence on the unity of the novel's plot with an appreciation of its harmonization of the forms of comedy and the novel, they seek to recover the virtues of the Chicago School of criticism divested of its overemphasis on Aristotle. In their discussion of Allworthy's change of heart, they reflect that Fielding could easily have "flip[ped] back a few pages to insert a line about Allworthy receiving a letter."[64] It may seem odd to consider that the novel uses an "offstage" when it can "go" there itself, but when Fielding's narrator gestures "offstage," this does not signify the novel's repudiation of the theater but rather its extension by other means.

Fielding used the theater to project a new kind of fictional space, an arena beyond the page, where characters may or may not undergo the revolutionary changes of heart or mind that otherwise tax representation by evoking the author's authority. Scott Black has been rightly critical of the New Historicist tendency to see Fielding's refusals to describe internal changes as clearing the way to a better understanding of character or self-fashioning; instead, Black, like Fletcher and Benveniste, sees Fielding using comic theater within and alongside the novel to produce new forms of narration.[65] Rather than cultivating readers' identification with characters, Fielding prevented their collapse by modulating the distances between readers and what occurs, and can be said to occur, on the page. Both Fielding and Richardson constructed readers' experiences of their novels in relation to the theater; they did so differently, but both contributed to the legacy of techniques that subsequent novelists inherited and further refined. The dialectic between them that McKeon argues produces novelistic realism lies instead at the heart of readers' experiences of the novel, a genre that includes realism but cannot be entirely identified with this mode. In *Evelina*, Frances Burney fused both Richardson's and Fielding's treatments of rereading, and in *Pride and Prejudice*, Jane Austen transformed rereading into cognitive revision and affective realization.

When Evelina receives the duplicitous letter that Willoughby has written under Orville's forged signature, she encloses or transcribes it in a letter to her friend Miss Mirvan (letter XXVII). Discussing the replacement of her initial delight at discovering that she is loved by "Orville" by astonishment, indignation, and shame provoked by the improprieties that the letter expresses, Evelina exclaims, "Upon a second reading, I thought every word changed,—it did not seem the same letter,—I could not find one sentence that I could look at without blushing."[66] Though she does not isolate a single feature of the letter, she repeats three times that it has been utterly transformed. This lack of description covers the discrepancies between those readers who may already have found the letter to be suspicious and those who, like Evelina, read it naively at first. The insistence on its complete transformation, like Fielding's "Lennard," points backward and prompts a return to read it again, Richardsonian fashion, through Evelina's eyes.

At the center of *Pride and Prejudice*, in chapter 35, Elizabeth Bennet receives a long letter from Darcy, which is reproduced; in chapter 36, she reads it, and even though, after the first time through, she "put it hastily away, protesting that she would not regard it, that she would never look at it again," she reads it again.[67] In this scene of rereading as revision, Austen describes Elizabeth's expostulations, refusals, and recognitions as she changes her opinions; the narrative can freely concentrate on the feelings the letter has inspired in Elizabeth because of the inclusion of Darcy's letter, to which readers can refer back——or not. Austen thus moves beyond the reading lessons provided by her precursors, giving greater prominence to the Darcy whom Elizabeth has internalized in her mind and heart than to his embodiment in the letter he sends.[68] Although his letter remains the agent that produces her change, readers are not required to reread along with Elizabeth, although they may. Austen developed the narrative flexibility that allowed readers to follow the transformations that Elizabeth's rereading prompts without requiring us to mirror her act of rereading.

What is at stake here is not just the falling away of Richardson's and Fielding's didacticism, though that is surely part of it, but also the development of the capacity for narrative distance to be mobile, flexible, and variable within texts. Austen's debts to Richardson have been fully acknowledged; by contrast, as Jill Campbell notes, the opposition of Fielding to Austen has come naturally to a critic like D. A. Miller, who is interested in formal questions of style but also wants to maintain a commitment to ideological critique and the identity categories that have privileged male heterosexuality within literary history.[69] But Austen's pyrotechnical manipulations of narrative distance also derived from Fielding even as she maximized readers' capacity to identify with characters, which she inherited from Richardson.

For example, a Fieldingesque moment occurs in *Persuasion*, when Anne Elliot goes with her sister Mary to visit the Musgroves for the first time.

> To the Great House accordingly they went, to sit the full half hour in the old-fashioned square parlour, with a small carpet and shining floor, to which the present daughters of the house were gradually giving the proper air of confusion by the grand piano forte and the harp, flower-stands and little tables placed in every direction. Oh! Could the originals of the portraits against the wainscot, could the gentlemen in brown velvet and the ladies in blue satin have seen what was going on, have been conscious of such an overthrow of all order and neatness! The portraits themselves seemed to be staring in astonishment.[70]

The point of view of the painted ancestors through which the disordered parlor is gently critiqued is not Anne's. The clever animation of the portraits to bring out the differences between the past and the present at first would seem to offer a kind of comic appropriation of the Gothic convention of the living portrait inaugurated by Walpole. But the gesture involves instead the narrative occupation of two spatially opposite perspectives: first to survey the contents of the room from the point of view of the portraits and then to look back at the portraits "staring in astonishment." The omniscient narrator intrudes with the apostrophic "Oh!" to introduce a non-character-based perspective that coexists with other, more familiar narrative devices, including (but not limited to) free indirect discourse, to manage readers' identifications with character and to render the changing ways Anne experiences the discrepancy between the past and the present. Indeed, the power of the novel derives from Austen's coordination of Anne's experience of this discrepancy with that of readers, which are not identical. Although Fielding has long been appreciated for his "clockwork" management of plot and has been both lauded and reviled for his voluble narrator, his inauguration of the sort of perspectival play that encourages, if it does not force, the divergence of readers' perspectives from characters has been marginalized in accounts of the later psychological novels that privilege characters' consciousness and readers' identifications with them.[71] Austen's Fieldingesque "Oh!" foreshadows Thackeray, Eliot, Dickens, and Trollope more vividly than it does Henry James, James Joyce, or Virginia Woolf, who explicitly rejected the tyranny of ordinary readers and downgraded the cozy narrator's address to readers as middlebrow.[72] The segregation of the history of the theater from the history of the novel has also helped to efface Fielding's legacy. Both Richardson and Fielding undertook to shape novel readers' experiences in more direct ways than did subsequent novelists, who did not have to; significantly they did so with reference to the theater.

THE PROMISE OF EMBARRASSMENT

Frances Burney's Theater of Shame

W HEN D. A. MILLER OBSERVED of Jane Austen's style that "it obeys an overwhelming urge to give correctness a *theatrical form*," he disclosed the dialectic between of self-display and self-erasure that underwrites his production of her style as Style itself.[1] For Miller, nowhere is this more evident than in her use of the free indirect style, which offers a third term between narration and character, "a kind of turnstile that helps to organize the boundary, and recycle the binary, of an antithesis. Organize? Say rather flaunt: free indirect style gives a virtuoso performance, against all odds, of narration's persistence in detachment from character, no matter how intimate the one becomes with the other."[2] Miller's personification intuits the theatrical roots of free indirect discourse, whose full disclosure helps to explain its innovation in the novels of Frances Burney. Throughout her career, Burney's writings (plays as well as novels) depended on a dialectic between shame and the theater that was crucial to her narration of female development.

When I call Burney's use "innovative," I do not mean that she invented free indirect discourse; the project to counterbalance the novelty of the novel with awareness of its debts to the genres of drama and the conventions of theatrical presentation can have no such investment in "firsts." Her uses, however, call for a new account that emphasizes the technique's relationship to the stage. The directions in which she took it are most visible in her second novel, *Cecilia* (1782). She also developed another narrative device, a reversal of perspective by 180 degrees, that had a significant presence in *Camilla* (1796) but whose theatricality crystallized in her last novel, *The Wanderer* (1814), in which it pivots on a proscenium. These contributions to narrative technique are best appreciated in the context of the generative relationship between shame and theater that dominated her whole career but whose significance, I propose, is not just biographical. She distilled the ideas of entertainment associated with Colley Cibber into narrative form.

She mediated both the comedy of manners and melodrama to subsequent novelists, including Austen, and therefore assumes a central place in the theatrical history of the novel. This chapter treats all of Burney's novels; the next one looks at her legacy to Austen and Elizabeth Inchbald.

It was Austen who signaled the transformative capacity of shame that lay at the heart of Burney's novels when she described Elinor Dashwood and Edward Ferrars's entry into "a most promising state of embarrassment" when they first sit down together, having accidentally been granted the opportunity to resume their long-interrupted courtship toward the end of *Sense and Sensibility*.[3] But Burney's influence on Austen should not be her only claim to fame: her achievements in narrative loosen the identification of free indirect discourse with Austen, who now, along with Shakespeare, stands at the stripped-down center of the English canon, and significantly enriches our catalog of literary technique.

Burney's first three novels, like Austen's six, had mapped the marriage plot onto narratives of female development. The divergence of her last one from this pattern has made it almost completely inassimilable into the version of the history of the novel that culminates in Austen, even though, published the same year as *Mansfield Park*, with which it shares scenes of amateur theatricals, *The Wanderer* also may have influenced Austen's later writing.[4] On top of the amateur theatricals, the theater thoroughly imbues *The Wanderer*; many scenes involve performance, and its leading female characters embody opposing performance styles. Burney's last novel is continuous with her earlier work, even as it explores extending their concerns into the post-Revolutionary period. More a melodrama of manners than a comedy of manners, *The Wanderer* thus makes possible a new genealogy for the novel in which Austen remains a major figure but that, by providing a more varied account of narrative form, also accommodates their Jacobin contemporaries. Though the Jacobin use of literature to convey political ideas and the radicalism of their politics have led critics to treat them separately from Burney and Austen, they shared developments in narrative technique that are best understood in the context of melodrama, as I show in chapter 5.[5]

But the comedy of manners also passed from Richardson and Fielding to Austen, who completed its migration to the novel, through Burney. In *The Visit*, the most sophisticated of the dramatic sketches included in Austen's *Juvenilia*, she comically telescoped the conventional courtship plot from flirtation to marriage by means of a shortage of chairs that forces lovers to sit on each other's laps at the briefest of formal dinners.[6] In a miraculously compressed five pages, Austen cleared the way to replace the physical choreography of gesture by an internal psychological portraiture, though a choreography—indeed dramaturgy—of perspectives at the center of her novels remained associated with the language of gesture.

Whereas Austen abandoned playwriting, however, Burney continued to write plays throughout her career; her diaries frequently dramatized passages in dialogue; she even returned late in life, after the prospect of a dramatic production had faded, to tinker with the construction and timing of the scenes of her plays.[7] In Burney, the theater spawned techniques of narration and styles of psychological portraiture that Austen brought to the next level of sophistication.[8]

When Miller observed that "what being a character in Austen means" is to have all one's secret vanities and self-deceptions identified, ridiculed, corrected—in short to be "slapped silly by a narration whose recipient is kept from even noticing"—he detected but did not fully exploit a connection between shame and Austen Style.[9] He called into view the bond that Austen's narration makes with readers at characters' expense, or over their heads, a crucial aspect of Emma's developmental trajectory in the novel that takes her name. If at first Emma does not recognize that she is in need of correction and is thus incapable of being embarrassed, she learns and evolves; as the embarrassment that readers experience on her behalf comes increasingly to be shared with her, any discomfort that may accompany the initial schadenfreude disappears. Whereas not all development in Austen turns on embarrassment, it does so in Burney, where the links among mortification, theater, and narration are explicit.

Austen moved her readers and characters closer to each other over the course of the plot (and the heroine's) development, at least in *Emma*, where she orchestrated a slow but steady convergence of their positions. Burney, by contrast, modulated readers' distance from the action only at crucial points in the plot. Though she cultivated readers' intimacy with her heroines, she did not, unlike Austen, seek to dissolve readers' discomfort. Indeed, Burney's readers can find it difficult to reconcile the prim didacticism of her novels with the relentlessness, even cruelty, of some of their episodes. Development in Burney therefore gets measured more overtly than in Austen by milestones delivered in recognition scenes and set pieces. As the theatricality of these markers suggest, her narrative innovations and the relations they elicit between readers and characters grew together out of the configuration of theater and shame that lies behind their affective punch.

THE THEATER OF SHAME

A parade of shameless minor characters prances across the pages of Burney's novels. They prompt as well as measure her heroines' development. A typical scene in Burney will involve the heroine's visit to the theater or some other performance. Perhaps she will be in the company of a shameless character, or she may encounter one there, where she will have a double experience: not only her own proper response to the performance but also mortification on behalf of the companion who is incapable of such a response. The secondhandedness of the heroine's shame suggests that her capacity for aesthetic appreciation lies in her ability to entertain vicarious experience. Aesthetic appreciation is thus offered as both an equivalent to and a prerequisite for moral development; both are indexed by the heroine's susceptibility to shame.[10]

Surprisingly often, the shameless characters are in loco parentis. Burney's heroines are susceptible to shame because they find themselves in double binds as the children of well-meaning parents or guardians who, for one reason or another, are unavailable or inadequate and unassailable to critique, even when they are not explicitly shameless. In London, as Evelina is separated from her valued guardian, Mr. Villars, she must depend on her preposterous grandmother, Mme. Duval, and the outrageous husband of her chaperone, Captain Mirvan, until the belated recognition of her reluctant father is secured. Orphaned at the outset of the novel, Cecilia has three equally problematic guardians who are supposed to guard her financial interests and help her to fulfill the terms of an inheritance dictating that she may marry but never give up her name. Harrell is a reckless gambler who kills himself when faced with financial ruin; Briggs a miser; and Delvile, the aristocratic father of the man Cecilia loves but cannot marry. Camilla's distant parents, the Tyrolds, are virtuous, but they leave her and her siblings in the care of their incompetent rich uncle, Sir Hugh, who visits ruinous physical, emotional, and financial circumstances on them. Ellis/Juliet, the wanderer of the last novel, is vulnerable to a range of mortifying social difficulties, including repudiation by her own aristocratic relatives, until circumstances permit her to be restored to her proper family lineage in the end. The heroines are constrained: to remain grateful and dutiful, they cannot be ashamed of their parents or guardians; they must instead be ashamed of themselves, even when their own behavior does not warrant it. The shame-susceptibility of the heroines makes them educable, eligible for improvement, and able to manage adversity within the strict codes of proper femininity.

Where we find scenes of shame in Burney, there we also find theatricality, a rule of thumb suggested by the frequent coincidence of shamelessness in the heroines' guardians and the frequent occurrence of embarrassing scenes at the theater (or other kinds of performance). It should not be surprising to find psychobiographical roots to the theater's status as a site of shame. Burney received early encouragement from David Garrick, Richard Brinsley Sheridan, and others to develop the natural ear for dialogue they detected in *Evelina* by writing a comedy.[11] Though she won initial approval for the project from her father and her mentor, Samuel "Daddy" Crisp, the two daddies subsequently censured and censored her efforts.[12] Burney persisted in writing plays, penning three more comedies as well as four tragedies over the course of her career, but the only one to be produced was a flop.[13] They were only published in 1995.

Among feminist critics who consider Burney, Nora Nachumi has persuasively contextualized her thwarted career as a dramatist with regard to the difficulties women writers faced writing for the stage, and Emily Hodgson Anderson has explored the manifestation of these difficulties in her novels.[14] Indeed, Burney's theatricality has received ample critical attention, from the local observation of the frequent appearances that performances make as settings or topics of conversation to a recent book-length semiotic analysis of the language and gestures of acting in her novels.[15] But the generative combination of shame and theatricality that shaped her narrative style has not yet fully been recognized; its significance is neither purely biographical nor related only to gender. Instead, the connections between shame and theatricality in Burney anchor a history of the novel from Richardson and Fielding to Austen and Inchbald.

Theatrical and other entertainments structure the development of Evelina, the eponymous heroine of Burney's only novel in letters, significantly subtitled "The History of a Young Lady's Entrance into the World": from her first letter from London to Mr. Villars commending Garrick's performance as Ranger in *The Suspicious Husband*, her experiences of theatrical and musical performances of many kinds display her natural taste, whether she finds herself in like-minded and appreciative or oblivious company.[16] A set piece at the theater early in the novel explicitly lays out Burney's equation of manners and morals as these are filtered through a performance of Congreve's *Love for Love*. Lovel, the insensitive fop, pretends he does not know what play is being performed since he only comes to the theater to make an appearance; Willoughby, the rake, draws flattering but inappropriate parallels between Evelina and Congreve's coquette, Miss Prue; Orville, the true gentleman, is attuned to the discomfort that the racy content of the play has caused Evelina, Miss Mirvan, and her mother and so discusses the exemplary character of Angelica (80–83).[17] Later, attending an opera with her arriviste cousins, the Branghtons, causes Evelina acute discomfort in advance of the performance since they quibble over what to wear and the price of admission, as well as during it since they talk instead of listening (90–94). In these instances and others like them in this as well as the other novels, Burney is interested in the sources of shame that provoke the heroine and the transfer of discomfort, shame, or embarrassment to her from the others who may not feel it themselves and from her to readers. The intensity of this interest can be gauged, perhaps, by the extraordinary frequency of the word "provoke" and its variants in *Evelina*: it appears forty times, which amounts to once in about every nineteen pages and is twenty to thirty times more often than in any other novel published that same year.

Provocation has a special relationship with shame. In part, this is due to the structure of shame itself, which, according to the affect theorist Silvan Tomkins, "is the most reflexive of affects in that the phenomenological distinction between the subject and object of shame is lost"; "close to the experienced self, it generates the torment of self-consciousness."[18] Shame, in other words, when it provokes affective transfer, does so along the axis of identity. Provocation's relation to shame, however, also takes a specifically theatrical form because of the embodiment of shameless theatrical entertainment by Colley Cibber.

Cibber had provoked both Henry Fielding and Alexander Pope into repudiations in *The Author's Farce* and *Shamela* and in the four-book *Dunciad*, respectively.[19] His style long retained its provocative powers. In a notebook sketch for *Valmouth* (1919), for example, Ronald Firbank channeled Cibber, writing "STEEN-KIRK" in all capitals near a description of an unkempt household in which the housemaid finds a "man's peruque [*sic*] behind a great bookstand," thereby appropriating the two props most clearly associated with him: the scarf with which Lady Easy covers her sleeping husband's head so that this unfaithful man can wake up to virtue in *The Careless Husband* (1704) and the giant wig he sported in performances as Lord Foppington.[20] In *Brighton Rock* (1938), to take another example, Graham Greene reflected Cibber's sustained association with popular culture, calling the person to be spotted in the novel's version of the newspaper-sponsored game of Lobby Lud "Kolley Kibber."[21] Though most accounts of the theater's role in the Georgian period have centered on Garrick, it was Cibber who embodied the aesthetics of popular entertainment in the bourgeois public sphere, as Elaine McGirr and Darryl Domingo have each recently shown.[22] He retained these associations into the twentieth century.

Burney's response to Cibber not only reflects his popularity in the later eighteenth century but also strikes one of the major chords of her oeuvre: the orchestration of shamelessness, theatricality, and shame to narrate the aesthetic and moral development of her heroines, through which the comedy of manners passed onto Austen and Inchbald. Considerably less skeptical than Pope's or Fielding's, her response was nevertheless filtered through theirs: she borrowed some of their disdain even as she accepted the bourgeois morality he had embraced. Like Fielding, Burney incorporated into a novel Cibber's *The Provok'd Husband* (1728), one of the most popular plays of the century.[23] Both did so to illustrate attitudes toward performance more generally, though in each case, we catch a glimpse of the persistent problem of the relations between aesthetic form and moral force that Cibber towed in his wake.

In the aftermath of a puppet performance in book 12, chapter 6, of *Tom Jones*, the landlady finds her maid Grace, pointedly named after the sober-minded lady of Cibber's play, "on the Puppet-show Stage in Company with the Merry-Andrew, and in a Situation not very proper to be described."[24] By having Grace use the stage as a platform for sexual intercourse, Fielding exploited the difficulty of telling if her sexual arousal in response to what is shown on stage is the opposite or an extension of the imagined responses of her more refined counterparts. In selecting the stage for her tryst, and the Merry-Andrew for her partner, moreover, Grace would appear to take to its logical conclusion the argument voiced by the puppet master, that behavior represented on the stage inspires like-minded behavior in its audience. Part of Fielding's joke, however, is that Grace is inspired by what she has *not* seen, for the puppet master, trumpeting the virtues of the puppet stage as a vehicle for rational entertainment, disdains all lowness and has cut the play accordingly. Grace, however, justifies her actions to the landlady, explaining that she has taken the puppet Lady Townly as her role model.[25] Fielding thus offers an extreme and ironic version of the monkey-see, monkey-do theory of aesthetic response that had animated the reform of the stage codified by Jeremy Collier and put into practice by Cibber, as I explored in chapter 2.

Though *The Provok'd Husband* was an important play to Burney, it seems to have taken her a while to figure out how to use it. As Margaret Doody has demonstrated, the scenes of its amateur performance in *The Wanderer* were revised and recycled versions of ones she had originally drafted for *Camilla* and scrapped.[26] She had celebrated the style of spectatorial immersion that Fielding associated with Cibber (and Richardson) when she showed Evelina longing to join Garrick onstage in her rhapsody about *The Suspicious Husband*: "I would have given the world to have had the whole play acted over again. And when he danced—O how I envied Clarinda. I almost wished to have jumped on the stage and joined them" (*Evelina*, 26). Burney here reversed the direction of Fielding's response to Garrick in another theatrical scene in *Tom Jones*, when Partridge expresses his preference for the performance of the actor playing King Claudius over that of "Squire" Hamlet.[27] In this ironic appreciation, Garrick's natural acting style elicits Partridge's imaginative crossing of the proscenium to bring the Prince of Denmark down into the ranks of the English gentry. Whereas Partridge brings Garrick off the stage, however, Evelina imaginatively projects herself onto it. Burney thus abstracted the climb of Grace, the maid, onto the stage, to refine sexual into aesthetic pleasure.

Though Burney did not discuss Fielding much herself in the pages of her journals and diaries, she recorded the people around her drawing the comparison between her work and his and finding hers to be superior in elevation and morality.[28] Notably, her pleasure in reading Fielding's plays also made her feel dirty:

"I must own I too frequently meet with disgust in all Fielding's Dramatic Works, to laugh with a good Heart even at his Wit, excellent as it is & I should never think myself wading through much dirt to get at it."[29] Burney is uncomfortable with the "wading through dirt" that Fielding demanded, and her laughter is adulterated by disgust and her pleasure in reading by shame and self-reproach.

Burney did not mention Cibber by name in the journals and diaries, though she recorded "Daddy" Crisp's recommendation of his *Apology* when she was composing her first comedy, *The Witlings*.[30] She saw a performance of Cibber's *Careless Husband* on March 27, 1777, and later recounted bits of dialogue in her diary; she also acted parts of it with Maria Allen and Jenny Barsanti, "amid 'tremendous mirth'; there Mr. Crisp and Hetty, [acting out a scene from *Evelina*], danced a minuet, as Madam Duval and Mr. Smith."[31] In comparison to the discomfort prompted by Fielding, including the terrible stage fright she records during a family performance of *Tom Thumb*, her enjoyment of Cibber was less compromised.[32]

Though Burney found Cibber's manipulation of laughter and shamelessness in the name of morality more appealing than Fielding's disgust-inducing lowness, she also must have registered Fielding's (and Pope's) critique of Cibber's shameless self-promotion from the standpoint of a classicized and thus elevated aesthetics. Thirty years after Fielding's and Pope's attacks on Cibber and thereafter, Burney could use Cibber's comfortable bourgeois morality to offset Fielding's vulgarity; meanwhile, her aspirational aesthetics allied her with Fielding (and Pope), whose satire she could use to distance herself from Cibber's pandering as an entertainer. She assuaged their different disturbances to feminine modesty by playing Cibber and Fielding off each other, working laughter, shame, and shamelessness together to depict her heroines' aesthetic and moral educations.

The development of Burney's heroines in the theater of shame vectored shame's capacity to break down the boundaries between its subjects and objects, to recur to Tomkins's language, toward readers. Finding narrative form for the theatricality of shame, she cultivated the intimacy between readers and characters in *Evelina* and *Cecilia* and found ways, in *Camilla* and *The Wanderer*, to sustain that intimacy while pushing it beyond vicarious identification with any single character. The narrative techniques she developed derive from her development of the capacity to modulate the degrees of distance between a more omniscient and a more limited third-person perspective. These contributions to narrative form took specific shape as her career developed. The narrative functions of shameful or shame-inducing theatricality marked the limits of epistolary form in *Evelina*, which Burney thereafter abandoned; provided the enabling conditions for her development of free indirect discourse in *Cecilia*, whose theatrical roots become clear upon consideration of the remarkable exploitation of asides in her belated comedy of manners, *Love and Fashion* (1800); and crystallized in *The Wanderer* the perspectival reversals that pivot on a proscenium that she had initially explored in a less explicitly theatrical manner in *Camilla*.

EVELINA, CECILIA, THEATRICALITY, AND NARRATIVE INNOVATION

In *Evelina*, not only is the theater of shame the scene of social and moral development; it also marks the representational limits of epistolarity, as can be seen in the recognition scenes between Evelina and her father, Sir John Belmont, that constitute the emotional climax of the novel. Shame is the dominant chord of their interactions: Evelina Anville's progress toward marriage hinges on her obtaining paternal recognition, but Belmont has consistently refused to acknowledge her legitimacy or even to see her, believing that he has already done his duty to the child of Lady Belmont. The novel will revalue this paternal neglect, retrospectively redeeming him once it is revealed in the end that a nurse switched her own daughter for Evelina and that Belmont had indeed raised this child in the belief that she was the product of his marriage; this clarification, however, can only follow once he has seen Evelina, who physically resembles her mother to a remarkable degree. His recognition is finally enabled by Evelina's capacity to absorb his shameful abandonment of Evelina's mother by being more ashamed at provoking his feelings than he is for his own neglect.

Evelina narrates this episode to her guardian, Mr. Villars, in volume 3, letter 17:

> "Come forth, then, my dear," cried [Mrs. Selwyn], opening the door, "come forth, and see your father!" *Then, taking my trembling hand, she led me forward.* I would have withdrawn it, and retreated, but *as he advanced instantly towards me*, I found myself already before him. What a moment for your Evelina!—an involuntary scream escaped me, and *covering my face with my hands, I sunk on the floor.* He had, however, seen me first; for *in a voice scarce articulate* he exclaimed, "My God! Does Caroline Evelyn still live!"
>
> Mrs. Selwyn said something, but I could not listen to her; and, in a few minutes, he added, "Lift up thy head,—if my sight has not blasted thee,—lift up thy head, thy image of my long-lost Caroline! Affected beyond measure, *I half arose, and embraced his knees, while yet on my own.* "Yes, yes," cried he, *looking earnestly in my face*, "I see, I see thou art her child! She lives—she breathes—she is present to my view!—Oh God, that

> she indeed lived!—Go, child, go," added he, *wildly starting, and pushing*
> *me from him,* "take her away, madam,—I cannot bear to look at her!" And
> then, breaking hastily from me, *he rushed out of the room.* (372, my
> emphases)

Evelina's nonconfrontational passivity enables Belmont to experience the remorse
necessary for him to restore her name. Disappointing as it may be to readers who
seek a more recognizable feminist Burney, the moral of the story seems to be that
only proper female delicacy will elicit this conferral of patriarchal legitimacy.[33]
Strikingly, Burney delivers this moral in a scene whose sentiment is heightened by
its being a theatrical tableau.

As the passages I emphasized in the quotation indicate, description becomes
stage direction because of the way it punctuates dialogue. These virtual stage directions, moreover, describe the father and daughter in postures that would have
been familiar to Burney's readers from the stage.[34] This invocation of the theater
at the moment of the most sentimental pressure illustrates its centrality to Burney's writing.

This configuration repeats when Evelina makes a second visit to her father
some ten pages later. She once again kneels at his feet, crying out, "It is your child,
if you will own her!" (385). Sir John bursts into tears in recognition of how he had
mistreated Evelina's mother, rises up, crosses the room, and banishes her from his
presence. Begging for his blessing before obeying, she shows him the last letter
from her mother. When he challenges her as to whether she knows its contents,
she answers, "it has never been unsealed" (385). He then reads it, sinks down on
his knees before her, and when she raises him up, once again recognizes her as his
and gives her his blessing.[35]

Burney does not interrupt the choreography of this tableau to give us the
letter, even though its contents presumably would help to narrate Belmont's reform
into a caring father. The scene does not, in regular epistolary fashion, have us read
alongside Belmont; it does not do so because readers have already read the letter:
Burney produced it earlier in the novel when Mr. Villars sent it enclosed to Evelina (338–340). Intent on wringing every last bit of feeling from the father's recognition of the daughter, Burney departs from epistolary convention. Granting
readers early access to the letter despite its never having been unsealed, she rup-
tures the epistolary frame.

The elevated emotional temperature of the scenes of paternal recognition
pushed Burney beyond the governing fiction of epistolary form: the idea that characters and readers encounter events and information at the same time, perhaps
the main source of the power of Richardsonian writing to the moment. She for-

goes this kind of synchronization of characters' and readers' responses, but she provides another kind of seamlessness (what film theorists would call suture) in the scenes of tableaux. When the child kneels to her father and then again when the father kneels to the child, Burney solicited readers to respond as they would in the theater. Theatrical modes of presentation are here called in to support an epistolarity stretched to the breaking point. In *Evelina*, Burney turned to the stage for resources that were not otherwise available to her in epistolary form.[36] The subsequent novels are all narrated omnisciently, though in them, theater continues to supply resources for narrative in surprising ways, in, for example, her development of free indirect discourse.

Free indirect discourse is frequently hailed for its sophisticated capacity to provide readers with access to characters' mental states, and it has even been celebrated as the hallmark device of the novel itself. Blakey Vermeule gives a good overview of various accounts of free indirect discourse, but her interest in the access it gives to characters' minds leads her to minimize other aspects of the device.[37] Franco Moretti, by contrast, tunes into the ways it functions as "a technique of socialization, not individuality": in vacillating between two idioms or perspectives, that of the narrator and that of characters, free indirect discourse both accesses characters' subjectivity and objectifies characters to show the way they see themselves. When Jane Austen's Elizabeth Bennet "observes her own life from the outside as if she were a third person, the grammar of the free indirect style is really the message."[38] Both Vermeule and Moretti adopt Ann Banfield's linguistic account of free indirect discourse as "unspeakable sentences," an excellent description of syntax stretched across mixed idiolects that is a feature of writing and not speech.[39] But Burney's development of free indirect discourse suggests that the narrative device had theatrical roots.

Burney, like other authors, often used free indirect discourse to blur the distinctions between the narrator and a character; occasionally she used it to cross the boundaries that exist between one character and another. Both uses serve to alter readers' distance from the action. An example of the first type, drawn from *Cecilia*, occurs in a passage in which Burney charts the movements of Cecilia's mind and the progress of her feelings as she wonders whether she should listen to Miss Belfield's confession of love for Mortimer Delvile, the man with whom Cecilia has also fallen in love.

> The next day Miss Belfield was to tell her everything by a voluntary promise; but she doubted if she had any right to accept such a confidence. Miss Belfield, she was sure, knew not she was interested in the tale, since she had not even imagined that Delvile was known to her. She might hope, therefore, not only for advice but assistance, and fancy that while

she reposed her secret in the bosom of her friend, she secured herself her best offices and best wishes for ever.

Would she obtain them? No; the most romantic generosity would revolt from such a demand, for however precarious was her own chance with young Delvile, Miss Belfield she was sure could not have any.[40]

Burney's account of Miss Belfield's motivations is produced through Cecilia's responses to them.[41] The momentum of Cecilia's emotional progress culminates in the question, "Would she obtain them? No." The narrator ambiguously addresses this question to both readers and Cecilia. The question and its answer, moreover, are close enough in proximity as well as content to Cecilia's own thoughts to be a question she addresses to herself. By the end of the last sentence, the involuted syntax makes it unclear who is skeptical of Miss Belfield's chances with Delvile: the narrator, Cecilia, or both. Readers are thus taken into the confidence that Cecilia desires to withhold her best wishes from Miss Belfield, even if she is pained to recognize her own lack of generosity or, perhaps, may not even recognize it herself.

This example of free indirect discourse uses an indeterminate mode of interrogative address to affectively align readers with Cecilia, thus bringing them closer together, at the same time as the narrator addresses readers over Cecilia's head, thus wedging them apart. Burney finely coordinates readers' positions, using free indirect discourse to manipulate in opposite directions affective and cognitive responses: readers are granted cognitive superiority over the character at the same time as we share her emotions. This narrative distance-modulating effect anticipates Austen.

Margaret Doody draws an example of the second type of free indirect discourse from *Cecilia*, in which Mr. Delvile's exaggerated sense of his own greatness penetrates the narrator's description of his response to Cecilia. Upon first meeting him, she is offended by his "air of haughty affability," but he attributes "the uneasiness which his reception occasioned, to the over-awing predominance of superior rank and consequence."[42] As Doody says, "Most of Mr. Delvile exists in his own mind."[43] Burney's application of Delvile's vocabulary to Cecilia's experience of him accomplishes two things at once: by making it difficult to pinpoint the boundary between Cecilia's experience of Mr. Delvile and his experience of himself, Burney establishes that he is as incapable of vicarious experience as she is susceptible to it. Burney thus aligns readers with her heroine's capacity for vicarious experience, bringing us closer to the heroine at the expense of another character. This use of free indirect discourse is theatrical insofar as it transposes into a compressed narrative device the dynamic of secondhand shame that occurs in the scenes Burney so frequently sets at the theater. The first kind of free indirect discourse is also theatrical, as emerges more clearly from a comparison to her use of asides in *Love and Fashion*, which has an astonishing number of them.

ASIDES AND FREE INDIRECT DISCOURSE

At first glance, asides addressed to an audience would seem to be quite different from free indirect discourse addressed to readers. For one, narrators' direct addresses in the "dear reader" mode of Fielding, Thackeray, or Trollope are usually located at the opposite end of the spectrum from narrators whose lack of audibility or visibility is understood as the height of sophistication, irony, and, by Miller, even as Style itself. Miller explicitly contrasted Austen's impersonal and divine omniscience to the overly embodied point of view assumed by the clubby narrators of Fielding and Thackeray or the maternal, all-forgiving voice of George Eliot.[44] Second, asides are spoken by characters who thereby take the audience into their confidence, whereas the grammatical "unspeakability" of free indirect discourse has been used to associate it with the representation of thought rather than speech. The comparison, however, flows from the structural similarity implicitly observed though not exploited by Miller when he noted that Austen's narration slaps characters silly without them even being aware of it. Free indirect discourse, like asides (even those between characters), is used to convey cognitive privilege to readers or audience members, as Burney's use clarifies because it exploited her theatergoing readers' thorough familiarity with the position they usually occupied in the audience.

Asides could be considered a prototypically theatrical device especially insofar as, in breaking the fourth wall, they make evident that the normative posture of the audience is that of overhearing. But asides are also novelistic insofar as they allow the audience the kind of access to characters' thoughts that is usually provided by narrators, whether in free indirect discourse or not. Moreover, like free indirect discourse, asides can function in two distinct ways: to reveal a character's thoughts and to allow for special acts of communication to take place between characters. Theatrical prints that visually distilled characteristic styles of performance often represented moments of asides, not just because of the frontal postures of the actors but also because they thereby provided viewers with the opportunity to relive or imagine one of the key pleasures of theatergoing when they were taken into the confidence of the characters onstage. In figure 4.1, for example, Frances Abington is depicted in the character of Lady Betty Modish from Cibber's *Careless Husband*, speaking an aside.

Before the Restoration, dramatic characters' thoughts could be conveyed in soliloquy, but the neoclassical attack on the absurdity of self-addressed speeches

Figure 4.1. Frances Abington as Lady Betty Modish, I. Taylor, published T. Lowdnes (1777) (Permission of the Harry Ransom Center)

prompted a steep decline, though it did not eliminate them completely. François Hédelin, abbé d'Aubignac, recognizing that the stage could not do without soliloquies entirely, recommended limiting their length to a dozen words or one verse.[45] In a history of the soliloquy, James Hirsh observed another important difference between those of the Renaissance and the Restoration: Renaissance soliloquies could be overheard by other characters, whereas Restoration soliloquies functioned as interior monologues and thus could not be overheard.[46] For Hirsh, Descartes's model of mind helps to explain this rerouting from speech to thought in utterances taking the form of soliloquies or asides. An informal survey of asides over the course of the eighteenth century suggests that the appearance of the novel may also have been an influence.

The neoclassical strictures on asides took hold more firmly in tragedy than in comedy, though the overall number in comedies, itself quite variable, declined between 1675 and 1722: Wycherley used 72 in *The Country Wife* (1675) and 71 in *The Plain Dealer* (1676), Congreve used 3 in *Way of the World* (1700), Cibber used 39 in *The Careless Husband* (1704) and 43 in *The Provok'd Husband* (1728), Steele used 20 in *The Conscious Lovers* (1722).[47] An uptick later in the century, with Goldsmith using 28 in *She Stoops to Conquer* (1773) and Sheridan using 35 in *The Rivals* (1775) and 53 in *School for Scandal* (1777), was dwarfed entirely by the remarkable 119 in Burney's *Love and Fashion*.[48]

If Goldsmith's and Sheridan's asides responded to what the novel could do, they nevertheless remained less novelistic than Burney's. In a revival of the traditional vice figure who takes the audience into his confidence, for example, Sheridan gave the two-faced Joseph Surface more asides than any other character in *School for Scandal*. Most of these are concentrated in act 4, scene 3, which also features the famous screen discovery scene. The play thus subordinates the supposed truths spoken by Joseph in his privileged communications with the audience to what is visibly exposed for all to see. In Sheridan's exploration of the differences between what can be said and what can be shown, he ultimately retained the stage as the adjudicator of truth: it is the platform that levels the cognitive superiority that is momentarily granted to the audience, a privilege that novels handled differently.[49]

By contrast, in *Love and Fashion*, not only are Burney's asides novelistic, but they are novelistic in two different ways: most often, characters use them to abrogate the position of the narrator; at some moments, though, they also share with free indirect discourse the capacity to give audiences or readers epistemic privilege by expressing thoughts or wishes that a character does not know or own. This more unusual use locates *Love and Fashion*, a belated comedy of manners, at a crossroads of the theater and the novel.

Hilaria Dalton, the play's comic heroine, wants to marry for love and fashion, but Valentine Exbury, the young man she loves, has no money and worries that she cannot tell the difference between them. Readers of *Camilla* will recognize these concerns as lightweight, shorthand versions of those plaguing Edgar Mandlebert. To a certain extent, the play, which Burney composed after the novel appeared in 1796, could be considered a miniature version of it. In act 5, scene 2, Burney allows the play's lovers the uninterrupted tête-à-tête permitting the mutual self-clarification that was denied to Edgar and Camilla until the final chapter of this five-volume, ten-book novel.

The play also registers the pressure of other contemporary novels. For example, it includes a supposed ghost whose haunting effects are rendered comic because they are actually produced by people using the hidden staircase and private door to one of the rooms. Burney thus provides a dramatic version of Radcliffe's explained supernatural. It also includes a Strange Man who wanders around the grounds telling people's fortunes but who is revealed in the end to be a bailiff there to arrest Valentine for debt. In the course of his wanderings, the Strange Man encounters a Woodcutter and a Haymaker, rustic characters who, in country accents, praise love for its greater satisfactions than money. Burney thus populates a landscape just beyond the purview of the cottage to which the Exbury family has retreated in order to curb their expenses, the play's set. She thereby elaborates a range of socioeconomic positions beyond the usual dyad of masters and their servants to provide a social panorama of the kind more usually associated with the novels of Maria Edgeworth or Burney herself than with the eighteenth-century stage.

Burney used asides mainly for comic effect to reveal the discrepancy between characters' expectations and what they can safely say or in response to what is said to them, allowing characters uniformly, no matter how minor or from which social level, the ability to reveal themselves to the audience over the heads of the other characters. Like the example of the second type of free indirect discourse that blurs the boundaries between characters, this use of asides brings the audience closer to one character at the expense of the others. In act 3, scene 1, for example, the Strange Man tells the maid Innis's fortune in the presence of the butler Davis and the valet Dawson, both of whom consider themselves eligible suitors and neither of whom can recognize themselves in the unflattering physical description the fortune-teller gives. After each description, Davis and Dawson each react in asides, a pattern of utterance that repeats five times.

The scene of the play that is built most exclusively on asides in which characters reveal more than they themselves understand turns on the attempt of the kindly Lord Exbury to induce remorse in his spendthrift son, Mordaunt, whose debts have caused the family to move to the haunted cottage. Shame has a pivotal function in this scene, but comically, it fails to have its improving effect on this prodigal son.

At the beginning of the scene, Lord Exbury lays out his disappointed expectations mainly in asides:

> MORDAUNT: I am afraid I have made you wait, my lord.
> LORD E: Not much. (*aside*) What unfeeling ease!
> M: Not that you can have anything of consequence to do with your time, to be sure, in a place such as this.
> LORD E: (*aside*) Astonishing! his courage almost diverts me of self-command! (act 4, scene 2, lines 169–174)

They proceed in a similar fashion until Lord Exbury is overpowered and begins to reprimand his son, at which point Mordaunt begins to respond in asides.

> LORD E: Various are the excuses, and many the palliations for the indiscretions of youth, where repentance follows misdeeds, and error is succeeded by calamity: but so impenetrably are you hardened that you seem indifferent to the consequences of your faults, as to their heinousness.
> M (*aside*): I am frightened to death lest I should drop off to sleep before he has done!
> LORD E: The smallest appearance of concern would soften us all; one single moment of contrition subdues us completely.—
> M (*aside*): He'll never forgive it if I do! (act 4, scene 2, lines 204–213)

Mordaunt appears so immune to his father's reproach that he is actually capable of nodding off during it. Though his emotional apathy is (presumably) uttered in tones of languor because he is falling asleep, he uses the vocabulary of agitation: "I'm frightened to death." The comedy derives not only from the juxtaposition between the feelings he expresses and his behavior but also from the fact that, virtually unconscious, he speaks here only in asides. Asides direct the shame that Mordaunt cannot experience toward the audience, which experiences it on his behalf. As he verges on sleep, moreover, Mordaunt perhaps prepares to enter the zone of unconscious remorse from which Cibber's Sir Charles Easy had awakened to virtue in *The Careless Husband*. Asides might here be said to function like the first type of free indirect discourse, in which feelings of which a character cannot properly be said to be aware are conveyed to readers in an idiom shared between the narrator and the character, with an undecidable degree of complicity or participation of the character.

Burney's asides bring out that audience members' or readers' capacity for experiencing vicarious emotion does not depend on, though it can include, an identificatory relationship with a character: rather, it is positional. The similarities between asides and free indirect discourse suggest, moreover, that though the sentences Burney writes in free indirect discourse may draw their narrative force from an unspeakable syntax, their provenance in the theater of shame gives them a performative in addition to a grammatical dimension: they position readers visà-vis the action in places, postures, and attitudes that are not and cannot be fully congruent with those of the characters. The comparison with her use of asides suggests that Burney used free indirect discourse to locate readers in an imagined theater, thus reproducing the preferred scene of the heroines' socialization, but with the additional capacity for moving us closer to or farther away from the action or in different directions simultaneously according to appeals to our affective or cognitive responses.

Free indirect discourse, however, is not the only device Burney used to modulate readers' distance from and involvement with her novels and their characters. In *Persuasion* (1816), when Austen's narrator extolls readers first to adopt the perspective of the portraits on the walls from which to view the disorder of the Musgroves' parlor and then to look back at the staring portraits themselves, the theatricality of the perspectival reversal is easy to overlook. In *The Wanderer*, by contrast, similar reversals are explicitly theatrical. In Burney's last novel, by virtue of its thoroughgoing theatricality, she provided a proscenium to organize reversals of perspective that she had earlier explored quite extensively in *Camilla*.

CAMILLA, THE WANDERER, PERSPECTIVAL REVERSAL, AND MELODRAMA

Camilla and *The Wanderer* are both excruciatingly long and repetitive and, for those reasons, were seen even in their own time as only partial successes, if that. Burney responded to critics of *Camilla* who had objected to its length and didacticism by producing a significantly shorter second edition; she tried to persuade herself that similar objections to *The Wanderer* were politically motivated.[50] The theatrical frame of reference, however, should not be taken as the source of these novels' failure; rather, it makes it possible to perceive their experimentation with narrative devices for cultivating intimacy with and affective investment in a flawed heroine like Camilla or a constrained character like Ellis/Juliet.

Burney organized readers' access to the worlds that her novels describe with their theatrical experiences, and her own, in mind. By the later 1790s, moreover, repetition had become a way to signify the subordination of characters to their circumstances in the melodramatic modes associated with both the Gothic novel and the Sturm und Drang drama. Burney's heroines each more or less passively withstand the recurrent tests to which those who misjudge them subject them, only to emerge morally triumphant in the end, though quietly so. Like her Jacobin contemporaries, Burney used repetition to signify social determination, though she also boosted the negative associations of melodrama in *The Wanderer* by personifying its energies in its Wollstonecraftian antiheroine, Elinor Joddrel.

Camilla, a novel of prolonged missed opportunity, turns on the almost universal recognition that Camilla Tyrold and Edgar Mandlebert love each other and belong together and on their consistent misunderstandings, first of themselves and then of each other—even after they have become engaged to each other. They keep looking past each other, misrecognizing each other's motivations and feelings, and failing to find occasions to explain themselves to each other, even though they appreciate each other's true worth. In the first half of the novel, these opportunities are missed by chance or because of social manners or gender norms; in the second half, self-knowledge and the knowledge of others become convoluted as individual motivation and self-consciousness still do nothing to facilitate mutual understanding. Instead, as both Camilla and Edgar try to perform to and against each other's expectations, the accumulation of failed recognitions only makes matters worse.

Dedicated to exposing the lovers' mortifying failures to understand themselves and each other while providing descriptions that make readers understand what each one does and does not see, this novel is designed to probe the discrepancy between readers and characters. It relentlessly explores the narration of limited perspective, in which characters' self-consciousness cannot produce illumination, notwithstanding such a high degree of plot repetition that its main narrative arc is reprised in full. After having failed to inspire signs of love from Edgar by means of an extended flirtation with the foppish Sir Sedley Clarendel, Camilla flirts first with Hal Westwyn and then with Lord Valhurst and still does not succeed in winning Edgar back. Instead she inadvertently validates his suspicions that she may be a "confirmed coquette."[51] The pattern of misrecognition between the lovers that structures the narrative as a whole is echoed at the local level by many episodes that are structured by reversals of perspective between characters including, but not limited to, the lovers. The description of what a character sees is followed immediately by a description from the opposite perspective.

In a virtuoso reading of *Camilla* that is finely attuned to its investment in economic matters, Deidre Lynch has proposed that "spectacle suspends story."[52] She captures the dialectic between women's objectification on the marriage market and their subjectification as consumers. Of Burney's treatment of the double logic of the commodity, Lynch observes that Camilla must learn to turn down its invitation, to look at herself in the mirror and say, "That's not me."[53] But this look in the mirror, whether it elicits recognition of the reflection that looks back or demurral, rests on a perspectival reversal. The exchange of glances and stares and the rhythms and reversals of direction in what is seen do not oppose spectacle but rather constitute it. Spectacle, moreover, does not so much interfere with or suspend story as augment it. Lynch's treatment of spectacle is not essential to her argument, but it threatens to cancel the role of theater in Burney's narrative experiment and, in so doing, to make the novel both more familiar and easier to dismiss as flawed. In Burney, spectacle's ordinariness does not mitigate its intense shame-inducing capacities; instead it emphasizes them, as can be seen in the episode in Southampton in which Mrs. Mitten and Camilla go shopping.[54]

Mrs. Mitten takes Camilla along the High Street, proposing that they enter each shop to ask for directions as a pretext for checking out the goods. Mrs. Mitten "boasted to Camilla, that, by this clever device they might see all that was smartest without the expence of buying anything" (607). But this perusal with no intention to purchase first attracts the attention of the shopkeepers and then inspires alarm that the women are shoplifters. Burney stages the shopkeepers' perspective as the reverse of the women's.

The men follow the women out onto the street.

> Mr. Firl, a sagacious old linen-draper, who concluded them to be shop-lifters, declared he would keep aloof, for he should detect them best when they least expected they were observed.
>
> Mr. Drim, a gentle and simple haberdasher, who believed their senses disordered, made a circuit to face and examine them, frequently, however, looking back, to see that no absconding trick was played him by his friends. When he came up to them, the pensive and absorbed look of Camilla struck him as too particular to be natural; and in Mrs. Mitten he immediately fancied he perceived something wild, if not insane. In truth, an opinion preconceived of her derangement might easily authorise strong suspicions of confirmation, from the contented volubility with which she incessantly ran on, without waiting for answerers, or even listeners; and his observation had not taught him, that the loquacious desire only to speak. They exact time, not attention.
>
> Mrs. Mitten, soon observing the curiosity with which he examined them, looked at him hard in return talking the whole time in a quick low voice, to Camilla, upon his oddity, that, struck with a direful panic, in the persuasion she was marking him for some mischief, he turned short about to get back to his companions; leaving Mrs. Mitten with precisely the same opinion of himself which he had imbibed of her. (608–609)

What characters see and how they process it leads Burney's narrator to pronounce judgment on their limitations, which, ironically, are shown to be symmetrical. As the men circle, face, and retreat from the women, these reversals of perspective escalate the tensions of the episode. The men, having wagered on the women's business, pursue them to a bathing house, where they are subjected to an even more humiliating confrontation. Edgar, who happens to be in the neighborhood, rescues them and gathers more negative impressions of Camilla's flightiness, but not before more reversals of perspective occur.

Lynch's opposition of spectacle to story means she must reconcile "the Frances Burney who describes the spectacle of consumption" with "the Frances Burney who narrates the ineffable psychological subtexts of selfhood," but the opposition is one of her own making.[55] *Evelina* systematically explored the various kinds of attention that different scenes of performance and entertainment elicit in order to accord its heroine the natural capacity for aesthetic appreciation that her entry into the world will refine and on which basis she will deserve marriage to Orville. The hurdles Cecilia and Camilla must overcome as they proceed to integrate aesthetic and economic matters make their trajectories more complex. Consequently, it takes them longer to obtain the romantic and social validation they deserve. But in all three novels, shopping provides the training ground for the kinds of subjectivity Burney explored not only because of the relations to commodities that it required or enabled, for which Lynch supplies a brilliant and thorough account, but also because of its resemblance to theater, as her own formulation, "the spectacle of consumption," suggests. The image in figure 4.2, "Beauty in Search of Knowledge," depicts the self-possessed Beauty on her itinerary as she negotiates public streets and semipublic spaces such as the circulating library or the theater; it thus captures the similarities between shopping and cultural consumption that borrowing from the circulating library or attending theatrical performances entailed.

The novel was not for Burney the only literary expression of the virtual subjectivity that it also helped to constitute. Nor did it constitute such virtual subjectivity alone. The theater was not opposed to the novel in Burney's project; it was its ally. This subjectivity, moreover, was constituted by shame: Camilla, having contracted "debts from mingled thoughtlessness, inexperience and generosity" (737), is "overwhelmed with [an] internal shame" (761), compounded by the similarity between her conduct and that of her shameless male relatives, her brother Lionel and her cousin Clermont. She emerges from the resulting state of debilitation morally improved. The perspectival reversals that recur in *Camilla* provide a mechanism for investing narration in various embodiments that make possible its freedom from any particular embodiment. Burney's commitment to perspectival reversal as a

CIRCULATING LIBRARY

BEAUTY in SEARCH of KNOWLEDGE.

London Printed for R. Sayer & J. Bennett. Map. Chart & Printsellers N°53 Fleet Street 30th Dec 1782

Figure 4.2. "Beauty in Search of Knowledge," after print by John Raphael Smith, published by Sayer and Bennett (1782) (© Trustees of the British Museum) way to organize narration dictated a high degree of repetition, much of it deriving from the structural similarity of the episodes, a feature *Camilla* shares with *The Wanderer*, in which the spatial organization of the perspectival reversals obtains a more explicit theatricality: in *The Wanderer*, the pivot on which they occur often enough is an actual or virtual proscenium.[56]

Melodrama thoroughly infuses the plot of *The Wanderer*, which deals with the consequences of the French Revolution. Burney's familiarity with the new stage fashions at the turn of the eighteenth century stemmed not only from the aborted attempt to produce her comedy *Love and Fashion* in 1800 but also from consistent play-going: she saw at least five new plays in the London season of 1797–1798, including Matthew Lewis's *The Castle Spectre*, his dramatic adaptation of *The Monk*, and comedies by George Colman the Younger and Thomas Holcroft.[57] Between 1802 and 1812, when she was trapped with little money on the outskirts of Paris due to the Napoleonic conflicts, she nevertheless went occasionally to the theater, to the opera, and to the Boulevards at least once.[58] The amateur theatricals of *The Wanderer*, like those of *Mansfield Park*, let characters explore their romantic feelings for one another under the cover of their parts. In Burney, the inset play also helps to develop the contrast between the two styles of female performance that dominate the book: the self-effacing recessive style of the shame-susceptible Ellis/ Juliet; the wanderer of the title; and the self-aggrandizing, projective style of the shameless Elinor Joddrel.

Ellis/Juliet is awkwardly positioned as a refugee from France with no money and no name she feels able to acknowledge, and she is powerless to refuse the demands of her hosts, on whose goodwill she relies utterly. She is cast against her wishes in the role of Lady Townly in Cibber's *Provoked Husband*. Her performance combines reticence and good manners and somehow telegraphs her aristocratic blood to the assembled members of the audience, which includes Lord Melbury and Lady Aurora Granville, to whom she is related, as the novel's conclusion reveals some eight hundred pages later. Elinor, in marked contrast, eagerly assumes the role of stage manager and even imagines herself also taking the role of the vulgar Lady Wronghead.

Understandably, readers have described the striking contrast between the performance styles of Ellis/Juliet and Elinor as an opposition to be grasped either in political or gender terms, with the main interpretive problem being how to collate the two.[59] This allegorization, however, occludes a view of the women as partners. They form an awkward and impossible love triangle with Albert Harleigh; their rivalry expresses a mimetic desire that is also an engine that drives the plot. Their interactions in and around the theater echo and, through repetition, amplify the dynamics of Burney's earlier works, but they also complicate, if not refuse to establish, the single stable relationship of vicarious identification between readers and the heroine that *Evelina* and *Cecilia* had solicited (on the basis of the heroine's capacity for experiencing secondhand shame) and *Camilla* had complicated. The dynamic female contrast and the technique of perspectival reversal come together in two of the four scenes of Elinor's attempts at suicide.

Burney's perspectival reversals offer a sequence in which the view of what a character sees is immediately followed by a description of what can be seen in her. Burney exploits this reversal most fully first in a theatrical scene in which as much of the action occurs in the audience as on the stage. A proscenium thus supplies the axis for 180-degree reversal from what can be seen on the stage to what can be seen from the stage, a narrative equivalent of the shot-reverse-shot of classic cinema. Abrupt perspectival shifts that alternate between what each character sees and what can be seen in them creates fast-paced action. This emotion-packed scene features Elinor's second failed suicide attempt.

Elinor's first suicide attempt had elicited Ellis's promise never to marry Harleigh, although this does not prevent subsequent attempts, which she stages in increasingly elaborate scenarios designed to secure Ellis and Harleigh as witnesses. These suicide scenes are thus not only dramatic, that is to say, emotionally overcharged, but also theatrical, in that Elinor is their dramaturg. Her second suicide attempt occurs in the public rooms of a hotel, where Ellis is reluctantly about to give a concert on the harp. She enters the rooms trembling with trepidation, "seating herself behind a violincello-player, and as much out of sight as possible, till necessity must, of course, bring her forward."[60] Elinor, on the other hand, thoroughly embraces the opportunity for self-staging. She enters elaborately disguised as a strange deaf and dumb man in foreign clothes. "Wrapt in a scarlet cloak [which was] open at the breast, to display a brilliant waistcoat of coloured and spangled embroidery, [he wore] a small, but slouched hat, and a cravat of enormous bulk [which] encircled his chin" (357), Elinor is dressed in the style of the fashionable young men of the Directoire known as the *Incroyables* (see figure 4.3).

Elinor's disguise as a deaf-mute alludes to stage melodramas, which often featured characters with physical or intellectual disabilities, including the one frequently taken as the first, *Çoelina, ou l'enfant du mystère* (1800) by Guilbert de Pixérécourt.[61] Translated into English by Thomas Holcroft, *A Tale of Mystery* (1802) featured a deaf-mute character who identified the villain in the nick of time. Burney thus affiliates Elinor not only with Jacobin feminism but also with melodrama.

The disguised Elinor plants herself directly in Ellis's line of sight. Suspecting that this might be "Elinor disguised, and Elinor come to perpetrate the bloody deed of suicide" (359), Ellis faints. As Harleigh leaps up to help her, Elinor reorients

LES INCROYABLES.

Figure 4.3. Horace Vernet's *Les Incroyables* from *Modes Parisiennes* (The incredibles, Paris fashions, 1795) (© Trustees of the British Museum)

attention away from the action on the stage, crying out, "Turn, Harleigh, turn! and see thy willing martyr!—Behold, perfidious Ellis! Behold thy victim!" (359). She then plunges a dagger into her breast. These thrilling reversals in perspective use narrative to extend the resources of the theater in a direction they cannot go (because the audience has only its point of view of the stage) even as they are made possible by the stage. This sort of reversal of perspective may be more familiar to us from its use in film. Hitchcock gives a similar one in the climactic scene of *The 39 Steps*, also set in a theater, from the point of view of the audience to the point of view from the stage.[62]

These reversals in perspective focus on Harleigh as he first helps Ellis and then Elinor. "His presence of mind was sooner useful than that of any of the company; the ladies of which were hiding their faces, or running away; and the men, though all eagerly crowding to the spot of this tremendous event, approaching rather as spectators of some public exhibition, than as actors in a scene of humanity.

[121]

Harleigh called upon them to fly instantly for a surgeon; demanded an arm-chair for Elinor, and earnestly charged some of the ladies to come to her aid" (359–360). Harleigh is differentiated from the rest of the audience because of his activity: he is an actor, whereas they are spectators, as befits his traversing the proscenium. Burney does not here counterpose the theater to some more authentic realm of behavior—indeed, the diction suggests the opposite: that any action occurs in the "scene of humanity." The theater here is not a metaphor, but neither is it only a setting. Rather, it provides a set of conditions for narrative exploration or, perhaps more precisely, a toolkit for narrative composition. If Elinor's interruptive, upstaging performance relieves Ellis of the need to perform, by the same token Ellis's fainting helps make possible the bungling of Elinor's suicide attempt. And Elinor's swoon, as Emily Anderson points out, enables Harleigh to have the surgeon intervene and save her life.[63] These plot-advancing actions occur in a mise-en-scène in which Harleigh and Elinor project themselves onto the stage to complete, rather than offset, Ellis's recessive performance.

Another version of this scene in another failed suicide attempt features similar reversals of perspective, though these occur in a virtual rather than an actual theater. Elinor has lured Ellis, now Juliet, and Harleigh from their separate locations to a remote church. Dressed in a white shroud, having prepared her own tombstone, Elinor hopes that the backdrop to her suicide will serve double duty as the altar for the couple's wedding. Having released Juliet from her vow not to marry Harleigh, Elinor exclaims, "Here is the spot! Here stands the altar for the happy;—here, the tomb for the hopeless" (580). Harleigh interferes with Elinor's attempt to shoot herself, though she tries again; once again, she is foiled by Harleigh.

Rapid shifts in perspectives describe what Elinor stages and what Harleigh and Juliet see. Although the line between actors and audience members is blurred by the absence of an actual stage in this episode, Burney nevertheless uses the directionality of perspective to produce similar effects to those of the earlier suicide attempt in the theater. Harleigh and Juliet's failure to exchange glances produces an awkward and shame-filled moment that gives Elinor the opportunity for one last attempt to shoot herself and Harleigh the chance to prevent it.

> Juliet stood motionless, pale, almost livid, and appearing nearly as unable to think as to speak. But the feelings of Harleigh were as much too actively alive, as her's seemed morbid. Agitation beat at every pulse, flowed in every vein, throbbed even visibly in his heart, which bounded with tumultuous triumph, that Juliet, now, was liberated from all adverse engagements: and though he sought, and meant, to turn his eyes, with tender

pity, upon Elinor, they stole involuntarily, impulsively, glances of extatic felicity at the mute and appalled Juliet.

The watchful Elinor discerned the distraction, which he imagined to be as impenetrable as it was irresistible. Shame mingled with despondence; and she disengaged herself from his hold; but, suspicious of some new violence, he hovered over her with extended arms; and presently caught a glimpse of a second pistol, placed behind the tablet, and, as nearly as possible, out of sight. Her intention could not be doubted; but, forcibly anticipating her movement, he seized the destined instrument of death, and, flying to the porch, fired it also into the air. (581)

Even the clunky efforts to tell us what may lie beyond the characters' self-knowledge, for example, that Harleigh mistakenly imagines his distraction by Juliet to be imperceptible to Elinor, does not create much of a lag. This scene, like the earlier one, is excruciating because Burney seeks to maximize readers' discomfort at the same time as she would put us at a remove from the dramaturgy of the primary stage manager, the shameless Elinor, now shamed. "Now confounded; [Elinor] reddened with confusion, trembled with ire, and seemed nearly fainting with an excess of emotion; but she forced a smile and said, 'Harleigh, our tragic-comedy has a long last act! But you can never, now, believe me dead, till you see me buried. That, next, must follow'" (581). In Elinor's suicide scenes, Burney pushes her interests in shame and theater to the extreme in order to reveal their mutual interdependence at the level of narrative content as well as technique.

Burney would seem to invite us to dismiss Elinor's melodramatic self-dramatizations—indeed, she virtually disappears from the novel after she recovers from this last suicide attempt. But however negatively her theatricality is valued, Elinor functions in a complex mise-en-scène that does not and indeed cannot afford to repudiate the theater itself. None of the characters is free from the need to perform, or from theater's aesthetic pleasures, even though theater is also the vehicle through which other emotions and values are conveyed in narrative. The full meaning of theater in Burney's novels cannot be reduced to its affiliation with one character or another or to the experience of having been thwarted in her attempts at theatrical production; instead it must be understood as a potential setting, as well as a set of cues for descriptions of scene, action, and characters' speech, which operate together in a complex narrative structure.

Burney's free indirect discourse and perspectival reversals deliver the process of her heroines' socialization as the penetration of individual experience (their moral development) by social concerns (their recognition by others and their acquisitions of taste, manners, and sometimes title). As interested as her novels may be in individual mental processes, they are equally interested in depicting the social world, which they often do by representing it in microcosm at the theater. Her heroines' socialization, moreover, is rendered in narratives that exhibit a generic hybridity across the different media and social spaces of the theater and the novel to provide a sensitive registration of the ways they exist in their own minds, which may or may not be reflected back at them by the other inhabitants of their worlds or coincide fully with the views of readers. The plot repetitions of the later novels stem from Burney's interest in narrating the determination of characters by circumstance, which can offer a new measure of their development. The Jacobin novelists Elizabeth Inchbald, Thomas Holcroft, and William Godwin explored the doctrine of necessity by experimenting with plot repetition and different narrative perspectives that reflected not only the influence of melodrama but also that of Burney—notwithstanding their political differences. Putting Burney and her theatricality back into the history of the novel accommodates elements of the novel that have otherwise seemed anomalous.

IN "BY THE FIRESIDE," a 1933 essay only published in English in 2015, Walter Benjamin offered a highly compressed version of his idea of "story" in a review of the German translation of Arnold Bennett's *The Old Wives' Tale* (1908). Reflecting on Moritz Heimann's remark, "A man who dies at the age of thirty-five is a man who dies at the age of thirty-five every day of his life," he reserved judgment on its truth in the world but applied it nevertheless to the novel.

> The reader meets characters "the meaning of whose lives" he must be able to grasp. Thus somehow or other he must know in advance that he will learn about their deaths; if need be only in a metaphorical sense, i.e. the end of the novel—but, even better, in their actual deaths. How do they signal that death awaits them, a specific death, moreover, that will occur at a particular point in the novel? That is the question the reader finds so irresistible, and which binds him to the text, just as he is hypnotized by the flames in the hearth.[1]

In "The Storyteller" (1936), for which "By the Fireside" served as a sort of rehearsal, Benjamin returned to Heimann's remark to retool his treatment of the novel reader alone by the fireside. "In this solitude, the reader of the novel seizes upon his material more jealously than anyone else. He is ready to make it completely his own, to devour it, as it were. Indeed he destroys, he swallows up the material as the fire devours the log in the fireplace. The suspense which permeates the novel is very much like the draft which stimulates the flame in the fireplace." The suspense that comes from readers' need to know in advance about characters' deaths remains: "What draws the reader to the novel is the hope of warming his shivering life with a death he reads about."[2]

In "The Storyteller," the novel could become the "earliest symptom of a process whose end is the decline of storytelling" because of its "essential dependence on the book," that is, print, even though story persisted, as Benjamin illustrated with the example of Leskov.[3] Although in "By the Fireside," the attention to media was more attenuated, he produced an arresting comparison of the experience of the solitary novel reader to the consumer of the other genres: the reader of novels sits alone by the fire; the member of the audience at a play "subside[s] into the crowd and shares its response"; and the reader of poetry "is willing to turn into a partner and lend his voice to the poem."[4] Benjamin thus crystallized generic and media differences on the way toward illuminating the difference that print makes, from which, perhaps paradoxically, emerged a depiction of an entity that persists across media and genre: story.

Benjamin's examination of the generic and media distinctions crucial to the experience and organization of literature suggests that they are historically contingent, that they take shape under the aegis of particular cross-generic and intermedial configurations. His scene by the fireside embeds aspects of story by dramatizing them and thereby indicates one answer to the irresistible question: novels often signal the meaning of characters' lives, that is, their deaths by theatrical means. This chapter concludes my investigation of the cross-generic and intermedial relations of the novel and the drama in the eighteenth century by demonstrating that Elizabeth Inchbald and Jane Austen each adapted dramatic, indeed melodramatic, conventions to signal the meaning of characters' lives and thereby refined the narrative techniques of the novel.

Inchbald, for example, took techniques from the melodramatic stage to signal characters' deaths. Those techniques were taken up almost immediately by her fellow Jacobin and sometime friend William Godwin and polished later by novelists committed to structures of determinism and overdetermination, including Anthony Trollope, Charles Dickens, and Thomas Hardy whom I discuss in a brief coda. The fates of Austen's characters are bound up not with death but with marriage, yet she, like Inchbald, incorporated techniques from melodrama in order to subordinate the comedy of manners' emphasis on marriage to the narration of female development.[5] Melodrama played a role in the generic disambiguation of the novel from the drama notwithstanding, indeed perhaps because of, its cross-generic, multimedia, and multimodal nature. It is no accident that when Benjamin adapted the insights of "By the Fireside" for "The Storyteller," he used melodramatic tropes to depict the devouring vampiric novel reader shivering by the fire.

Inchbald and Austen are an unlikely pair, but bringing them together provides some advantages.[6] Though their politics were different, their gender politics were similar insofar as each explored the compulsory nature of marriage and its consequences for women. Their theatricality also took different forms: Inchbald's experiences as a working actor and playwright equipped her to find narrative equivalents of stage practices, whereas Austen more often exploited dramatic conventions for reading purposes, though direct borrowings from the stage can also be found in her novels. Together they revise the history of the novel, pushing against the realism paradigm, Inchbald from beyond its confines, Austen from within them, with consequences for any history of the novel that remains cognizant of the persistence of generic and media crossings.

In Inchbald's "Remarks" on the 125 plays included in *The British Theatre*, Longman's popular anthology (1806–1808), she frequently observed the differences between reading plays and seeing them performed; yet she also wrote scenes, as I argued in chapter 2, for an audience of novel readers.[7] Austen's novels not only reflect the significance of the elocutionary movement, as Patricia Michaelson has observed; her orchestration of free indirect discourse and dialogue also discloses the design to be read aloud.[8] Inchbald and Austen each illustrate intermediary and intermedial practices between performance and print in their novels and elsewhere, even though Inchbald also polemicized about the differences between plays and novels, and Austen, now second only to Shakespeare in the English canon, has come to serve metonymically for the novel itself.

The traditional view that Austen is antitheatrical has not gone unchallenged. Penny Gay has established the significance of the experience of the theater across Austen's novels, though most other critics interested in the topic have gravitated toward her incorporation of the amateur theatricals into the first third of *Mansfield Park*.[9] Fanny Price's reluctance to participate has been equated with her author's attitude toward the theater, notwithstanding corrective readings by Daniel O'Quinn, Ros Ballaster, and others, a conflation underwritten by the identification of Austen with the form of the novel itself.[10] This latter alignment flows from Austen's sophisticated use of free indirect discourse, a technique critics from across the spectrum agree lies at the heart of the novel for its unique capacity to represent characters' minds.[11] But this conjoining of Austen with free indirect discourse has served to obscure that, at key moments, the thoughts and feelings of Austen's characters are not narrated at all. Readers understand that which is not narrated because it is delivered by stage effects, including mise-en-scène, dialogue, and asides.

Although the first line of *Pride and Prejudice*, "It is a truth universally acknowledged . . . ," is remembered by all its readers, less frequently acknowledged is that it introduces two whole chapters of practically unadorned dialogue, as Michaelson observes. Remarking that such extended dialogue may be unprecedented, she also notes trenchantly that free indirect discourse gives an especially oral quality to Austen's writing.[12] When Ann Banfield described free indirect discourse as unspeakable, her observation of its grammatical divergence from ordinary language attested to its literariness but did not preclude its sentences from being read aloud.[13] Indeed, the combination of dialogue and free indirect discourse across Austen's oeuvre attests to her theatrical imagination and to her enlistment of the theatrical imaginations of her readers. Yet treatments of Austen have tended to flow from a presumed opposition between the novel and the stage, just as treatments of Inchbald have reflected this same assumption from the opposite direction. Her two novels, *A Simple Story* (1791) and *Nature and Art* (1796), have been analyzed in relation to her stage career in accounts that, though productive, have depicted the attractions of the novel as opposed to those of the stage.[14]

Inchbald and Austen intersect most prominently in *Mansfield Park*, in which the play produced by the Bertrams and their friends is Alexander von Kotzebue's *Lovers' Vows* in Inchbald's translation. Austen was familiar with it: she may have seen it performed at the Theater Royal in Bath, and as O'Quinn has acutely observed, the roles she assigns to her novel's characters resonate ironically with their fates.[15] Their intersection prompts a revisionary account of melodrama, which frames the three sections of this chapter. In the first section, I consider Inchbald's reflections on the political differences between novels and plays alongside the distinction in other theoretical statements of the time—differences belied to a certain extent by the hybridity of her own work. I explore her significant influence on Godwin in the second section. In the last section, I turn to Austen, whose annexation of dramatic conventions for the reading experience in key moments of *Sense and Sensibility*, *Mansfield Park*, and *Persuasion* amplifies the ambiguities of the politics of generic distinction that the Jacobins had introduced. At these moments, which lay bare the registration of the compulsory nature of marriage even as they probe the limits of realism, Austen comes to resemble Inchbald. Writing novels that incorporated melodramatic elements on the cusp of a greater separation of novels from plays, Inchbald and Austen together permit the history of the novel as it was shaped by the stage over the long eighteenth century to return, in conclusion, to the Benjaminian idea of story.

THE MELODRAMATIC MOMENT

Theater historians usually locate the origins of melodrama in the wake of the French Revolution and identify the first as Guilbert de Pixérécourt's *Çoelina, ou l'enfant du mystère* (1800). An astonishing success with 374 performances in Paris and almost 2,000 in the provinces, the play was almost immediately translated into

English by Thomas Holcroft as *A Tale of Mystery* and performed at Covent Garden in 1802.[16] Though musical interludes, especially songs, had long been used in drama, the simultaneous accompaniment of speech and action by music in the form that has since been naturalized for us via the film soundtrack was an invention of melodrama. The distinctive use of music to accompany action as a constant mood indicator and amplifier and the inclusion of pantomime gestures had also been features of Jean-Jacques Rousseau's earlier play *Pygmalion* (1763), subtitled a "melo-drame" and introduced at Weimar by Johann Wolfgang von Goethe.[17]

Rousseau incorporated music and pantomime to bring his play into closer alignment with the performance modes of the fairgrounds, where spoken drama was forbidden, but this did not prevent its adoption by the Comédie Français in 1775. The full deregulation of the French stage only occurred after the Revolution in 1791.[18] Meanwhile, notwithstanding the rigorous application of stage licensing in London during the turbulent 1790s, generic experimentation proliferated, helping to break down the alternation in the repertory of comedy and tragedy and to undermine the economic stability of the patent house system.[19] Theater historians have emphasized the significance of the history of regulation to melodrama, but that history cannot completely explain its emergence, which reflects the coalescence of multiple sources and pressures, as is always the case with generic and formal change.[20]

As Robert D. Hume has pointed out, the dual monopoly of the patent stage in London made impossible the maintenance of a strict separation by venue of spoken drama from musical entertainment, pantomime and farce: whereas spoken drama was prohibited from the illegitimate stage, the licensed stage incorporated all performance types.[21] Indeed, musical theater had been performed almost continuously on the licensed stage, as the performance history of *The Beggar's Opera* (1728), extraordinarily popular across the century, attests. During the 1760s, various other styles of musical theater were developed. The "whole show" included three or four hours of entertainment, the main piece, pantomime, farce, and musical entertainments; but these performance elements were segmented, whereas melodrama could amalgamate them all into a single play. As Richard Bevis has observed, the musicalization of comedy contributed to its spectacularization before the turn of the nineteenth century.[22] *The Castle Spectre* (1797), the dramatic adaptation of Matthew Lewis's *The Monk* (1796), for example, featured music by Michael Kelly to accompany spectacular scenic and lighting effects, a combination that has led some critics to question the differences between Gothic drama, also popular in the period, and melodrama.[23] The kinds of plots that were prominent in melodrama, moreover, made their way onto the London stage via the runaway success of Kotzebue's Sturm und Drang plays.

The critical reception of Inchbald's controversial *Lovers' Vows* centered on the impropriety of Amelia's imposition of her choice of a husband on her father and served to reinforce its popularity: the play was staged many times every year between its initial production in 1798 and the 1820s.[24] Inchbald's ignorance of German required her to use literal translations in adapting Kotzebue, an extra effort reflecting his astonishing popularity.[25] *The Stranger*, for example, about an adulterous wife who repents and receives her husband's forgiveness, was performed twenty-six times in the 1798–1799 season, during which Godwin saw it five times; as David O'Shaughnessy has demonstrated, it inspired his novel *St Leon*.[26] Other adaptations and translations of Kotzebue staged in that season alone included *The Birth Day* by Thomas Dibdin, *The Count of Burgundy* by Alexander Pope, *The East Indian* by Matthew Lewis, *The Horse and the Widow* by Thomas Dibdin, *Pizarro* by Richard Brinsley Sheridan, *Family Distress* by Henry Neuman, and *Sighs* by Prince Hoare. The box-office appeal of Kotzebue was such that some London stage managers paid him to supply manuscripts likely to achieve success in Britain even before they appeared in Germany. According to Carlotta Farese, British Kotzebuemania stemmed from his presentation of daring subject matter in a sentimental fashion and his supply of juicy roles readily adopted by such powerhouse actors as Sarah Siddons, John Philip Kemble, and Edmund Kean.[27] Also significant, however, were the plays' integration of affectively intense and prototragic action alongside low comedy and their provision of happy endings.

To contextualize melodrama within the dramatic and novelistic crosscurrents of the 1790s as the product of cross-border traffic between France, England, and Germany is also to reveal its transcendence of the theater. Peter Brooks traced the form's appearance in the novels written after 1830 by Honoré de Balzac and Henry James, thereby laying the grounds for its treatment as a mode among whose features he included the "secular occult," a manner of presenting what earlier tragedy had treated as sacred, and other thematic and stylistic expressions of a Manichaean worldview in plots about victimization that centered on pitiable characters persecuted by aristocratic villains.[28] Brooks looked for its resurgence in later novels, but it is worth observing that the traffic between the novel and the stage was synchronic and involved cross-Channel translation as well. English Gothic novels not only were adapted for the English stage but were also translated and dramatized in France.[29] Stage melodrama specialized in demonstrating the subordination of nonheroic characters including people of the lower orders, the blind, the deaf, the mute, and even animals to circumstances whose pathos, whatever their causes, was amplified by multimedia means. Though novelists including Inchbald and Austen may have been skeptical of the Gothic, with its reliance on the supernatural, and disdainful of its exploitative conventionality, they nevertheless gave novelistic form to much of what had been signified on the melodramatic stage by means of multimedia representation.

Insofar as melodrama can be taken to signify a multimodal and spectacular entertainment that problematized the neoclassical alternatives of tragedy and comedy and brought out in newly significant ways the differences between print and performance, it worked alongside the novel to usher in a modern organization of literature. The attempt to shoehorn the novel into the neoclassical domain of Poetry on the basis of its resemblance to drama was rendered obsolete, and two ways of treating the relationship between drama and novels could then come to the fore. On the one hand, both were consigned together to the domain of the popular, most famously by William Wordsworth in the preface to the *Lyrical Ballads* when he jointly excluded "frantic," that is, Gothic, novels and "German," that is, melodramatic, plays from serious literature. On the other hand, drama and novels were opposed to each other by others, including Inchbald, who articulated the different capacities of each based on their contrasts even as her own authorial innovations reflected their sustained and mutual influence on each other.

In "To the Artist" (1807), Inchbald reoriented the claim Thomas Holcroft had made for the aesthetic unity of the novel on the basis of its similarity to drama. In the programmatic preface to his 1780 novel *Alwyn; or, The Gentleman Comedian*, Holcroft had depicted the modern novel as "another kind of work. Unity of design is its character. In a Novel, a combination of incidents, entertaining in themselves, are made to form a whole; and an unnecessary circumstance becomes a blemish. [Furthermore,] the legitimate Novel justly deserves to be ranked with those dramatic pieces whose utility is generally allowed."[30] Inchbald accepted Holcroft's advocacy for the aesthetic legitimacy of the novel on the basis of its similarity to drama, but she went on to reflect on novels' and plays' different political uses. It is worth paying close attention to her formulations since, in them, she clarified some of the reasons novels and plays came to be understood in terms of their differences rather than their similarities even as she also demonstrated some of the reasons novels took up the techniques of the melodramatic stage.

Inchbald's essay describes how to write a novel by means of an extended consideration of its different capacities from drama. It ends, "The Novelist is a free agent. He lives in a land of liberty, whilst the Dramatic Writer exists but under a despotic government.—Passing over the subjection in which an author of plays is held by the Lord Chamberlain's office and the degree of dependence which he has on his actors—he is the very slave of the audience. He must have their tastes and prejudices in view, not to correct, but to humour them."[31] Inchbald has been understood here to celebrate the freedom of the novelist from the state censorship to which the dramatist was subjected, yet she was equally if not more interested in the playwright's enslavement to the audience. For Inchbald, the obligation to present social harmony was a powerful constraint on the dramatist, one that operated not so much in the domain of stage licensing, in censorship, or in the playwright's accountability to regulation but in her accountability to her audience.

> The great moral inculcated in all modern plays constantly is—for the rich to love the poor. As if it was not much more rare, and a task by far more difficult—for the poor to love the rich. And yet [w]hat dramatic author dares to expose in a theatre, the consummate vanity of a certain rank of paupers, who boast of that wretched state as a sacred honour, although it be the result of indolence or criminality? What dramatist would venture to bring upon the stage a benefactor living in awe of the object of his bounty? Who, moreover, dares to exhibit upon the stage, a benevolent man, provoked by his crafty dependent to become that very tyrant, which he unjustly had reported him? (165)

Apart from observing the rare occurrence of the poor loving the rich, Inchbald does not here analyze directly the difficulty posed to dramatic representation by it; instead she switches gears to discuss the impossibility of staging the inverse possibility: the ungrateful poor. She does so, she implies, because both the grateful and the ungrateful poor would reveal how little the poor have to be grateful for in the first place; both scenarios would thus expose social inequality, a recognition that might cause the audience discomfort. The absence of such scenes thus illustrates the dramatist's enslavement to the audience and its demand for pleasure.

The stage could not issue a critique of the conventional definitions of honor and tyranny both because of the drama's predictable plots and limited scenarios and because of the kind of understanding that plays elicited from their audiences. Whereas dramatic representation of the rich landlord's charity would serve only to reinforce complacency, readers, by contrast, would be able to extrapolate from novelistic treatments of the wretched or crafty pauper an understanding of the conditions contributing to his position: the unfair and unequal distribution of wealth. Here Inchbald would draw a formal distinction between stage and novelistic representation. As she observed, "The giver of alms, as well as the alms-receiver must be revered on the stage.—That rich proprietor of land, Lord Forecast, who shall dare bring him upon the boards of a theatre, and show—that, on the subject of the poor, the wily Forecast accomplishes two most important designs? By keeping the inhabitants of his domain steeped in poverty, he retains his vast superiority on earth; then secures, by acts of charity, a chance for heaven" (166). The stage's capacity to produce critique was limited by an inability or lack of will to expose Lord Forecast's designs, in the absence of which the audience could mistake his charity for benevolence without recognizing that it actually perpetuated his power. Stage representation, according to Inchbald, could not produce critique because it did not require explanations for the conditions it represented. The stage could not or did not move its audience from the situation it presented to the exposure of underlying structural social conditions because it assumed or presented those conditions as natural.

But the formal distinction Inchbald would draw was, in fact, contingent. "Situation," it turns out, had its own special sense in the theatrical context. Patrice Pavis has observed that over the course of the eighteenth century, "dramatic situation" came to replace the "dilemma" of classical drama theory.[32] Melodrama brought into visibility relations between terms such as "situation" and "effect," as can be seen in Coleridge's reflections on Matthew Lewis's dramatic adaptation of *The Monk* as *The Castle Spectre* in a letter of January 23, 1798 to Wordsworth: "The merit of *The Castle Spectre* consists wholly in it's [sic] *situations*. These are all borrowed, and all absolutely pantomimical; but they are admirably managed for stage effect." For Coleridge, the play's reliance on "situations" is the essence of its "*theatric* merit."[33] Distinct from plot, on the one hand, and effect, on the other, "situation" places characters in relation to one another in a particular setting, and the relations and the setting both develop resonant capacities to amplify "effect" (as well as affect). Coleridge's understanding that Lewis's "stage effect" rises out of his "situations" is echoed in Edward Mayhew's 1840 treatise *Stage Effect*. "To theatrical minds the word 'situation' suggests some strong point in a play likely to command applause; where the action is wrought to a climax, where the actors strike attitudes, and form what they call a 'picture,' during the exhibition of which a pause takes place; after which the action is renewed, not continued, an advantage of which is frequently taken to turn the natural current of interest."[34] Mayhew, like Coleridge, analytically distinguished "situation" from "effect" even though, or perhaps because, the two are so closely bound up in melodrama.

"Situation" here means something like the moment worthy of being frozen into a tableau. Insofar as it follows sequentially from the action, it can be seen as its consequence rather than its foundation, though as the culmination of the action, it also recapitulates its foundation. "Situation" thereby represents a double temporal logic that retrospectively recasts sequence as causality. Both Inchbald and Austen used dramatic situation in their novels and found ways beyond tableaux to capitalize on its powers. Inchbald's adaptation involved the development of new narrative techniques for signaling the powerful effects of determinism, whereas for Austen, situations are to be found in her mise-en-scène of characters, most often in drawing rooms, in configurations that permit the exchange of glances, smiles, and gestures to communicate in the absence of being narrated at all.

In melodrama, audience recognition could supersede in importance the recognition that the Aristotelian (and neoclassical) hero underwent. Though Inchbald was skeptical of the capacity for dramatic situation to engage stage audiences politically, she nevertheless adapted it for novels where it could prompt readers to a fuller investigation of causes. Deeming novels to be more politically effective than plays, she found in them the narrative means for raising readers' consciousness in a mode of presentation that nevertheless retained the stamp of the stage. Austen's famous irony often takes the form we call dramatic irony; she exploited this kind of recognition, though not to the political ends Inchbald desired. Inchbald, by contrast, sought in novels to make dramatic irony into a political instrument, as did Godwin when he adapted the ideas of *Political Justice* in *Caleb Williams*. David O'Shaughnessy has suggested that the possibility of disseminating those ideas in the theater was on Godwin's mind before he turned to the composition of his novel.[35] The novel, moreover, reflected Godwin's substantial interests in writing for the stage, as well as Inchbald's influence. Yet if politics were significant to Godwin's understanding of the differences of genre and media, it is curious to observe that such differences recede in his descriptions of reading.

For Godwin, the experience of reading was crucial and crucially diverse.[36] He used the term "tendency" to distinguish the messages that readers actually received from those that were designed.[37] Varied uptakes by readers lay beyond authors' control, as Godwin illustrated in "Of Choice in Reading" (1797) with the example of Nicholas Rowe's play *The Fair Penitent* (1703) that thereby suggests theatrical presentation could fix interpretation more effectively than reading. "The moral deduced from this admirable poem by one set of readers will be, the mischievous tendency of unlawful love, and the duty incumbent upon the softer sex to devote themselves in all things to the will of their fathers and husbands. Other readers may perhaps regard it as a powerful satire upon the institutions at present existing in society relative to the female sex, and the wretched consequences of that mode of thinking."[38] On the one hand, Godwin's identification of Rowe's play as a poem shows the uneven application of distinct generic terms in the period. When Coleridge treated Shakespeare's drama as poetry, he emphasized its reception by reading, but here Godwin harked back to the older, neoclassical, sense of poetry that included drama, read as well as performed.[39] On the other, though the scene of reception, even by reading, remained theatrical for Godwin, as is suggested by his selection of a play as his example, and though theater remained for him the presumptive site of literary experience, as O'Shaughnessy has convincingly established, the instability of reading captured by "tendency" puts a strain on this theatrical base.[40]

The disjunction between novels and plays in Inchbald's "To the Artist" made explicit the breakdown of the homology between reading novels and seeing plays performed, yet neither she nor Godwin was entirely able to shake off its hold. She discussed the differences between reading plays and seeing them performed with some regularity in her "Remarks" and understood that the play-going and play-reading public was also an audience of novel readers.[41] Godwin's and Inchbald's theatricality shaped not only their notion that the novel could be a vehicle for political ideas but also the way their novels expressed politics and used melodrama to do so.

It is curious to observe that the contrast Benjamin drew between the novel reader, who reads alone by the fireside, and the playgoer, who joins the crowd, earmarked the political potential of theater on which Berthold Brecht capitalized—especially because Brecht's understanding depended on the opposite configuration of the one Inchbald had proposed. For Brecht, theater had revolutionary potential, but for Inchbald, the novel could convey the critique that could not be staged. This reversal indicates the importance of investigating the formulations of generic and media distinctions both as they change and as they are reflected in the composition of plays and novels. The ensemble of literary techniques inspired by the theater, in general, and melodrama, in particular, to be found across novels at the beginning of the nineteenth century suggests, furthermore, that they were not yet as disambiguated from plays as they would later come to be.

Media differences would come to have increasing weight, but other factors also helped to shape the divergence of novels from plays, including the separation of popular plays and novels from serious literature that Wordsworth had endorsed and the privilege granted to individual silent reading over sociable reading aloud. Indeed, the differences between reading alone and reading in company affect the political valences of joining the group. Group reading aloud occurred in homes as well as in public and semipublic meeting places, as can be seen in Dorothy Wordsworth's diary description of the enjoyment she and her brother took at a tavern after their walk which William had depicted as solitary in "I Wandered Lonely as a Cloud"; together they there perused "a volume of Enfield's Speaker and an odd volume of Congreve's plays."[42] Other people may also have listened to and enjoyed or perhaps even participated in that scene of tavern reading, though Dorothy doesn't mention it. It is worth wondering what would it have taken to transform this gathering into a political assembly, in the Wordsworths' time as well as in Brecht's.

MELODRAMATIC NARRATION IN THE JACOBIN NOVEL

Inchbald's novel *A Simple Story* (1791) has a two-part structure: in the first part, Miss Milner seduces and marries her guardian, the former Catholic priest Dorriforth, who, having been freed from his vows of chastity to pursue his obligations to the Church by propagating more Catholic members of the gentry, has assumed the title of Lord Elmwood; in the second part, their daughter, Matilda, overcomes the obstacles that her father has placed on her when he took her in after her mother's adultery and death, most prominent among which is the rule that he can never lay eyes on her since, in an echo of Burney's *Evelina*, she looks exactly like her mother.[43] The double transformation of Dorriforth/Elmwood, first from priest and guardian into husband and then from too severe into loving father, unifies the two parts.

Most readers of the novel have not granted Dorriforth/Elmwood the centrality he deserves for many different reasons, including biographical evidence pointing to the composition of the two parts of the novel in separate periods of Inchbald's life, the feeling of some readers that the second part is inferior to and even possibly an apology for the first part's audacity in portraying a female character like the seductive Miss Milner, and a tendency to assume that female—indeed feminist—writers' works must turn on their female characters.[44] But the novel's central concern with the transmission of relations across generational lines makes Dorriforth/Elmwood's role pivotal, and his changes are reinforced by the resemblance between mother and daughter.

In *Nature and Art* (1797), Inchbald again took up the transmission of relations across generational lines in the story of two brothers, Henry and William, who begin in poverty, and their sons, also named Henry and William, in whom the sibling bonds of obligation compromised by rivalry are recapitulated and exacerbated by William's social ascent. The two Henrys of this didactic novel have their characters and values shaped by Nature, that is, the world away from "civilization" to be found in the colonies, while the two Williams are formed by Art, that is, the socially structured, mannered, and moneyed world of the English gentry. In both novels, repetition reveals the circumstances that determine character and with which character is integrated. In both, temporally discontinuous events are linked as a series by their reappearance across generations. Inchbald reinforced the unity of this serial discontinuity, a feature that Martin Meisel has identified as the hallmark of melodrama, in various ways.[45] Retrospective revision of circumstances, the understanding induced by repetition that provokes questions about the givenness of situation, provides a "tendency" aimed at readers; when this understanding includes characters, they share it only incompletely.

A number of critics have connected Inchbald's description of characters' mental states in a sequence of alternatives, especially at moments of crisis, to the stage's language of gesture.[46] For example, when Dorriforth/Elmwood ponders Miss Milner's return from the forbidden masquerade in *A Simple Story*, his agitation is described as follows: "What passion thus agitated Lord Elmwood at this

crisis, it is hard to define.—Perhaps it was the indignation at Miss Milner's impru-
dence, and the satisfaction he felt at being on the point of revenge—perhaps his
emotion arose from joy, to find she was safe—perhaps it was perturbation at the
regret he felt that he must upbraid her—perhaps it was one alone of these sensa-
tions, but most probably, it was all of them combined."[47] Diane Osland has seen
this offering up of a series of motives or explanations for behaviors that are at times
analogous and amplificatory and at other times contradictory as "old-fashioned";
Emily Hodgson Anderson has depicted it as destabilizing the codes of performed
gesture that presumed emotional clarity to clear the way for ambiguous feeling
and the expression of a transgressive feminist agenda.[48] But with this refusal to
specify, Inchbald's translation of the gestural language of performed emotion into
narrative also insists on the discrepancy between characters' self-understanding
and the greater comprehension, even if it was not wholly certain, that was available to readers.[49]

Other theatrical aspects of Inchbald's narration that raise the affective temperature of the novel along with readers' consciousness include the tableau at the
climactic moment when Matilda faints in her father's arms that inaugurates his
reform from obdurate into loving father, a moment that Lytton Strachey singled
out in his appreciation of the novel to illustrate Inchbald's achievement of the
"effects of rarest beauty," and the act drop that covers the seventeen-year gap sepa-
rating the two parts of the novel.[50] In addition to these direct adaptations of
theatrical elements, Inchbald orchestrated the novel's serial discontinuity through
narrative means that aimed to intensify readers' affective involvement while also
granting them cognitive superiority to the characters.

For example, in the scene of Miss Milner and Elmwood's wedding, with
which the first part of the novel ends, Miss Milner discovers on that joyful day,
"even on that very day" (219), that the ring Lord Elmwood has put on her finger
is "a—MOURNING RING" (220). Portentous and heavily symbolic, this collapse of
affective extremes—the joy of marriage and the horror of death—onto a single
item produces an "excruciating shock" for Miss Milner, who experiences the intense
discomfort for a moment, a moment that resounds for the reader (220). However,
the reader appreciates, though Miss Milner does not, the prophetic significance
of the ring, in part because "MOURNING RING" are the last words of the first half of
the novel and they are capitalized and in part because the second half opens, after
an address to the reflective reader, with an extremely compressed version of what
has occurred in the seventeen-year hiatus. "Actuated by a wish, that the reflective
reader may experience the sensation, which an attention to circumstances such as
these, must cause; he is desired to imagine seventeen years elapsed, since he has
seen or heard of any of those persons, who, in the foregoing volumes have been

introduced to his acquaintance—and now, supposing himself at the period of those seventeen years, follow the sequel of their history" (221). We are then told, "The beautiful, the beloved Miss Milner—she is no longer beautiful—no longer beloved—no longer—tremble while you read it!—no longer virtuous" (221), and two pages later, she dies.

This management of the shift from the mother's story to the daughter's allows readers greater recognition than the characters possess not only because of the explicit instructions, the imperative to "tremble while you read," but also because of the temporal alternations in the final paragraphs of the novel's first part. The recognition described and prompted by the chapter's final words is a revisionary one, and not only because the anticipated joys of marriage are now tinged with dreadful apprehension. Having married the couple in a private ceremony, Sandford encourages them to fix the date for their legally recognizable public wedding as quickly as possible. Elmwood, who had been scheduled for a long journey, cancels his plans. The alternation of temporal expectations of increasingly shortened intervals compresses intensity into the instant to convey and amplify the ringing foreboding of the ring as bringing both joy and horror at once. Three sentence-long paragraphs lead up to the section's final words:

> Never was there a more rapid change from despair to happiness—than was that, which Miss Milner, and Lord Elmwood experienced within one single hour.
>
> The few days which intervened between this and their legal marriage, were passed in the delightful care of preparing for that happy day—yet, with all its delights inferior to the first; where every joy was doubled by the expected sorrow [of Elwood's imminent departure].
>
> Nevertheless, on that first wedding-day, that joyful day, which restored her lost lover to her hopes again; even on that *very* day, after the sacred ceremony was over, Miss Milner felt an excruciating shock. (219–220)

The temporal compression produced by these sentences offers readers an experience analogous to Miss Milner's shock, but she is overwhelmed by that which we can also understand.

The most affectively charged moments of this novel derive not from its representation of private emotional experiences rendered in the vocabulary of the internal mental processes undergone by characters, in what has come to be considered the special territory of the novel, but instead from the telegraphic communication of Miss Milner's "excruciating shock" that evokes the gestural language of stage, the tableau of Matilda fainting in her father's arms in the climactic recognition scene that produces his second transformation, and other narrative equivalents of dramatic devices designed to intensify readers' emotions about characters' affecting circumstances while granting us superior recognition—all features of Inchbald's narrative realization of the aesthetics of melodrama.

When the novel, in conclusion, marries off Matilda, now recognized and forgiven by her father, to Rushbrook, his nephew and the heir he had appointed in her place during her emotional exile, it both gestures toward and revises the comedy of manners, using melodrama to do so at the level of both plot and narrative technique. Rushbrook rescues Matilda from a botched kidnapping, a plot element that Inchbald had parachuted in from the Gothic that quickly establishes without needing any more narrative development the urgency of her marriage and his qualifications for the receipt of her love. Melodrama, furthermore, aids in the novel's comic resolution and modifies its presentation. The marriage can only be realized by readers' surmise. "Whether the heart of Matilda, such as it has been described, could sentence him to misery [by refusing to marry him], the reader is left to surmise—and if he supposes that it did not, he has every reason to suppose their wedded life was a life of happiness" (294). Readers are engaged to surmise and imaginatively project, even if it comes about through hypothesizing the opposite "sentence [of] misery," exactly that ending. *A Simple Story* actually ends two sentences later when Inchbald, speaking over the characters' heads directly to readers, recommends "A PROPER EDUCATION" for women as well as men. The explicitly didactic message recommends reading, including novels, and its emotional power derives from a narrative that borrows much from the stage, though with its all-caps format, it exploits the visual resources of print, as had the all-caps climactic ending of the first half of the novel in "MOURNING RING."[51]

Inchbald's second novel, *Nature and Art*, is even more explicitly didactic: in it, she develops another technique for addressing readers over the heads of the characters: by directly addressing characters. In *Nature and Art*, the narrator occasionally interrupts the flow of the action to address characters. For example, Hannah, the beautiful daughter of a cottager, does not receive a letter from William, the son of privilege and her seducer, for five months, and the narrator proclaims, "Yet, Hannah, vaunt!—he sometimes thought on thee—he could not witness the folly, the weakness, the vanity, the selfishness of his future wife, without frequently comparing her with thee. When equivocal words and prevaricating sentences fell from her lips, he remembered with a sigh thy candor—that open sincerity which dwelt upon thy tongue, and seemed to vie with thy undisguised features, to charm the listener even beyond the spectator" (99). Inchbald here tells readers something Hannah cannot know by addressing her. She thus offers a kind of dramatic irony since what is emphasized is not only William's regret for the differences between

Hannah and his wife but also Hannah's lack of awareness of his kind thoughts. This direct address thus operates along lines opposite to free indirect discourse: in free indirect discourse, a narrator renders a character's thoughts in an idiom located indeterminately between the narrator's and the character's, making it hard to tell if the thoughts are being endorsed or critiqued by the narrator; here, the narrator seemingly wants to bring to Hannah's awareness thoughts she is incapable of having. By addressing Hannah about things she cannot know at the moment and, indeed, does not come to know over the course of the novel, the narrator is also dramatizing the futility of narration to enlighten the character, if not readers.

In stranger instances of the narrator's direct address of a character, the interruption does not communicate anything *readers* do not already know. For example, when Hannah contemplates suicide, the narrator sums up the events that have brought her to this point, with which readers are already familiar:

> Unhappy Hannah! The first time you permitted indecorous familiarity from a man who made you no promise, who gave you no hope of becoming his wife, who professed nothing beyond those fervent, though slender, affections which attach the rake to the wanton; the first time you descended from the character of purity, you rushed imperceptibly on the blackest crimes. The more sincerely you loved, the more you plunged into danger: from one ungoverned passion proceeded a second and a third. In the fervency of affection you yielded up your virtue! In the excess of fear, you stained your conscience by the intended murder of your child! And now, in the violence of grief, you meditate—what?—to put an end to your existence by your own hand! (110)

The narrator here supplements readers' pity for Hannah by giving words to her confusion even as she recapitulates the plot. Hannah is here presented as incapable of articulating what the narrator expresses on her behalf. The direct address of Inchbald's narrator to characters aims over their heads; it is designed to prod readers into examining the causes for situations with which both they and the characters are already familiar.

Providing no new information and firmly didactic, this example aims to raise consciousness, to prompt readers to political critique. The ejaculation "what," a vocalization of the narrator, cuts two ways: on the one hand, it turns from Hannah to readers, taking the form of a stage aside and insisting that we share her outrage; on the other, in ventriloquizing Hannah's shock for her, it brings this passage into proximity to free indirect discourse and exposes one rationale for Franco Moretti's exploration of its incompatibilities with didacticism.[52] The narrator's direct address to characters is designed to push readers to recognitions beyond that which can be accomplished by drama, though it does so in a kind of stage whisper.

Both of Inchbald's novels imaginatively transform stage practices into novelistic narration, as critics have observed even if they have not noted all the manifestations enumerated here. But the characterization of the relation between the novel and the stage as an opposition, in conjunction with *A Simple Story*'s fairytale-like structure and *Nature and Art*'s didacticism, has made her fiction seem more anomalous than it needs to be and her legacy to the history of the novel consequently difficult to perceive. *Caleb Williams* is equally strange, though Godwin has proven easier than Inchbald to incorporate into the mainstream history of the novel. Critics have hailed it as the first psychological novel or a protodetective novel of sorts; but its first-person narration is less fully controlled than this characterization can capture, for Godwin vacillates between more than one "I" speaker. The frequent treatment of the novel's theatricality as merely metaphorical has served to normalize it and bring it into line with dominant accounts of novelistic realism, but Inchbald's remarkable influence, not limited to plot repetitions, puts it into a different light.

Godwin explained his choice of the first-person voice in the preface to *Fleetwood* included in the 1832 edition of Bentley's "Standard Novels": it provided a more immediate and thoroughgoing account of characters' motivations. "I began my narrative, as is the more usual way, in the third person. But speedily I became dissatisfied. I then assumed the first person, making the hero of my tale his own historian; and in this mode I have persisted in all my subsequent attempts at works of fiction. [I] employ[ed] my metaphysical dissecting knife in tracing and laying bare the involutions of motive, and recording the gradually accumulating impulses, which led the personages I had to describe primarily to adopt the particular way of proceeding in which they afterwards embarked."[53] This choice brought along a notable technical difficulty, namely, how to represent that which lies beyond the narrator's cognitive horizons. John Bender and Blakey Vermeule have each noted this problem, explaining the narrator's access to characters' mental states by Godwin's invention of a godlike perspective.[54] But as Pamela Clemit has pointed out, "The concept of universal psychological states is altogether foreign to Godwin's view of the individual as an indivisible member of society." "Godwin['s] appeal [is] to the reader [and not character] as the true arbiter of political justice," as is especially evident in the published ending, which, in contrast to the manuscript ending, puts the burden on readers to come to the understanding that Caleb achieved only too late.[55] Having explained Godwin's philosophical and literary commitments, however, Clemit has little to say about their narrative form or the techniques Godwin used to give readers a perspective beyond Caleb's.

Godwin's solutions are most evident in the revisions between the novel's first and third editions, in which he more explicitly located his first-person narrator and more overtly signaled the narrative organization that flowed from this choice.[56] For example, having included the elements of Falkland's past that preceded his engagement of Caleb Williams by having Mr. Collins, Falkland's long-time steward, relate them, Caleb explains in the first edition of the novel, "I shall join to Mr Collins's story various information that I afterwards received from other quarters, that I may give all possible perspicuity to the series of events. To the reader it may appear at first sight as if this detail of the preceding life of Mr Falkland were foreign to my history. Alas, I know from bitter experience that it is otherwise. To his story the whole fortune of my life was linked; because he was miserable, my happiness, my name, and my existence have been irretrievably blasted" (9). In the third edition, after the first sentence, Godwin added the following explanation: "To avoid confusion in my narrative, I shall drop the person of Collins, and assume to be myself the historian of our patron" (314). This is the most explicit but not the only instance of Godwin explaining the discrepancies between what Caleb can know and the story he tells.

The final chapter of volume 1 begins with a short preamble that treats the trial of Mr. Falkland for the murder of Barnabus Tyrrel, a murder he has actually committed, as Caleb comes to ascertain, but of which he is acquitted. "I shall endeavor to state the remainder of this narrative in the words of Mr. Collins. The reader has already had occasion to perceive that Mr. Collins was a man of no vulgar order; and his reflections on this subject were uncommonly judicious" (94). The second volume recapitulates this claim, opening with Caleb's announcement, "I have stated the narrative of Mr. Collins, interspersed with such other information as I was able to collect, with all the exactness that my memory, assisted by certain memorandums I made at the time, will afford. I do not pretend to warrant the authenticity of any part of these memoirs except so much as fell under my own knowledge" (103). These announcements contravene our conception of how first-person narration works, an achievement that critics, following Ian Watt, take already to have been accomplished by Defoe and Richardson. The progress narrative implicit in the dominant histories of the novel makes it difficult to explain Godwin's apparently wobbly reinvention of the wheel. But Godwin's narration draws attention to the different ways the characters understand their circumstances, differences both from one another and, especially in the case of Caleb, from themselves at different points in time.

Godwin uses more than one "I" speaker to move readers to affectively experience and understand the determination of character by circumstances, to which the situation of Caleb and Falkland's confrontation in the novel's concluding scenes gives climactic expression. Caleb Williams's explanations of his access to information about events he has not experienced cannot stand out as direct addresses because the whole novel is narrated in the first person. Yet the novel's interest in rendering characters' subordination to circumstances that they can only grasp incompletely, that is, the givenness of situation, is complemented by the direction of readers' attention to characters' limitations.

Ronald Paulson has remarked that it is difficult to imagine *Caleb Williams* without the precedent of *A Simple Story*, especially when it comes to plot repetitions. The doctrine of necessity, the belief that "the characters of men originate in their external circumstances," as Paulson, echoing Gary Kelly, observed, drove the integration of plot and character in Jacobin fiction to produce one source of novelistic unity.[57] The aesthetic unity and political efficacy of the novel prized by the Jacobins was shaped first by Holcroft's comparison of novels to drama and then by Inchbald's contrast between them, though in both cases, novels also incorporated dramatic situation. The plot repetitions subordinating characters to circumstances in each are narrated so that they prompt readers, if not characters, to investigate causes. Godwin, like Inchbald, found narrative equivalents to melodramatic stage effects to highlight the subordination of characters to circumstances and thereby to enlighten readers, if not characters, to structures of social oppression.

Though the didacticism of the Jacobin novelists can make it seem as though they reached a dead end, some later, ostensibly more sophisticated, writers took up the direct address of characters by the narrator, some examples of which I discuss in the coda. Inchbald's and Godwin's adoption for novelistic narration of techniques from the melodramatic stage and their legacy to other novelists interested in overdetermination problematize histories of the English novel that see them as anomalous interruptions that should be consigned to the wild hinterlands of Romanticism. In "What Is a Romantic Novel?," Robert Miles acknowledges that the double marginalization of the Romantic novel, both within the history of the novel and within the history of Romanticism, stems, in part, from the predominance of female novelists in the Romantic period. In response, he would recover a separate tradition of the "philosophical romance" inaugurated by Godwin, who inherits what Robert Kiely called an "obtrusive theatricality" from Horace Walpole and Ann Radcliffe. For Miles, Godwin's narratives need to be distinguished formally from the work of Jane Austen.[58]

Samuel Taylor Coleridge, however, offered a different genealogy for the Gothic, identifying its roots in Samuel Richardson when he condemned Charles Maturin's play *Bertram* for leaving its rake alive and unpunished at the end. Behind the melodramatic stage lay *Clarissa*, which had generated "the whole literary brood of Otranto."[59] For Miles, Austen's inventive use of free indirect discourse maps readers' experiences onto those of her heroines, whereas the philosophical romances of Godwin and his daughter Mary Shelley exhibit parabolic plots that, in the style of Brecht's epic theater, pull away from the category of character, which, after Austen, makes it impossible for them to be included in the novel's main line. But Coleridge's alternative genealogy of Gothic lets us see that when Austen and Inchbald transmuted Richardson's domestic fiction, which, for them, had already partially been mediated through Burney, they distinguished the virtues of marriage encoded in the comedy of manners from the narration of female development and other matters of social determination by means readily associated with stage melodrama.

Though Austen's politics were different from the Jacobins' and her sense of the moral purpose of novel-reading muted in comparison to Inchbald's and Godwin's, Austen also made recourse to melodrama to clear the way for the narration of her heroines' developments. Austen's occupation of a central position in the dominant histories of the novel thus permits a critique of the faulty opposition of the novel to the theater that Inchbald and Godwin also exemplify by means of their exclusion from the novel's dominant histories. Notwithstanding their political differences, Austen, like Inchbald and Godwin, turned to the theater as a resource for novelistic narration that supported but is not wholly reducible to the category of character.

AUSTEN'S THEATRICAL NARRATION

Jane Austen's narrative economy is often praised, as is her psychological realism, yet the first relies on the stage and the second is haunted by the generic expectations and dramaturgies of the comedy of manners and melodrama. Her narrator intrudes visibly on the action of her novels much more discreetly than do those of her Jacobin contemporaries.[60] Her most memorable appearances occur in *Northanger Abbey*, where they are associated with her theoretical program for the novel, but these are not her only appearances: the concluding chapter of *Mansfield Park* is narrated in an unusually extended first person, and other more subtle intrusions take the form of interjections and parenthetical asides in that novel and elsewhere. The narrator's asides and gestures toward that which remains unnarrated turn readers into spectators in *Sense and Sensibility*, *Persuasion*, and *Mansfield Park*, where, as we shall see, they serve alongside free indirect discourse in the alignment of heroines' with readers' perspectives and produce other effects, most prominent among which is the registration of the compulsory nature of marriage. Austen's use of melodrama to modify the emphasis placed on marriage in the comedy of manners is most visible in *Sense and Sensibility*.

Although Marianne Dashwood finds it to be a pity that Edward Ferrars has no taste for drawing when her sister, Elinor, finds this activity to be so enjoyable, "his great pleasure in the performances of other people," as Elinor recognizes early in the novel, represents the "innate propriety and simplicity of [his] taste."[61] At the level of plot, *Sense and Sensibility* validates Elinor's admiration of Edward and the compatibility of their tastes when it allows them to marry in the end. But taste also turns out to be central to the novel's operations on other levels: it is the fulcrum on which sociability and morality are balanced, not just for Elinor and Edward but for the novel's entire cast of characters, who are each presented in terms of taste—and not merely from Marianne's overheated point of view. For example, Sir John Middleton's satisfaction "in settling a family of females only in his cottage" is described as "the real satisfaction of a good heart" and elaborated as follows: "He had all the satisfaction of a sportsman; for a sportsman, though he esteems only those of his sex who are sportsmen likewise, is not often desirous of encouraging their taste by admitting them to a residence within his own manor" (39). Austen's sly analogy between Sir John's pursuits of women and his pursuits of game exhibits a characteristic lightness of touch that turns on the resonant "onlys": his settlement of the exclusively female Dashwood household "only in his cottage" suggests a limit to his magnanimity by emphasizing female vulnerability to male predation, but his sportsman-like esteem only for other sportsmen also signifies that he will protect his own domain. In the economical vocabulary of taste, Austen depicts Sir John Middleton as both generous and interested primarily in his own amusement.

In this early moment in Austen's novel, and in this early novel in her career, she tells us straight out that taste, as both the exercise of aesthetic judgment and the expression of preferences of other kinds, brings the like-minded together at the same time as it maintains the appropriate boundaries between them. Characters' interactions illustrate both trajectories: as they move toward one another close enough to achieve intimacy, they must maintain the degree of distance that, like Sir John's, ensures their satisfaction. These movements are made legible not only by means of figurative language and wordplay but also in scenes in which they are dramatized. Austen's theatrical imagination calls on that of her readers, as can be seen in the novel's greatest set piece, when Edward interrupts an awkward tête-à-tête between Lucy Steele and Elinor.

Lucy is in the middle of insisting that her dear friend Elinor share her happiness at being so well liked by Mrs. Ferrars, Edward's tyrannical mother, who, as

Elinor perfectly understands, would never approve of Lucy's secret engagement to Edward had she known of it. Mrs. Ferrars has been gracious to Lucy merely to keep Edward and Elinor apart. Edward's arrival interrupts Lucy's torture of Elinor, obliging the women to turn from dialogue to less direct modes of communication. The cross-purposes at which Elinor and Lucy operate have been described briefly between their speeches, but Austen turns to a more elaborate narration to contrast Elinor's exertions to make Edward comfortable to Lucy's "determin[ation] to make no contribution to the comfort of others" (275), exertions that extend even to the point of leaving Edward and Lucy alone in the room together when Elinor goes to fetch Marianne. Edward, Lucy, and Elinor each hope for the relief supplied by the introduction of another person, but Marianne's entrance causes even greater consternation. She exacerbates "the very circumstance which they would each have been most anxious to avoid" (274) because, ignorant of Lucy and Edward's engagement, Marianne addresses Edward as Elinor's suitor.

The drawing room here functions as a stage set: characters' exits and entrances, gestures and movements, at first speak louder than their words, but soon speech once again resumes its powers to cut through and against speakers' and interlocutors' thoughts and desires, thereby revealing characters' natures as well as their positions in relation to each other. Having set the scene, Austen can then deliver Marianne's comments, no matter how banal, in dialogue. Austen briefly narrates the "unexhilarating" (277) effect of commendations that aim to extend Edward's visit in the vain hope that Lucy will leave but instead prompt Edward to try to depart. For the most part, however, Marianne's speeches speak for themselves.

Marianne's inadvertent excruciations distribute discomfort differently to Elinor and Edward, who feel the awkwardness of both the situation and Marianne, and to Lucy, who shamelessly faces down her rudeness. When Marianne draws Edward aside "to whisper her persuasion that Lucy could not stay much longer," the narrator comments sardonically on her failure to see that "Lucy would have outstaid him if his visit had lasted two hours" (278). The dramaturgy of the scene distills the essence of Elinor's dilemma. She must keep her distance from Lucy's fake intimacies in order to preserve the possibility of a real intimacy with Edward; her maintenance of these boundaries makes it possible for her both to suffer and to survive Marianne's excessive closeness to Edward.

This dramatization of characters' positions does not always require the narration of the discrepancy between characters' actions and desires. Indeed, in characters' unspoken thoughts, *especially when they are not narrated*, we see the extent of Austen's theatrical imagination. Characters are put into relation, but the boundaries between them, as well as those between what they say, how they act, and how they feel, underlie the social vision that the novel endorses in its conclusion, when it ranks among Marianne's and Elinor's achievements "as [not] the least considerable, that though sisters, and living almost within sight of each other, they could live without disagreement between themselves, or producing coolness between their husbands" (431). The harmony of their social world is measured in conclusion by negation.

Persuasion presents a more sophisticated because more seamlessly integrated use of mise-en-scène cheek by jowl with free indirect discourse. Anne Elliot's understated recognition that Captain Wentworth still loves her in volume 2, chapter 8, gains emotional resonance because it recapitulates in miniature the history of their relationship. Readers recognize, though Anne does not, this echo effect, which is produced by the orchestration of characters' movements in the theatrical space of the concert hall. The scene begins with Wentworth and Anne exchanging what might seem to be mere formal niceties, a conversation that nevertheless conveys to Anne the conviction that Wentworth never cared for Louisa Musgrove and that "he had a heart returning to her."[62] She teases these implications out of his expression of surprise that the bookish Benwick would marry such a nonintellectual woman. Although Anne's reflections are given in the free indirect style, their rhythm is determined by the dramaturgy of the scene. When Anne and Wentworth meet before the concert begins, for example, Anne feels empowered to interact with Wentworth notwithstanding the hostile presence of her father and sister because they stand behind her where she cannot see them. "He was prepared only to bow and pass on, but her gentle "how do you do?" brought him out of the straight line to stand near her, and make enquiries in return, in spite of the formidable father and sister in the back ground. Their being in the back ground was a support to Anne; she knew nothing of their looks, and felt equal to everything which she believed right to be done" (197). Social obligations determine their separation in the concert hall, and Anne sits beside Mr. Elliot, who engages her in protracted tête-à-tête conversation. This configuration provokes Wentworth's jealousy, as Anne comes to recognize by the end of the scene, when he leaves the concert after telling her that there is "nothing worth [his] staying" (207). The characters thus physically re-enact over the length of a concert the pattern of their initial courtship, in which Anne, acquiescing to Lady Russell's bad though well-intentioned advice, had refused Wentworth despite being in love with him, an episode that occurs "more than seven years" (30) before the opening of the novel, narrated in free indirect discourse in volume 1, chapter 4, as Anne recollects the pain of their parting.

Much in the chapter turns on the relation between Anne's thoughts and her sensory awareness of her present moment as she strains to hear snatches of the conversation that occurs behind her back, in which Sir Walter and Lady Dalrymple discuss how handsome Wentworth is, for example, or as she tries to catch Wentworth's eye from across the room. Significantly, the most extended passages of dialogue occur between Anne and Mr. Elliot, even though what they say is almost entirely insignificant. This feature reprises the dialogue between Marianne Dashwood and Edward in *Sense and Sensibility*. In *Persuasion*, however, the focus remains resolutely on Anne, as Austen dramatizes the distracting noise through which Anne seeks to discern the signal: Wentworth's nonverbal and perhaps unconscious communication of his feelings. Austen here exploits both characters' and readers' experiences of theatrical space, but the homologies between reading novels and seeing plays, and their discrepancies, both for characters and for readers, are also visible at the dramatic center of the novel, which is explicitly marked as melodramatic.

At the novel's center is Louisa Musgrove's fall. Observing that Austen interrupts her narration of this scene with a parenthetical aside, "(it was all done [even if not told] in rapid moments)," Emily Rohrbach has emphasized the discrepancy between "the long time of reading and the short clock time of the 'story' (*récit*)" as the means by which Austen "makes us conscious that [she] could have done it differently, that she had multiple modes of narration among which to choose."[63] For Rohrbach, the brief aside turns readers into onlookers at the Gothic spectacle of the corpse-like young lady, but here she captures without fully recognizing the degree to which Austen borrows from the stage. "Captain Wentworth knelt with [Louisa] in his arms, looking on her with a face as pallid as her own, in an agony of silence" (Austen, *Persuasion*, 118): the characters here assume a posture familiar from the stage. The interruption of the frightful event by Austen's aside insists on readers understanding more about the scene than do its participants, who are affectively carried away: this combination is characteristic of melodrama. Austen's exploitation of readers' and characters' experiences of theatrical space, the homologies between reading novels and seeing plays, and their discrepancies, for readers as well as for characters, are even more evident in *Mansfield Park*, where they are also more explicitly connected to melodrama.

In that novel, Austen recapitulates the dramatization of taste as the grounds on which like-minded relationality is achieved while characters' autonomy is enforced. But if, in *Sense and Sensibility*, manners and morals converged, as they also do for Anne and Wentworth in *Persuasion*, though not for Benwick and Louisa Musgrove, their divergence in *Mansfield Park* helps more fully to expose the work of Austen's theatricality. Even those readers who use Fanny Price's unwillingness to participate in the amateur theatricals of *Mansfield Park* as evidence for Austen's antitheatricality do not admire her. Readers do not like Fanny because of her recessive nature, but over the course of the novel, she emerges from a position that is more or less objectified to one that is more fully embodied. If it has been difficult to resist associating the heroine's perspective on the theater either with that of the novel itself or with its author, this is because Austen uses the theater to narrate her development.

In the first volume, the novel delivers Fanny's point of view symbolically: when she is not melting into the sofa in the drawing room at Mansfield, and thereby rendered invisible to the others, she is alone on a garden bench looking out over the ha-ha at Sotherton and thereby aligned with the perspective privileged by the garden's—and the narrative's—design.[64] At first, Mary Crawford cannot tell if Fanny is "out." Her emergence into the world and into an embodied existence in the novel is achieved by means of the disarticulation of manners from morals that begins with the expression of her feelings for Edmund.

When Edmund advises Fanny to wear William's ornamental cross on the necklace that Mary Crawford has given her to her coming-out ball because he "would not have the shadow of a coolness arise between the two dearest objects [he has] on earth," Fanny responds, "She was one of his two dearest—that must support her. But the other!—the first! She had never heard him speak so openly before, and though it told her no more than what she had long perceived, it was a stab;—for it told of his own convictions and views. They were decided. He would marry Miss Crawford. It was a stab, in spite of longstanding expectation; and she was obliged to repeat again and again that she was one of his two dearest, before the words gave her any sensation."[65] In the long passage of free indirect discourse, Austen tracks Fanny's movement from stabbing jealousy to another sensation. The passage continues, "Could she believe Miss Crawford to deserve him, it would be—-Oh! How different would it be—how far more tolerable! But he was deceived in her; he gave her merits which she had not; her faults were what they had ever been, but he saw them no longer" (307). Fanny's ability to feel her newly acknowledged position of elevation in Edmund's esteem involves the derogation of Mary Crawford as an appropriate love object for him. Moreover, she would find Edmund's choice more tolerable if only she could think better of Mary. Fanny, we are led to believe, would find it easier to suppress her own feelings and accept her second-place status in Edmund's affections if Mary deserved him more. This distinctive combination of feeling and judgment that D. W. Harding identified as "regulated hatred" is premised on the moral condemnation of Mary.[66] The imagined possibility of Mary's greater deserts promises a self-abnegation that, because it is only imagined, permits a self-assertion that leverages Fanny into visibility, a visibility more fully dramatized in two related scenes that consist primarily of dialogue. The first, like the set piece in *Sense and Sensibility*, takes place in the Bertram drawing room;

the second occurs during a private walk that Edmund and Fanny take in the shrubbery.

Edmund does not see that Henry Crawford would make a bad choice for Fanny both because it pleases him to imagine that he could keep his "two dearest objects" close if he were to marry Mary and Henry were to marry Fanny and because he believes that Fanny would improve Henry. Yet at stake in Edmund's misguided view of Henry is not just the virtue, or lack thereof, of both men's self-interest but also the presumed association of manners and taste with good judgment and sound morals. Both the Crawfords are lively, witty, and pleasing, yet their valuation of the sociable and aesthetic dimensions of life does not guarantee their appreciation of the good. Fanny's sounder perceptions of their limitations come to be vindicated by their bad behavior; before their exposure, however, Fanny's views are more subtly realized through Austen's theatrical narration. Fanny, now embodied, can fully emerge as the novel's perspectival center as aesthetic taste comes to be dissociated from moral judgment in the scene in which Henry Crawford reads aloud from Shakespeare's *Henry VIII* to the assembled family members.

Crawford is an excellent reader; and though Fanny listens, "determined to be interested by nothing else" than her work, "taste was too strong in her," and "she was forced to listen" (389). Having scrutinized Henry's progress with Fanny, Edmund asserts on their walk together that she and Henry are not as dissimilar as she may think: "You are quite enough alike. You *have* tastes in common. You have moral and literary tastes in common. You have both warm hearts and benevolent feelings; and Fanny, who that heard him read, and saw you listen to Shakespeare the other night, will think you unfitted as companions?" (403). Edmund, however, also concedes that Henry's suit would have been more successful if he had known her as well as Edmund himself does: "Between us, I think we should have won you" (402). To a certain extent, Edmund here courts Fanny both on Henry's behalf and through him for himself, a double registration whose possibility had been opened in the earlier scene by the double registration of the word "constancy."

After Henry's dramatic reading, he and Edmund discuss the importance of elocution and eloquence for clergymen, a conversation in which Henry participates with Fanny's attention in mind, as Austen indicates in parenthetical stage directions and ellipses-signaling asides. Henry confesses, "'For myself, at least, I must confess not being always so attentive as I ought to be—(here was a glance at Fanny) that nineteen times out of twenty I am thinking how such a prayer ought to be read, and longing to have it to read myself—Did you speak?' stepping eagerly to Fanny, and addressing her in a softened voice; and upon her saying, 'No,' he added, 'Are you sure you did not speak?'" (393–394). Though Henry goes on to display a surprising degree of thoughtfulness about preaching styles, even admitting to "a sort of envy" (395) for the position, he qualifies his interest: "I do not know that I would be fond of preaching often; now and then, perhaps, once or twice in the spring, after having been anxiously expected for half a dozen Sundays together, but not for a constancy; it would not do for a constancy" (395). For Patricia Michaelson and Abigail Williams, Henry and Edmund's discussion, to which Fanny has listened attentively, and the selection of the reading from *Henry VIII* attest to the importance of the elocutionary movement: scenes from that Shakespeare play were included in Enfield's manual *The Speaker* (1774).[67] For them, this episode attests to Austen's provision of speech lessons for women in a novel exploring female accomplishments that was designed to be read out loud. Both rightly observe the powerful gendered constraints on public female performance, yet this serves in each to support a stricter segregation of drama from novel in Austen than I believe is warranted. Having listened attentively throughout, Fanny understands what Edmund does not: the significance of Henry's constancy, or lack thereof, as it applies to his affections as well as his behavior more generally. *Unspoken and unnarrated*, the association of manners and morals, this episode insists, cannot be grounded in the aesthetic domain alone.

Mansfield Park had experimented with subordinating the marriage plot to a more intense narration of development. Marriage is not the goal it had been in *Sense and Sensibility* and *Pride and Prejudice*: its achievement is strangely marginalized, merely reported among the other "just deserts" meted out by the narrator in the final chapter, which begins by embracing "my Fanny," who "at this very time, I have the satisfaction in knowing, must have been very happy" (533). The actions that have cleared the way to Fanny's happiness, however, have been delivered in the most indirect fashion. Edmund reports to Fanny in their walk in the shrubbery that serves as their courtship his discovery that Mary Crawford is insufficiently moral to make him a good wife. The conclusion and denouement, including their marriage, are then delivered in narrative summary. This muted treatment of climactic action appears odd if one is reading for the (marriage) plot but makes more sense once the novel's goal fully to bring out Fanny is recognized.

Austen's subordination of the marriage plot to the narration of Fanny's development amplifies the strikingly reserved portrait of the pleasures of marriage depicted at the end of *Sense and Sensibility*. Both novels produced modifications to the conventional comedy of manners ending using melodrama, which provided a necessary, if tonally discordant, source of energy for a quieter project: to separate the narration of female development from marriage. In the earlier novel, Colonel Brandon's past is melodramatic, as Clara Tuite has pointed out, which either qualifies him for Marianne's romantic imagination or disqualifies the romance of their marriage altogether.[68] In *Mansfield Park*, Austen exploited melodrama in her incorporation of *Lovers' Vows* to lay down in its casting a template for the bad romances that must be overcome. Aborted melodrama thus launches Fanny Price on the road to embodiment and marriage. In *Persuasion*, the compulsory nature of marriage determined by the comedy of manners is registered in the coordinated reflection in another drawing-room scene on the results of the three courtships the novel has followed with varying degrees of interest: those of Henrietta Musgrove and Charles Hayter, Louisa Musgrove and Benwick, and Anne and Wentworth. The comic discussion of the first one by Mrs. Croft and Mrs. Musgrove and the more serious consideration given to the second by Captain Harville and Anne call the future pleasures of these couples into question; against this backdrop, Wentworth writes his memorable declaration to Anne. Though the novel presses their happiness on us, even Anne's connubial bliss is qualified by the "tax of quick alarm" that she will have to pay for the glory of being a sailor's wife, as Austen puts it in the novel's final sentence (275).

In the canceled chapter of *Persuasion*, Austen permitted Anne and Wentworth a face-to-face *éclaircissement* that is comically and clumsily stage-managed by Admiral Croft. He drags Anne in off the street and maneuvers her into a room alone with Wentworth to investigate the truth of the rumor of her engagement to Mr. Elliot that has raised concern about the Crofts' tenancy at Kellynch. Once she denies the report, their reunion is established through exchanges of looks, gestures, and changes of color that rely on body language. The theatricality of the scene is continuous with that of the set piece of *Sense and Sensibility*. Wentworth's letter in the published ending is equally theatrical, though it measures the increase in narrative sophistication that Austen had acquired over the course of her career.

For Mary Favret, Wentworth's letter to Anne "shocks like a thunderclap"; the declaration of love he composes produces a revolution in the plot and carries a whiff of naval warfare that signifies the capacity of the most private, indeed intimate, letters to register public concerns, with implications for fictional letters as a vehicle for political interest in the novel as a genre.[69] For Michael McKeon, Austen produces "the third-person effect" through a similar letter: of Elizabeth Bennet's reading of Darcy's letter in *Pride and Prejudice*, McKeon observes, "reading letters privatizes the public activity of social knowledge and publicizes the private activity of self-knowledge."[70] For both critics, the novel itself has a special capacity, to recapitulate public, political, and ideological matters in the private, domestic sphere and to project back onto the world the significance of private behavior. This capacity flows from the reflective and reflexive capacity of novelistic realism, realized in moments that materialize and thematize writing and reading. Yet it must also be observed that the intimacy effects of Wentworth's letter derive as much from Austen's reliance on the stage.

Writing with his back turned to the company, "Captain Wentworth's hitherto perfectly quiet division of the room" into the two conversations is interrupted (Austen, *Persuasion,* 254). The slight noise of him dropping his pen "startle[s] Anne at finding him nearer than she had supposed" (254). Occupying the position that Anne had taken at the concert, Wentworth strives to hear Anne's discussion with Harville, in which her claiming the privilege of having loved the longest, even after hope has gone (253-54), moves Wentworth to make his own declaration. His note is the verbal culmination of the passion that his body language in the act of writing, his agitation upon leaving the room, and his quick return to give her the note have already conveyed.[71] Remaining alone in the room for "ten minutes only" after sinking into the chair he had occupied while writing to read, moreover, Anne is frozen in a tableau, as Austen describes the internal "agitation" of her "overpowering happiness" (258). In an influential formulation of the ways the realist novel produced its effects, Ian Watt suggested that the novel in letters delivered experiences of intimacy not possible on the stage, but Austen relies heavily on stage effects in order to enhance the intimacy of this letter. In *Persuasion,* as in *Sense and Sensibility* and *Mansfield Park,* moreover, even when marriage brings some women some happiness, its compulsory nature emerges at the threshold of realism, where Austen annexes stage conventions for the reading experience. Austen's celebrated realism, I am suggesting, is supported by this annexation of the theater in which the comedy of manners, modified by melodrama, is retooled for prose narrative, which depends, at climactic moments, on mise-en-scène to orchestrate the interweaving of dialogue and free indirect discourse.

Notwithstanding significant differences of politics and other matters, the comparison between Austen and Inchbald, by highlighting their shared theatricality and their shared gender politics, distinguishes two lines along which novels of female development evolved thereafter: the comedy of manners and the novel of social determinism. The status of the authorial hand marked by repetition, asides, and other forms of address by means of which the narrator is embodied; other ways of highlighting that which the novel presents as given, that is, dramatic situation, which align readers with character or experiences of their own embodiment: these bear the mark of the stage in both Inchbald and Austen, as did similar and other narrative devices in Burney and Fielding before them. The contributions made to the novel's emergence by the cultural dominance of the theater are not restricted to novels of female development, though I have concentrated on those to demonstrate the still underappreciated centrality of female authors to the canon and have compared such divergent authors to underscore the range of novels in which the debts to the stage can be found.

This analysis brings to the surface a set of related assumptions about the realist novel that are in need of revision: the presumed opposition of the theater to the novel that I have been arguing against throughout accompanies the assumption that the novel was consumed paradigmatically in sessions of private, individual, and silent reading. That Austen's novels were read aloud, as Patricia Michaelson and Abigail Williams each establish, and were designed to be puts discontinuous and sociable reading alongside individual silent reading as well as other forms of consumption for which literacy was not a prerequisite, such as the theatrical performance of adaptations and the acquisition of spin-off paraphernalia inspired by novels. Working from the places where the genres, novel and drama, intersect with their media, print and performance, makes it possible to recover the role of the theater in a different history of the novel that scholars, at work variously on the social life of books and the afterlives of characters, have recently undertaken.

I have sought to dismantle the opposition of the theater to the novel not only by observing the intermediary and intermedial experiences of the novel between print and performance but also by examining cross-generic and intermedial collaborations in novels as these supported the development of a range of narrative techniques. That one of these, free indirect discourse, has been taken as the hallmark of the novel's generic distinction discloses the stakes of misrecognizing as formal the historical contingency of such generic distinction: it reveals as a fantasy the notion embedded in the dominant histories of the novel that it achieved aesthetic autonomy.

According to the Watt/McKeon history of the novel, it subsumes other genres, most notably romance, into realism. "Novelization" is the name Mikhail Bakhtin gives to this process.[72] Though other accounts, including those of feminist literary history, may narrate it differently, they remain invested in the genre's aesthetic autonomy. But the idea that any literary genre (or any of the other arts, for that matter) fulfills its singular destiny when it achieves aesthetic autonomy is a fantasy deriving from a Hegelian aesthetics whose influence is still to be found in the prizing of objects whose form recapitulates their content. Whether or not it is possible to overcome the idealization of this fusion, perhaps the time has come to decouple it from literary history by treating the distinction of the genres and their media as less absolute, indeed, as contingent. Their distinctness is neither achieved for once and for all nor arrived at through a path that moves only forward, a recognition that demands a longer and more unified history of the novel that nevertheless remains open to the ways it was shaped by the other arts, not only by the stage.

STORY

Benjamin distinguished two kinds of novels: those, following Flaubert, interested in prosody; and those by Scott, Dickens, Thackeray, Stevenson, Kipling, and Bennett, interested in story. The psychological novel written by Flaubert's followers has been granted far greater prestige, especially in histories of the novel that have applied too strictly and exclusively an unwritten critical law of generic division. Accounts of the English novel have come to give Austen precedence over Flaubert, while the fairy-tale repetitions of Inchbald's *Simple Story*, if it is recollected at all, make it more easily assimilated to the domain of story. Benjamin promoted generic differentiation along the lines of media difference. "The Storyteller" depicts the salient characteristics of the novel, historically slow to emerge, as crystallized by print. Producers and consumers were dissociated from the scene of telling as well as from the place occupied by the storyteller in artisanal culture. Yet the novel did not completely destroy story, which remains present in some novels, short stories, and printed tales by Edgar Allan Poe, Robert Louis Stevenson, and others, in which "the soul, eye and hand are brought into connection."[73] Story's presence in print militates against strict generic division, even though it also highlights the media difference that informs Benjamin's description of the different experiences of the genres. But story also persists across media. The novel, as a result, cries out for a longer and more unified history that acknowledges the path it took to generic distinctness; generic distinctness, rather than aesthetic autonomy, means that this history remains accountable to the transportability of some of the novel's elements across media and genre.

The Novel Stage has told a part of this story. The ways theater mediated the development of narrative form over the course of the long eighteenth century, furthermore, makes up only part of the novel's relation to the stage. But to let Benjamin's emphasis on the novel-reading experience, like the experience of the other genres, reflect the increased power of the media of literature to inflect the genres makes it possible to resist the hypostatization in much criticism of our own time that treats novels as if they are only to be read and plays as if they are only to be performed. Print and performance did not compete for the same market share in the period any more than they do in our own time. Instead they fueled the desire for each other, as we should know from the contemporary enhancement of profits produced by cross-media adaptation and translation. Moviegoers and TV-series watchers buy the books that inspired them when books are their sources and then, quite possibly, turn around and also purchase the novelizations they spawn. Rather than narrowing, each format broadens the audience, even if the hierarchy of value is here measured by dollars rather than by any aesthetic criterion.

The persistence of story, its capacity for different kinds of mediation, and the possibility that generic distinctions will move in and out of focus and change over time make it worthwhile to recall the diversity of novels and their existence alongside the other genres of literature, and indeed other media of art, through which they continue to revitalize their capacities to represent and interest their readers. Novels of all kinds aim to deliver a wholly specific experience of the worlds they represent, and the specificity of this delivery will best be understood in terms of the persistence of story in a variable media ecology that will often include significant differences between the moment of production and the moment of consumption, differences that literary history, especially if it is carried out in a multimedia register, is equipped to characterize.

But dominant histories of the novel have equated its failure to fit into the extant categories of literature with its remaking of literature in its own image. Perhaps these overly streamlined accounts of the novel's powers that concentrate on the characteristics to which it, and seemingly only it, have given rise could be recognized as modernist or, at the least, the product of an institutionalized literary criticism that rewards the restriction of study to a single given period, genre, or author. *The Novel Stage* has offered another, messier, view of literary history that tells the story of the novel as it reflects the influence of the theater because the theater was the default aesthetic experience at the time of the novel's development.

My goal has not been to shatter the dominant paradigms of the novel—formal realism, domestic ideology, nobody's story—by splintering the genre into smaller subgenres: domestic fiction, female bildungsroman, comedy of manners, the novel of social determination. Rather, I have sought to challenge the adequacy of any single one of these accepted paradigms to account for the evolution of the novel's formally distinguishing marks. I have not discovered some new, as of yet uncharted archive of novels but have rediscovered the differences among already-familiar more and less canonical texts by adopting a binocular view: by emphasizing what novels borrowed from the theater, I have offered a way to refine our understanding of the emergence of the novel that proposes a dialectical relationship between collaborations across the categories of genre and media and the production of distinctions of genre and media. This dialectic provides a more unified history of the novel that remains open to its registration of the influence of the other arts. It is my contention that by broadening our approach to the novel to inquire after its multimedia relations, we sharpen our sense of what the novel was and continues to be capable of achieving.

The Melodramatic Address

W HEN ELIZABETH INCHBALD'S narrator addresses her character Hannah directly in *Nature and Art* (1797), it becomes tempting to abandon this didactic novel to the relative obscurity in which it has abided. Yet however ham-fisted, this naive mode of address also occurs in some celebrated novels by acknowledged masters, including Charles Dickens, Anthony Trollope, and, with some modification, Thomas Hardy. Narrators' direct addresses to characters dramatize an exchange between fictional entities that exist at different levels of fictionality; they thereby express an animation we do not find in novels of the twentieth century or our own day, for that matter, notwithstanding the vogue for fiction in the second person inspired by Jay MacInerney.

Direct addresses to characters rely on a paradox: though they elicit great sympathy for characters' miserable plights, they do so by pointing out these characters' limited capacity to comprehend their own situations—-despite the fact that the addresses directed to them are nominally aimed at their illumination. Instead, these addresses deliver to readers a combination of affective intimacy and cognitive distance, one that has been celebrated as the sole achievement of free indirect discourse. Adjacent to free indirect discourse, these addresses thus can elicit a more precise understanding of how the fetishized device works even as they underscore the theatrical roots of the novel as it is pulled in directions other than realism.

Narrators intrude on characters, at least in the examples I have found, at moments of heightened sentiment, indeed melodrama. Voluble narrators and melodramatic novels have been reviled separately, but the connections help to disclose the consequences of incorporating melodrama more fully into the history of the novel. Jenny Davidson has identified the "teleological orientation of the term 'novelistic' towards nineteenth- rather than eighteenth-century fictional practice," especially insofar as the "novelistic detail," since Ian Watt's account of formal realism, has insisted on a particular form of referentiality.[1] Having identified the bifurcated place the novel came to occupy in the modern organization of literature as one split along the lines of serious and popular, with only the former capable of being elevated to an art, this book has vindicated, to a certain extent, this teleology.[2] A consideration of a few examples of this mode of address in nineteenth-century novels, however, serves to outline the rest of the theatrical history of the novel as it diverges from psychological realism by emphasizing the mediations that support the category of character rather than seeing it as a reflection of the ways minds, or brains, work.[3]

In Charles Dickens's *Dombey and Son* (1848), the narrator exhorts the cruel Mr. Dombey to show love to his daughter, Florence: "Awake, unkind father! Awake now, sullen man! The time is flitting by; the hour is coming with an angry tread! Awake!"[4] Ventriloquizing a desire for Dombey's reform that readers are presumed to share, Dickens here could be thought of as refining Inchbald's use in *Nature and Art*:

> Unhappy Hannah! The first time you permitted indecorous familiarity from a man who made you no promise, who gave you no hope of becoming his wife, who professed nothing beyond those fervent, though slender, affections which attach the rake to the wanton; the first time you descended from the character of purity, you rushed imperceptibly on the blackest crimes. The more sincerely you loved, the more you plunged into danger: from one ungoverned passion proceeded a second and a third. In the fervency of affection you yielded up your virtue! In the excess of fear, you stained your conscience by the intended murder of your child! And now, in the violence of grief, you meditate—what?—to put an end to your existence by your own hand![5]

Inchbald's narrator here lists the events that have brought Hannah to the brink of suicide as a way of directing readers' attention to its cause. Appreciating Hannah's situation enhances the pathos of her condition. Despite the narrator's outraged ejaculation "what?" Hannah cannot hear. Her suicide is interrupted instead by Henry's appearance.

If Hannah cannot hear the narrator, Mr. Dombey will not listen. Dickens's narrator morally chastises Mr. Dombey to no avail, but readers are expected to respond because they share the view from the future that the narrator invokes in the continuous present, "the hour is coming," from which the character is excluded. Both Inchbald and Dickens thus give narrative form to characters' limitations; through the direct address of the character who cannot or will not respond, readers are also prompted to acknowledge that things might have evolved differently.

Can You Forgive Her?, the title of Trollope's 1865 novel, has been treated by Garrett Stewart as an instance of the "dear reader" mode of address, even though the titular question could as easily be one posed to the husbands-to-be on whose forgiveness the marriages of the novel depend.[6] More than a teaser asking what will happen next, the title probes the husbands' emotional capacities for forgiveness at the same time as it exploits readers' enjoyment of the lively women so that we, like their duller husbands, can come to accept imperfect marriages as the best possible outcome. Trollope's title, in other words, aligns us with the husbands, but it also opens a distance from them, eliciting from us a better understanding than they themselves can have, especially of the social constraints that demand emotional sacrifice—especially from women.

Trollope's title also points to a future beyond the ending of the novel.[7] Although the novel's marriages indicate that the men have answered "yes," Plantagenet Palliser's forgiveness is not absolute; his difficulties with Lady Glencora's impulsive sociability in later novels of the series return him to the initial circumstances of their marriage. Readers' forgiveness, meanwhile, cannot be guaranteed, notwithstanding the ultimately unenforceable moral pressure this novel exerts. It is worth noting here, as Trollope does in *An Autobiography* (1883), that he recycled the plot of *Can You Forgive Her?* from a failed play he wrote called *The Noble Jilt*.[8]

Other examples of narrators' direct addresses to readers share these characteristics: the alignment of readers and characters as addressees alongside the emphasis on their divergent understandings; the expression of moral, if not overtly didactic, messages; and the projection of a future orientation that involves imagining alternative outcomes that contribute to determinism at the level of plot. Narrators' addresses to characters signify contingency by theatrical means, even if, by virtue of having narrators, it would seem difficult to imagine such addresses occurring on the stage.[9] Although not all the novels in which these addresses appear can be considered melodramatic, they occur in close enough proximity to it to make the investigation of the connection worthwhile for what it can tell us about the formal contributions melodrama made to the history of the novel.

"The melodramatic address": a technique that aims not to represent characters' mental processes as these are both enabled and restricted by social (and grammatical) conditions, which is how free indirect discourse works, but rather to evoke alternative possibilities at the level of plot. This opening to alternative futures could be called "counterfictional" for the attention it draws to the shape of these novels' particular worlds at the limits of plot. Pointing to what did not, cannot, or will not happen, the narration of the "counterfictional," furthermore, is worth considering alongside Catherine Gallagher's description of the counterfactual novel.[10]

Counterfactuals "tell it like it wasn't," according to Gallagher, by imagining a history that did not happen often from the perspective of its losers or victims. Counterfictional moments also "tell it like it wasn't," even if the glimpse of what wasn't is brief and occupies a second-order terrain in which the "facts" themselves are wholly imaginary. In indicating what did not happen, these moments ask readers to imagine along with the novelist alternative fates for fictional characters in novels that were not written. Gallagher builds on Ian Watt's insight into the special status of referentiality in formal realism, which she augments with accounts from analytic philosophy to illuminate the ontological status of fiction.[11] Whereas Gallagher uses philosophy to help to explain fiction, I propose, by contrast, that fiction might have something to contribute to the philosophical problem of possible worlds—at least to our understanding of their affective prerequisites. When narrators' direct addresses to characters indicate alternative futures, they lay bare that the imagination of such possible worlds (in fiction and, perhaps, in philosophy as well) depends on the recognition of the pathos of characters' dilemmas.[12]

In *Little Dorrit* (1857), Dickens's most melodramatic novel, Mr. Dorrit, having hired Mrs. General to train his daughters as ladies, asks for her view of their temperamental differences. Mrs. General replies, "Fanny has force of character and self-reliance. Amy, none." The narrator then proceeds: "None? O Mrs. General, ask the Marshalsea stones and bars. O Mrs. General, ask the milliner who taught her to work, and the dancing-master who taught her sister to dance."[13] Like the addresses to Mr. Dombey and Hannah, this one refers to factors exceeding Mrs. General's awareness. Like the other examples, this instance is purely didactic: readers have reinforced the same lesson about Amy's value that Mrs. General is incapable of learning. But then Dickens adds a spectacular twist that plays on the status of what can happen in a novel.

The narrator continues, "O Mrs. General, Mrs. General, ask me, her father, what I owe to her; and hear my testimony touching the life of this slighted creature, from her childhood up!"[14] The narrator seems here to identify so completely with Mr. Dorrit that he ventriloquizes him using the first person. This ventriloquism threatens to show the novelist's hand: "I am Mr. Dorrit. No, I am the father of all these characters," the narrator seems to say, "with whom I fully identify despite their moral limitations." "Mr. Dorrit's" first-person response to the questions not really posed by Mrs. General is an idealization; that is to say, it expresses the narrator's wish and presumably also that of readers, for what we desire Mr. Dorrit to say. However, he does not say or even think it. The next sentence reads, "No such adjuration entered Mr. Dorrit's head."[15] When the narrator speaks as Mr. Dorrit, he also invites the reader to pass judgment on Mr. Dorrit for his failure to speak in this way, that is, for his failure to recognize Amy's strengths.

When the narrator ventriloquizes in the faux-theatrical address to Mrs. General a position not taken by Mr. Dorrit, he speaks through "Mr. Dorrit," though none of that character's distinctive vocalizations, his "hems" and other hiccups, appear, as they might be expected to, in free indirect discourse. Instead, by addressing readers by means of addressing Mrs. General, Dickens advances the narration of counterfictional possibility. The wished-for conversation that does not "actually" occur in the novel projects a parallel fictional world. Dickens here holds his creations at arms' length and invites us to see around them, which is one of the ways he opened the possibility for Amy Dorrit and Arthur Clennam to overcome the circumstances to which they have been subordinated and to remake themselves in however limited a way in the aftermath of the collapse of the House of Clennam. Robyn Warhol has observed similar moments of Dickens' narrative refusals, including an ostentatious refusal to describe in a syntax that takes the form of "not . . . , not . . . , not . . . , but . . ."[16] Warhol associates what she calls Dickens's "unnarration" with the shape of his plots, especially their openness to the possibility that things could have turned out differently, but she does not observe the modal connection between this way of imagining counterfictional possibility and melodrama.

Inchbald's and Dickens's narrators' addresses to characters are brief and intermittent rather than full-fledged examples of second-person narration, yet they disclose, perhaps, the appeal of the second person to contemporary writers, who may require more affective involvement with their characters than can easily be acknowledged without embarrassment.[17] By contrast, Inchbald simply and unapologetically increases the pathos of Hannah's situation when she lists plot events to tell the outrageous story of her degradation. Dickens, meanwhile, assumes that our affective involvement with characters will motivate our desire for the alternatives he provides in the counterfictional address of the narrator to the character. He thereby shows that the device can be quite playful.[18] "Necessity" may sometimes be less grim in Dickens than in Inchbald, but sometimes melodramas have happy endings.

Hardy's novels have been considered in relation to melodrama, so it is worth investigating his merger of this mode of address with free indirect discourse.[19] *The Mayor of Casterbridge* (1886) contains a series of ambiguously addressed hypothetical questions that provide Hardy with the means to project the possibility that things could have worked out differently. Blurring the possibility that the character is addressing him- or herself with the possibility that the narrator is addressing the character and/or readers, these questions merge one type of free indirect discourse with the melodramatic address.

Burney's *Cecilia*, as we saw in chapter 4, contains this sort of free indirect discourse in the form of a hypothetical question: "Would she obtain [Miss Belfield's confidence of her feelings for Delvile]? No; the most romantic generosity would revolt from such a demand, for however precarious was her own chance with young Delvile, Miss Belfield she was sure could not have any."[20] It is unclear if the narrator's question is addressed to readers or Cecilia. The syntax amplifies this lack of clarity by failing to specify who is skeptical of Miss Belfield's chances with Delvile: the narrator, Cecilia, or both. Readers are thus taken into the confidence that Cecilia desires to withhold her best wishes from Miss Belfield, even if she is pained to recognize her own lack of generosity or, perhaps, may not even recognize it herself. Here, although Burney opens for readers a privileged perspective on Cecilia, she does not open the plot up to alternative possible outcomes. By contrast, in Hardy's hands, this interrogative mode both indicates alternative directions along which plot events may unfold and exposes the futility of their pursuit.

Much of the determinism of plot and subordination of characters to circumstances in *The Mayor of Casterbridge* derives from its explicit theatricality. Casterbridge is frequently described as a stage, which is partly metaphorical and partly a conception of the setting as more than just a backdrop that allows Hardy to depict what does and does not happen in its marketplace as an interplay of glances. If Elizabeth-Jane had seen Michael Henchard using the alley door to gain access to Lucetta's apartment, she would have realized they were lovers; if Henchard had observed the eagerness with which Lucetta watches out the window for Farfrae, he would have learned that Farfrae was his rival. Readers see what the characters do not. Moreover, these failed awarenesses and absent knowledges are the means by which the plot can unfold with inevitability: things could have worked out differently—but they did not.

At the novel's conclusion, as Henchard contemplates how to tolerate the marriage of Elizabeth-Jane to Farfrae, the narrator issues the hypothetical questions, "But what if he were mistaken in his views, and there were no necessity that his own absolute separation from her should be involved in the incident of her marriage?" "He proceeded to draw a picture of the alternative—himself living like a fangless lion about the back rooms of a house in which his stepdaughter was mistress; an inoffensive old man, tenderly smiled on by Elizabeth, and good-naturedly tolerated by her husband. It was terrible to his pride to think of descending so low; and yet for the girl's sake he might put up with anything; even from Farfrae."[21] Imperfectly aligning reader, character, and narrator, Hardy's interrogatory mode renders Henchard's thoughts in a style that is indirect, though we would be hard-pressed to call it "free." The syntax mirrors Henchard's reasoning even if we have no grounds for determining whether the idiom is his since Henchard speaks so rarely; significantly, the narrator describes Henchard's imaginative efforts as "draw[ing] a picture."

As Henchard readies himself to return to Casterbridge to attend the wedding, Hardy's narrator repeats this intermediate mode of narration: "What if he had been mistaken in his views; if there had been no necessity that his own absolute separation from her he loved should be involved in these untoward incidents? To make one more attempt to be near her: to go back; to see her, to plead his cause before her, to ask forgiveness for his fraud, to endeavor strenuously to hold his own in her love, it was worth the risk of repulse, ay, of life itself."[22] The question, with its close verbal echoes of the earlier formulation, opens to view an alternative choice, the possibility of return, on which Henchard then embarks. The ensuing short clauses in the infinitive articulate his wishes, with the semicolons doing as much of the work of representing his thoughts as the words themselves. This example of free indirect discourse works as much at the level of punctuation as of grammar.

Even though Henchard reverses his earlier decision and returns to Caster-bridge, this change of heart is ultimately futile: not only does it fail to secure the rapprochement with his daughter that he so earnestly desires, but it also results in his humiliation and death. This intermediary narrative mode of interrogative address is the means by which Hardy, like Inchbald and Dickens before him, simultaneously renders an openness of the plot to alternative circumstances and registers the present inevitability of the way it unfolds. Perhaps the most curious aspect of this representation of counterfictional possibility is how close it comes to giving the game away entirely. Things could have worked out differently—if the author had wanted them to.

Hardy, like Inchbald, risked revealing the authorial hand in order to cultivate the pathos of characters trapped in social structures to which they contribute despite their best intentions, a pathos Dickens exploited when his narrator ventriloquized Mr. Dorrit (though it should be noted, the ventriloquism also offered the narrator what we might think of as plausible deniability for breaking the fictional frame through which we perceive that the social circumstances of the novel are determined by the novelist's imagination). Things could have worked out differently, but it would not have made any difference. This narrative mode holds out the hope that the film theorist Linda Williams has identified at the heart of melodrama, that it may not be too late; at the same time, it portrays too-lateness.[23] Melodrama: not just plot but relation to plot—the affectively and politically charged imagination of alternatives that serves to register the inexorable force of constraints in the present. Melodramatic address: one of the techniques by means of which readers and viewers are positioned to achieve this relation.

Perhaps the master of this technique is Trollope, though many of his novels cannot properly be classified as melodrama. *Barchester Towers* (1857), for instance, contains quite a few examples of the narrator directly addressing characters in which the connections between this device and the opening to alternative futures is made explicit, yet they occur in a comic vein. Nevertheless, Trollope's narrator himself refers more than once to the courtship plot of the novel as a melodrama.

He thereby both dismisses it and draws attention to the dependency of the novel on it. As D. A. Miller insightfully perceived, perhaps Dickens's melodramatic interest in institutions was not ultimately that different from Trollope's comic interest in bureaucracy.[24] Although Trollope had elevated the importance of character over plot in the *Autobiography*, plot retained a complex status displayed in the narrator's direct addresses to characters and expressed as well in the attitude taken toward melodrama.[25]

Plot may be dismissed by the narrator's interruptions of its forward momentum, in the suspension of suspense when readers are told early on not to worry that Eleanor Bold will marry Mr. Slope and in the accompanying reprimand for reading for the plot. Its determining force is nevertheless acknowledged, albeit playfully, in the narrator's direct addresses to characters. Confronting Mr. Harding for his failure to ask his daughter Eleanor about her feelings for the obsequious Mr. Slope, for example, the narrator poses a series of questions: "Ah, thou weak man; most charitable, most Christian, but weakest of men! Why couldn't thou not have asked herself? Was she not the daughter of thy loins, the child of thy heart, the best beloved to thee of all humanity? Had she not proved to thee, by years of closest affection, her truth and goodness and filial obedience? And yet, knowing and feeling all this, thou couldst endure to go groping in darkness, hearing her named in strains which wounded thy loving heart and being unable to defend her as thou shouldst have done!"[26] When Harding goes to Eleanor's room, however, having made up his mind not to ask how she feels about Slope, the narrator explores the alternative chain of events that could have ensued.

> And he, foolish, weak, loving man, would not say one word, though one word would have cleared up everything. There would have been a deluge of tears, and in ten minutes everyone in the house would have understood how matters really were. The father would have been delighted. The sister would have kissed her sister and begged a thousand pardons. The archdeacon would have apologized and wondered, and raised his eyebrows, and gone to bed a happy man. And Mr. Arabin—Mr. Arabin would have dreamt of Eleanor, have awoke in the morning with ideas of love, and retired to rest the next evening with schemes of marriage. But, alas, all this was not to be.[27]

If, in Inchbald and Dickens, the impetus behind the narrator's direct address to characters is to let readers know that things could have worked differently but it would not have made any difference, in Trollope, the claim is that if things had evolved differently, there would have been no novel. This claim, moreover, is explicit: contemplating what might have happened if Eleanor had cried when reprimanding Mr. Arabin, the narrator confesses, "Everything would have been explained, and Eleanor would have gone back to Barchester with a contented mind. How easily would she have forgiven and forgotten the archdeacon's suspicions had she but heard the whole truth from Mr. Arabin. But then where would have been my novel?"[28] In almost Wildean fashion, Trollope thus conveys both the utter triviality and the complete moral seriousness of his novel.

In a portrait of Trollope's modernity, Amanda Anderson has observed a "formal economy" in which the insouciant narrator of *Barchester Towers* stabilizes characters beleaguered by the wan moral absolutes of their world and immobilized by a commitment to their own characteristics, such as Mr. Harding's to his mildness or Mr. Slope's to his obsequiousness.[29] Taking the title *He Knew He Was Right* (1862) as a nice illustration that this commitment borders on the perverse, Anderson perceives that Trollope entraps characters as a way to empower plot, but she does not recognize that this also draws him close to melodrama. Instead, she identifies it, using Lionel Trilling's terms, as a symptom of his sincerity. Though she attempts to capture his light touch by claiming, "Everybody is wacky in Trollope,"[30] she remains immune to his playfulness, predisposed to miss the peculiar challenge that Trollope poses to academic criticism.

"But then where would have been my novel?" Readers are prodded into simultaneously accepting the moral insights of the novel and the triviality of the package in which they are delivered. The pleasure lies in embracing the realization that no real consequences would follow from the novel's nonexistence, except the absence of the pleasure and the insights it provides. Academic literary criticism has a tough time with (its own) triviality; and novel studies has a tough time with novels that do not identify their own seriousness with the realist project.

Though Trollope may have shared some of the disdain for melodrama of those who defended the elevation of the novel as an art against more conventional and popular forms, he, in turn, also received their condemnation for his voluble narrator, whose invitation to enjoy the novel's triviality as well as its moral seriousness may share more with melodrama than initially meets the eye. Combining conventionality and seriousness differently, melodrama has yet to be appreciated fully for its formal contributions to narrative, of which the narrator's direct address to characters is just one example.

ACKNOWLEDGMENTS

One thing that happens when you work on a project for a long time is that you go through many feelings about it, and not just once. When I first got excited about the novel's relation to the theater as a way to rethink its history, I proposed to fellow scholars with interests in the novel that they might want to explore the topic. When no one took it up, I realized that it was up to me: this was my question. As I came to understand its scope, I was challenged, delighted, overwhelmed, determined, sickened, sometimes by turns, sometimes all at once. Becoming more familiar with the question, seeing where it could go and what it could do, involved recognizing what it dragged in its wake, its limitations, and its apparent strangeness. It has therefore been particularly gratifying recently to encounter others working on the intersections of the novel and the theater from different points of view. Unlike when I started, there is now an ongoing conversation to participate in.

Erin Keating, Katherine Mannheimer, Rebecca Tierney-Hynes, Ros Ballaster, Jenny Davidson, and Lisa Freeman have been stimulating interlocutors in person, as Emily Anderson and David Brewer have been in print. Thinking in dialogue with them and their work has improved my project immensely. From the outset, it was also crucial that my questions, no matter how naive, were welcomed by theater historians and performance studies people, areas in which I am not trained. Daniel O'Quinn, Fiona Ritchie, Lisa Freeman, Brigid Orr, Laura Rosenthal, and Gillian Russell have been particularly supportive. Elaine Freedgood, whom I encountered late in the process, was a critical source of intellectual encouragement. This project has undergone many phases of development, and the conversation, support, and scholarship of many people has helped to shape it. It gives me great pleasure to acknowledge them here. Any errors are purely my own.

Considering the dominance of the theater in eighteenth-century aesthetic theory and experience, why were people working on the novel happy, when they did not ignore theater altogether, to construe it as the novel's opposite? Shortly after I first began to explore the question of the theater's influence on the novel, this historical problem converged with a methodological one: how to use the media concept in literary studies? Sustaining exchanges with Jason Camlot, especially as we prepared to team-teach a course on media and genre, and with Tina Lupton about the media concept helped shape my thinking about media and genre. Kevin Pask has influenced my understanding of literary history as, in part, the history of the idea of literature. The opportunity to engage with Michael McKeon, especially about the *Secret History of Domesticity*, was important to my understanding of the stakes that the history of the novel might (or might not) have in drama. Early formulations of this part of my argument appeared in a collection of responses to McKeon published in *History Compass* 10, no. 9 (2012). Mark Salber Phillips, whom I first met at the symposium held at McGill in 2007 about McKeon's book, helped me in later interactions to a better understanding of neoclassical aesthetics.

This project was supported in its early stages by a Social Sciences and Humanities Research Council of Canada individual research grant. One of its first offshoots, a workshop on "melodrama at the interface of media and genre," also received SSHRC funding, as well as internal support from Concordia University's Aid to Research Related Events and the Center for Interdisciplinary Studies in Society and Culture. Some of the results appeared in print in a dossier of essays in *Criticism* 55, no. 4 (2013), thanks to the encouragement of Jonathan Flatley and the editorial support of Renée Hoogland. For their particular intellectual generosity in participating in a pretty wide-ranging and at times inchoate set of conversations, I would like to thank Bonnie Honig, Chantal Nadeau, Lynne Huffer, Jose Quiroga, Colin Talley, Michael Moon, Jonathan Goldberg, Mitchell Merling, Adam Frank, Ned Schantz, Jonathan Flatley, Darren Wershler, Katie Russell, Johanne Sloan, Jason Camlot, and Ariela Friedman. Thanks also to Jordan Crosthwaithe, my research assistant for this project. And special thanks to Cristina Iovita for helping shape my understanding of melodrama altogether.

A number of people made significant contributions to the project in exchanges they may not even recall having. Early encouragement came from Elaine Hadley; Jonathan Kramnick prompted me to consider Rochester's deathbed conversion; Paula Backscheider insisted that I read Burney's *The Wanderer*; Joseph Roach made me understand the methodological divide between theater studies and literary studies when he graciously participated in a roundtable I organized at ASECS, on possible relations between theater and other literary media; Sandra Macpherson discussed the frustrating category of character with me, which Aaron Kunin later helped me to understand more completely.

Parts of this manuscript have already appeared in print, though they have been substantially revised: portions of chapter 4 appeared in an essay on Frances

Burney in *ELH* 82, no. 2, and portions of chapters 2 and 5 appeared in an essay on Elizabeth Inchbald included in a special double issue of *Eighteenth-Century Fiction* on Georgian theater and other media, coedited by Daniel O'Quinn and Gillian Russell. I am grateful to the review process at both journals, which helped me to improve the clarity of my arguments.

More recently, generous invitations to present parts of this project have sparked other fruitful conversations that have contributed to its final shape: Andrew Franta and Scott Black brought me to the University of Utah's English department; Paul Yachnin hosted a talk about rakish reform for his Conversions team at McGill, Isabelle Daunais and the NOVANOV/TSAR team heard parts of this project on different occasions. I benefited tremendously from sustained conversation about the novel as a member of that FQRSC-funded team. At Rutgers, it was a pleasure to intersect with fellow contributors to *Emergent Nation: Early Modern Literature in Transition*, edited with grace by Elizabeth Sauer and published by Cambridge in 2019. I got valuable feedback at the meeting of the Johnson Society of the West in Chicago thanks to Heather Keenleyside's kind invitation. Nancy Johnson and Anna Battigelli invited me to SUNY Plattsburgh for "Jane Austen and the Arts," where I got to have a chat with Barbara Benedict that redirected my interests in *Persuasion*. Monique Rooney invited me to present at the CUSPP at the Australian National University in Canberra and also to participate in the Intermedialities conference, for which I got the chance to develop my thinking about Aphra Behn. Vanessa Smith generously sponsored a talk to the Novel Network group at the University of Sydney, where Olivia Murphy's questions were particularly helpful. It was a great pleasure to get to meet Penny Gay, to whose work on Austen I owe a significant debt. The care taken by two anonymous readers for Bucknell University Press have made this a much better book.

Colleagues have made themselves available at various times to read drafts of chapters and provided feedback that helped to ground the project. I thank Danielle Bobker, Lisa Freeman, Jonathan Sachs, and Tina Lupton. Student research assistance from Nate Szymanski, Robin Graham, Niki Lambros, and Olivia Wood has been invaluable. I have received crucial intellectual support from Ned Schantz and Jason Camlot. In my personal life, I am lucky enough to count Michael Moon, Jonathan Goldberg, and John Emil Vincent as my brilliant friends. Without the joys of their company and conversation, I would have lost the sense that my thoughts have value to others many years ago.

My daughters, Emma Pask and Violet Pask, have grown into adulthood as I have labored on this project. Their continued love and support amaze me. Kevin Pask, my partner in life's adventures, has continued to believe in me and in the project even when I despaired. The first reader of these pages whose judicious eye prompted many improvements, he was also frequently called upon as a re-reader, in which capacity his contributions to the project have been immeasurable. I am truly grateful for so much love. I owe the inspiration and determination to keep at it to my mother, Esther Frank, an indefatigable source of energy and excitement. I dedicate this book to her with much love and admiration.

INTRODUCTION

1. Anna Larpent, quoted in John Brewer, *The Pleasures of the Imagination: English Culture in the Eighteenth Century* (New York: HarperCollins, 1997), 57.

2. Brewer, 197.

3. Abigail Williams, *The Social Life of Books: Reading Together in the Eighteenth-Century Home* (New Haven, CT: Yale University Press, 2017). In a personal communication (March 2017), theater scholar Daniel O'Quinn estimated that during the season in the second half of the century, London people of fashion, even those who were not particularly wealthy, would have seen two plays a week.

4. Ros Ballaster, "Rivals for the Repertory: Theatre and Novel in Georgian London," *Restoration and Eighteenth-Century Research* 27, no. 1 (2012): 5–24.

5. William Congreve, preface to *Incognita* in *Incognita and The Way of the World* ed. A. Norman Jeffares (Columbia: University of South Carolina Press, 1966) 34; Henry Fielding's "comic Epic-Poem in Prose," *Joseph Andrews*, ed. Martin C. Battestin (Middletown, CT: Wesleyan University Press, 1967), 4; Samuel Johnson, *Rambler* 4, 31 March 1750, in *Selected Writings*, ed. Peter Martin (Cambridge, MA: Harvard University Press, 2009), 173–75; Samuel Richardson, *Clarissa; or, The History of a Young Lady*, ed. Angus Ross (New York: Penguin, 1985), 1495.

6. Paula Backscheider, "Retrieving Elizabeth Inchbald," in *The Oxford Handbook of the Georgian Theatre, 1737–1832*, ed. Julia Swindells and David Francis Taylor (Oxford: Oxford University Press, 2014), 615.

7. Rebecca Tierney-Hynes, *Novel Minds: Philosophers and Romance Readers, 1680–1740* (New York: Palgrave Macmillan, 2012), 11–19.

8. Michael Fried, *Absorption and Theatricality: Painting and Beholder in the Age of Diderot* (Chicago: University of Chicago Press, 1988).

9. See Jan Fergus, *Provincial Readers in Eighteenth-Century England* (New York: Oxford University Press, 2007), 95–104. See also Matthew J. Kinservik, "The Dialectics of Print and Performance after 1737," in Swindells and Taylor, *Oxford Handbook of the Georgian Theatre*, 123–139.

10. Emily Hodgson Anderson, *Eighteenth-Century Authorship and the Play of Fiction: Novels and the Theater, Haywood to Austen* (New York: Routledge, 2009); Ballaster, "Rivals for the Repertory"; Nora Nachumi, *Acting like a Lady: British Women Novelists and the Eighteenth-Century Theater* (New York: AMS Press, 2008); Lisa A. Freeman, *Character's Theater: Genre and Identity on the Eighteenth-Century English Stage* (Philadelphia: University of Pennsylvania Press, 2001).

11. Wolfram Schmidgen, "Undividing the Subject of Literary History: From James Thomson's Poetry to Daniel Defoe's Novels," in *Eighteenth-Century Poetry and the Rise of the Novel Reconsidered*, ed. Kate Parker and Courtney Weiss Smith (Lewisburg, PA: Bucknell University Press, 2014), 92.

12. David Duff, *Romanticism and the Uses of Genre* (New York: Oxford University Press, 2009); Jon Klancher, *Transfiguring the Arts and Sciences: Knowledge and Cultural Institutions in*

the Romantic Age (New York: Cambridge University Press, 2013); Clifford Siskin, *The Work of Writing: Literature and Social Change, 1700–1830* (Baltimore: Johns Hopkins University Press, 1998). Yet some scholars of eighteenth-century print culture have used generic categories, including drama and satire, to productive effect, including David A. Brewer, *The Afterlives of Character, 1726–1825* (Philadelphia: University of Pennsylvania Press, 2005); Katherine Mannheimer, *Print, Visuality, and Gender in Eighteenth-Century Satire: "The Scope in Ev'ry Page"* (New York: Routledge, 2011); Freeman, *Character's Theater*.

13. Ian P. Watt, *The Rise of the Novel: Studies in Defoe, Richardson, and Fielding* (Harmondsworth, UK: Penguin, 1974); Michael McKeon, *Origins of the English Novel, 1660–1740* (Baltimore: Johns Hopkins University Press, 1987); Nancy Armstrong, *Desire and Domestic Fiction: A Political History of the Novel* (Oxford: Oxford University Press, 1987); Catherine Gallagher, *Nobody's Story: The Vanishing Acts of Women Writers in the Marketplace, 1670–1820* (Berkeley: University of California Press, 1994).

14. Robert Miles, "What Is a Romantic Novel?," *Novel* 34, no. 2 (2001): 180–201.

15. See Matthew Buckley, "The Formation of Melodrama," in Swindells and Taylor, *Oxford Handbook of the Georgian Theatre*, 457–478; Samuel Taylor Coleridge, *Biographia Literaria; or, Biographical Sketches of My Literary Life and Opinions* (Princeton, NJ: Princeton University Press, 1983), 207–233.

16. John Guillory, "Genesis of the Media Concept," *Critical Inquiry* 36, no. 2 (2010): 321–362.

17. Katherine Mannheimer, personal communication, March 2017.

18. Michael Booth, "Theater History and the Literary Critic," *Yearbook of English Studies* 9 (1979): 15–27.

19. Robert Hume, "Drama and Theater in the Mid and Later Eighteenth Century," in *The Cambridge History of English Literature*, ed. John Richetti (Cambridge: Cambridge University Press, 2005), 316–318.

20. Tracy C. Davis, "Nineteenth-Century Repertoire," *Nineteenth-Century Theatre and Film* 36, no. 2 (2009): 6–28.

21. Diana Taylor, *The Archive and the Repertoire: Performing Cultural Memory in the Americas* (Durham, NC: Duke University Press, 2003).

22. On the novel's continuities with older forms, see Margaret Doody, *The True Story of the Novel* (New Brunswick, NJ: Rutgers University Press, 1997); and Thomas Pavel, *The Lives of the Novel: A History* (Princeton, NJ: Princeton University Press, 2013). On the novel and the news, see Lennard Davis, *Factual Fictions: The Origins of the English Novel* (New York: Columbia University Press, 1983). On the novel and other "novel objects," see Julie Park, *The Self and It: Novel Objects in Eighteenth-Century England* (Stanford, CA: Stanford University Press, 2010).

23. Stuart Sherman, "Garrick among Media: The '*Now* Performer' Navigates the News," *PMLA* 126, no. 4 (2011): 966–982.

24. For Richardson as dramatic novelist, see Mark Kinkead-Weekes, *Samuel Richardson: Dramatic Novelist* (Ithaca, NY: Cornell University Press, 1973); for Richardson's antitheatricality, see Elaine McGirr, "Why Lovelace Must Die," *Novel: A Forum on Fiction* 37 (2003): 5–23; and Teresa Michals, "'Like a Spoiled Actress off the Stage': Anti-theatricality, Nature, and the Novel," *Studies in Eighteenth-Century Culture* 39, no. 1 (2010): 191–214.

25. On Cibber's bourgeois feminism, see Elaine McGirr, *Partial Histories: A Reappraisal of Colley Cibber* (London: Palgrave Macmillan, 2016).

26. William Godwin, *Four Early Pamphlets (1783–1784)*, introduction by Burton R. Pollin (New York: Scholar's Facsimiles and Reprints, 1977), 267–282. Doody observes that Godwin reread Burney in her introduction to *Cecilia; or, Memoirs of an Heiress*, by Frances Burney (Oxford: Oxford University Press, 1988), xxxvii.

27. Martin Meisel, *Realizations: Narrative, Pictorial, and Theatrical Arts in Nineteenth-Century England* (Princeton, NJ: Princeton University Press, 1983).

28. Many critics, including Monika Fludernik and Robert Kaufman, have insisted on understanding that novel's theatricality metaphorically and have thereby failed to recognize Godwin's deep investment in the actual theater. See Monika Fludernik, "Spectacle, Theatre, and Sympathy in Caleb Williams," *Eighteenth-Century Fiction* 14, no. 1 (2001): 1–30; Robert Kaufman, "The Sublime as Super-Genre of the Modern, or 'Hamlet' in Revolution: Caleb Williams and His Problems," *Studies in Romanticism* 36 (1997): 541–574. For a corrective, see David O'Shaughnessy, *William Godwin and the Theatre* (London: Routledge, 2015).

29. Walter Benjamin, "The Storyteller: Reflections on the Works of Nikolai Leskov," trans. Harry Zohn, in *Theory of the Novel: An Historical Approach*, ed. Michael McKeon (Baltimore: Johns Hopkins University Press, 2000), 79.

30. Walter Benjamin, "By the Fireside," trans. Rodney Livingstone, *New Left Review* 96 (December 2015): 53.

CHAPTER 1 — GENRE, MEDIA, AND THE THEORY OF THE NOVEL

1. Rosalie Colie, "Genre Systems and the Functions of Literature," in *Modern Genre Theory*, ed. David Duff (London: Longman, 2000), 148–166.

2. See the introductions to parts 1, 3, 4, and 7, in *Theory of the Novel: A Historical Approach*, ed. Michael McKeon (Baltimore: Johns Hopkins University Press, 2000), 1–4, 145–154, 179–184, and 355–362; Mikhail Bakhtin, *The Dialogic Imagination: Four Essays*, ed. Michael Holquist, trans. Caryl Emerson and Michael Holquist (Austin: University of Texas Press, 1982).

3. Wolfram Schmidgen, "Undividing the Subject of Literary History: From James Thomson's Poetry to Daniel Defoe's Novels," in *Eighteenth-Century Poetry and the Rise of the Novel Reconsidered*, ed. Kate Parker and Courtney Weiss Smith (Lewisburg, PA: Bucknell University Press, 2014), 92.

4. See Jonathan Kramnick and Anaheid Nercessian, "Form and Explanation," *Critical Inquiry* 43 (Spring 2017): 650–669.

5. Judith Kegan Gardiner, "The First English Novel: Aphra Behn's *Love Letters*, the Canon, and Women's Tastes," *Tulsa Studies in Women's Literature* 8, no. 2 (1989): 201–222.

6. For a range of recent approaches, see Cynthia Richards and Mary Ann O'Donnell, eds., *Approaches to Teaching Behn's "Oroonoko"* (New York: Modern Language Association of America, 2014); for classic essays, see Margaret Ferguson, "News from the New World: Miscegenous Romance in Aphra Behn's *Oroonoko* and *The Widow Ranter*," in *The Production of English Renaissance Culture*, ed. David Lee Miller, Sharon O'Dair, and Harold Weber (Ithaca, NY: Cornell University Press, 1994), 151–189; Ros Ballaster, *Seductive Forms: Women's Amatory Fiction from 1684–1740* (Oxford: Oxford University Press, 1998), chap. 3.

7. Janet Todd and Derek Hughes, "Tragedy and Tragicomedy," in *The Cambridge Companion to Aphra Behn*, ed. Janet Todd and Derek Hughes (New York: Cambridge University Press, 2004), 83.

8. In *Enlightenment Orientalism: Resisting the Rise of the Novel* (Chicago: University of Chicago Press, 2012), Srivinas Aravamudan makes an important case for Behn to be granted a more prominent place in the history of the novel on the basis of her engagement with various transcultural models of fiction rather than on her transmutation of her understanding of the stage (see 58–72).

9. Catherine Gallagher, *Nobody's Story: The Vanishing Acts of Women Writers in the Marketplace, 1670–1920* (Berkeley: University of California Press, 1994).

10. Catherine Gallagher, "The Rise of Fictionality," in *The Novel*, vol. 1, *History, Geography, and Culture*, ed. Franco Moretti (Princeton, NJ: Princeton University Press, 2006), 336–363.
11. Simon During, "Literary Academia: Simon During Reflects, Part II," *Politics/Letters Live*, 31 May 2018, http://politicsslashletters.org/features/literary-academia-simon-reflects-part -ii/.
12. Michael McKeon, *The Secret History of Domesticity: Public, Private, and the Division of Knowledge* (Baltimore: Johns Hopkins University Press, 2005), 506–547.
13. Brian Cowan, "The History of Secret Histories," *Huntington Library Quarterly* 81, no. 1 (2018): 130–133. See Rebecca Bullard and Rachel Carnell, eds., *The Secret History in Literature, 1660–1820* (Cambridge: Cambridge University Press, 2017).
14. Michael McKeon, *Origins of the English Novel* (Baltimore: Johns Hopkins University Press, 1987).
15. McKeon, *Secret History*, 390–392.
16. Philip Sidney's *Defence of Poetry* was written circa 1579, published posthumously in 1595.
17. William Shakespeare, *Hamlet*, act 2, scene 2, lines 396–398, in *The Riverside Shakespeare*, ed. G. Blakemore Evans (Boston: Houghton Mifflin, 1974).
18. See Vinton Dearing's commentary in *The Works of John Dryden*, vol. 11, ed. John Loftis, David Stuart Rodes, and Vinton A. Dearing (Berkeley: University of California Press, 1978), 463–464.
19. Nancy Klein Maguire, *Regicide and Restoration: English Tragicomedy 1660–1671* (Cambridge: Cambridge University Press, 1992), 35; McKeon, *Secret History*, 391; see also my "Tragedy, Comedy, Tragicomedy, and the Incubation of New Genres: 1660–1714," in *Emergent Nation: Early Modern British Literature in Transition 1660–1714*, ed. Elizabeth Sauer (Cambridge: Cambridge University Press, 2019) 66–79.
20. Rachel Carnell, *Partisan Politics, Narrative Realism, and the Rise of the British Novel* (London: Palgrave Macmillan, 2006), 49–51.
21. For examples, see Aphra Behn, *Oroonoko*, in *The Works of Aphra Behn*, ed. Janet Todd, vol. 3 (London: William Pickering, 1995), 67, 71, 69.
22. Behn, 57.
23. Laura Brown, "The Romance of Empire: *Oroonoko* and the Trade in Slaves," in *The New Eighteenth Century: Theory, Politics, English Literature*, ed. Felicity Nussbaum and Laura Brown (New York: Methuen, 1987), 41–61.
24. Aphra Behn, *The Fair Jilt*, in *The Works of Aphra Behn*, ed. Janet Todd, vol. 3 (London: William Pickering, 1995), 113.
25. Cynthia Wall, *The Prose of Things* (Chicago: University of Chicago Press, 2006), 137.
26. Anne F. Widemayer, *Theater and Novel from Behn to Fielding* (Oxford: Oxford University Press, 2015), 43–47. For other accounts, see Monika Fludernik, *Towards a "Natural" Narratology* (New York: Routledge, 2002), 106–120; and Maximillian E. Novak, "Some Notes towards a History of Fictional Forms: From Aphra Behn to Daniel Defoe," *Novel: A Forum on Fiction* 6, no. 2 (1973): 120–133.
27. Carnell, *Partisan Politics*, 73.
28. William Nelson, *The Dilemma of the Renaissance Storyteller* (Cambridge, MA: Harvard University Press, 1973), 48–49.
29. In *Spectator* 40, Addison identifies his other favorite tragedies as Otway's *The Orphan* and *Venice Preserv'd*, Nathaniel Lee's *The Rival Queens; or, The Death of Alexander the Great* and *Theodosius*, Dryden and Lee's *Oedipus*, and Dryden's *All for Love*.
30. Joseph Addison, *Spectator* 249 (15 December 1711), Donald Bond ed. (Oxford: Clarendon Press, 1965), 3: 311–312.

31. Richardson's *Vade Medum*, quoted in Darryl P. Domingo, *The Rhetoric of Diversion in English Literature and Culture, 1690–1760* (Cambridge: Cambridge University Press, 2016), 51.

32. See Elaine McGirr, "Why Lovelace Must Die," *Novel: A Forum on Fiction* 37, nos. 1–2 (2004): 5–23; and Teresa Michals, "'Like a Spoiled Actress off the Stage': Anti-theatricality, Nature, and the Novel," *Studies in Eighteenth-Century Culture* 39, no. 1 (2010): 191–214.

33. William Congreve, Preface to *Incognita in Incognita and The Way of the World*, ed. A. Norman Jeffares (Columbia: University of South Carolina Press, 1966) 34. Samuel Richardson, *Clarissa; or, The History of a Young Lady*, ed. Angus Ross (New York: Penguin, 1985), 1495. In addition to Fielding's "comic Epic-Poem in Prose," *Joseph Andrews*, ed. Martin C. Battestin (Middletown CT: Wesleyan University Press, 1967) 4, another example would be Samuel Johnson's reference to romance being written according to the rules of comic poetry in *Rambler* 4, 31 March 1750, in *Selected Writings*, ed. Peter Martin (Cambridge, MA: Harvard University Press, 2009), 173–175. Samuel Johnson, *Lives of the English Poets*, 3 vols., ed. George Birkbeck Hill (New York: Octagon Books, 1967).

34. On the nomenclature for the novel, see Cheryl Nixon, ed., *Novel Definitions: An Anthology of Commentary on the Novel, 1688–1815* (Peterborough, ON: Broadview, 2009), 46–63. For the range of prose called "novels," see Peter Garside, James Raven, and Rainer Schowerling, eds., *The English Novel, 1770–1829: A Bibliographical Survey of Prose Fiction Published in the British Isles*, 2 vols. (Oxford: Oxford University Press, 2000).

35. David Duff, introduction to *Modern Genre Theory*, ed. David Duff (New York: Longman, 2000), 6–8.

36. Yury Tynyanov, "The Literary Fact," in Duff, *Modern Genre Theory*, 30.

37. William Wordsworth, "Preface to the Lyrical Ballads," in *Lyrical Ballads, and Other Poems, 1797–1800* (Ithaca, NY: Cornell University Press, 1992), 740–760.

38. Thomas Hobbes, "Answer to Davenant's Preface to *Gondibert*," in *Critical Essays of the Seventeenth Century*, vol. 2, *1650–1685*, ed. Joel Elias Spingarn (Oxford, UK: Clarendon, 1908), 54.

39. On Wordsworth and the distinction between serious and popular, see John Guillory, *Cultural Capital: The Problem of Literary Canon Formation* (Chicago: University of Chicago Press, 1993), 128–129.

40. Johann Wolfgang von Goethe, *Wilhelm Meister's Apprenticeship and Travels*, 2 vols., trans. Thomas Carlyle (Boston: Dana Estes, 1839), 1: 335.

41. Inchbald's essay is reprinted in her novel *Nature and Art*, ed. Shawn Lisa Maurer (Peterborough, ON: Broadview, 2005), 165.

42. See Ros Ballaster, "Rivals for the Repertory: Theatre and Novel in Georgian London," *Restoration and Eighteenth-Century Research* 27, no. 1 (2012): 5–24.

43. See Emily Hodgson Anderson, *Eighteenth-Century Authorship and the Play of Fiction: Novels and the Theater, Haywood to Austen* (New York: Routledge, 2009); Nora Nachumi, *Acting like a Lady: British Women Novelists and the Eighteenth-Century Theater* (New York: AMS Press, 2008); Lisa A. Freeman, *Character's Theater: Genre and Identity on the Eighteenth-Century English Stage* (Philadelphia: University of Pennsylvania Press, 2001).

44. John Wilson Croker et al., eds., *Noctes Ambrosianae*, vol. 1 (New York: Worthington, 1863).

45. An unsigned review of Sardanapalus, *The Two Foscari* and *Cain*, from the *Edinburgh Review* (dated February 1822, issued April 1822, 413–452) by Francis Jeffrey first "Consider[ed them] as Poems" and then "As Plays." See the reprint in *Byron: The Critical Heritage*, ed. Andrew Rutherford (London: Routledge and Kegan Paul, 1970), 229. On Byron's relations to the stage, see Alan Richardson, "Byron and the Theatre," in *The Cambridge Companion to Byron*, ed. Drummond Bone (New York: Cambridge University Press,

2004), 133–150. On the staging of *Faust*, see Cyrus Hamlin, "Faust in Performance: Peter Stein's Production of Goethe's *Faust* Parts 1 and 2," *Theater* 32, no. 1 (2002): 116.

46. William Gifford, in Rutherford, *Byron*, 70.

47. Katherine Mannheimer, personal communication, March 2017.

48. Michael Booth, "Theater History and the Literary Critic," *Yearbook of English Studies* 9 (1979): 15.

49. Paula Backscheider, "Retrieving Elizabeth Inchbald," in *The Oxford Handbook of the Georgian Theatre, 1737–1832*, ed. Julia Swindells and David Francis Taylor (Oxford: Oxford University Press, 2014), 615.

50. Steele, quoted in Julie Stone Peters, *Theatre of the Book, 1480–1880: Print, Text, and Performance in Europe* (New York: Oxford University Press, 2000), 47.

51. Peters, 49, 74. Thomas Lockwood observes that all of Fielding's plays were printed at the time of first production and *The Tragedy of Tragedies* on the date of first performance in 1731. See Lockwood's general introduction to *The Wesleyan Edition of The Works of Henry Fielding Plays*, vol. 1 (Oxford, UK: Clarendon, 2004), xxiv.

52. Tom Keymer, "Mastering the Art of Understating Your Wealth," review of *The Literary Correspondence of the Tonsons*, ed. Stephen Bernard, *London Review of Books* 38, no. 9 (2016): 21.

53. The anonymous *The Disguise: A Dramatic Novel* (1771) was a novel entirely in dialogue. The author explained having adopted dialogue because epistolary form had grown too tedious, according to the entry in *Biographia Dramatica; or, A Companion to the Playhouse*, by David Erskine Baker, Isaac Reed, and Stephen Jones, vol. 2 (London: Longman, Hurst, Rees, Orme, and Brown, 1812), 165.

54. See Jonathan Brody Kramnick, "Reading Shakespeare's Novels: Literary History and Cultural Politics in the Lennox-Johnson Debate," *Modern Language Quarterly* 55, no. 4 (1994): 429–453; reprinted in *Eighteenth-Century Literary History: An MLQ Reader*, ed. Marshall Brown (Durham, NC: Duke University Press, 1999), 43–67.

55. Daniel Barrett, "Play Publication, Readers, and the 'Decline' of Victorian Drama," *Book History* 2, no. 1 (1999): 174.

56. On Sheridan's relation to print culture, see David Francis Taylor, *Theatres of Opposition: Empire, Revolution and Richard Brinsley Sheridan* (Oxford: Oxford University Press, 2012), 34–37.

57. Quoted in Barrett, "Play Publication," 176.

58. On "Novels and Plays," see Peters, *Theatre of the Book*, 75; on "Poetry and Drama," see Simon Eliot, "Some Trends in British Book Publication 1800–1919," in *Literature in the Marketplace: Nineteenth-Century British Publication and Reading Practices*, edited by John O. Jordan and Robert L. Patten (New York: Cambridge University Press, 1995), 25–27.

59. Barrett, "Play Publication," 178.

60. Quoted in Peters, *Theatre of the Book*, 83.

61. William St. Clair, *The Reading Nation in the Romantic Period* (New York: Cambridge University Press, 2004), 143–157, and appendix, 692–714. See also Don-John Dugas, *Marketing the Bard: Shakespeare in Performance and Print, 1660–1740* (Columbia: University of Missouri Press, 2006), 213–238.

62. Don-John Dugas and Robert Hume, "The Dissemination of Shakespeare's Plays circa 1714," *Studies in Bibliography* 56 (2003–2004): 261–275. See also Joseph Roach, *"The God of Our Idolatry": Garrick and Shakespeare*, exhibition catalogue for an exhibition at the Lewis Walpole Library (New Haven, CT: Yale University Press, 2012), 6.

63. Jan Fergus, *Provincial Readers in Eighteenth-Century England* (New York: Oxford University Press, 2007), 98–99.

64. Maximillian Novak, "The Politics of Shakespeare Criticism in the Restoration and Early Eighteenth Century," *ELH* 81, no. 1 (2014): 125, 139n12.

65. Michael Dobson, "Becoming Uncut: Enlightenment Hamlets and the Ontology of Performance" (plenary lecture at Shakespeare Association of America conference, Vancouver, 3 April 2015).

66. William Shakespeare, *Hamlet, Prince of Denmark: A Tragedy as Is Now Acted by His Majesty's Servants* (London, 1756).

67. Charles Jennings, preface to *Hamlet* (London: 1770), 4.

68. Richardson, *Clarissa*, 1497. Tom Keymer discusses Richardson's treatment of Shakespeare in "Shakespeare in the Novel," in *Shakespeare in the Eighteenth Century*, ed. Fiona Ritchie and Peter Sabor (New York: Cambridge University Press, 2012), 122–125.

69. Brian Vickers, *William Shakespeare: The Critical Heritage*, vol. 4, *1753–1765* (London: Routledge and Kegan Paul, 1976), 20–21.

70. Francis Gentleman, *The Dramatic Censor*, vol. 1 (London, 1770), 352–353.

71. Jane Austen, *Mansfield Park*, ed. John Wiltshire (New York: Cambridge University Press, 2005), 390.

72. Austen, 390–391.

73. Patricia Michaelson, *Speaking Volumes: Women Reading and Speech in the Age of Austen* (Stanford, CA: Stanford University Press, 2002), 180; Abigail Williams, *The Social Life of Books: Reading Together in the Eighteenth-Century Home* (New Haven, CT: Yale University Press, 2017), 205, 207–208.

74. Robert DeMaria Jr., *Samuel Johnson and the Life of Reading* (Baltimore: Johns Hopkins University Press, 1997), 3.

75. Gilbert Austin, *Chironomia; or, A Treatise on Rhetorical Delivery* (London, 1806), 190, 203, 202, 206.

76. John Guillory, "Genesis of the Media Concept" *Critical Inquiry* 36, no. 2 (2010): 326, 334, 340, 341.

77. For metaphorical treatments of theatricality in eighteenth-century aesthetic theory, see Michael Fried, *Absorption and Theatricality: Painting and Beholder in the Age of Diderot* (Chicago: University of Chicago Press, 1988); John Bender and Michael Marrinan, *The Diagrammatic Imagination* (Palo Alto, CA: Stanford University Press, 2010). For nonmetaphorical treatment, see Christof Menke, *Force: A Fundamental Concept in Aesthetic Anthropology* (New York: Fordham University Press, 2013); Laura Rosenthal, *Ways of the World: Theater and Cosmopolitanism in the Restoration and Beyond* (Ithaca, NY: Cornell University Press, forthcoming 2020).

78. See Michael McKeon, ed. *Theory of the Novel: A Historical Approach* (Baltimore: Johns Hopkins University Press, 2000).

79. See Michael McKeon, "The Eighteenth-Century Challenge to Narrative Theory," in *Narrative Concepts in the Study of Eighteenth-Century Literature*, edited by Liisa Steinby and Aino Makikalli (Amsterdam: Amsterdam University Press, 2017), 39–78; McKeon, *Theory of the Novel*, 179–183.

80. Erich Auerbach, *Mimesis: The Representation of Reality in Western Literature*, trans. Willard R. Trask (1953; repr., Princeton, NJ: Princeton University Press, 1974), 554–55; Mark McGurl, *The Novel Art: Elevations of American Fiction after Henry James* (Princeton, NJ: Princeton University Press, 2001); Nicholas Dames, "Theories of the Novel," in *The Cambridge History of Literary Criticism*, vol. 6, ed. M.A.R. Habib (New York: Cambridge University Press, 2013), 506–523.

81. Elaine Freedgood, unpublished paper, "How the Victorian Novel Got Realistic, (in a French Way), Reactionary and Great," (July 2016), 3. She develops these ideas in *Worlds*

Enough: The Invention of Realism in the Victorian Novel (Princeton, NJ: Princeton University Press, 2019) which is not yet in print.

82. For a persuasive account of the dependency of major nineteenth-century realist novels on the theater, see David Kurnick, *Empty Houses: Theatrical Failure and the Novel* (Princeton, NJ: Princeton University Press, 2011).

83. Freedgood discusses Genette's debt to the filmologist Etienne Souriau in "How the Victorian Novel Got Realistic," 17. See Jean-Louis Baudry, "The Apparatus: Metapsychological Approaches to the Impression of Reality in Cinema," in *Narrative, Apparatus, Ideology: A Film Theory Reader*, ed. Philip Rosen (New York: Columbia University Press, 1986), 299–318.

84. For a recent account that rehearses some of these objections, see McKeon, "Eighteenth-Century Challenge."

85. Fludernik, *Towards a "Natural" Narratology*, 98.

86. Fludernik, 106–120.

87. Monica Fludernik, "Narrative and Drama," in *Theorizing Narrativity*, ed. John Pier and José Angel Garcia Landa (Berlin: de Gruyter, 2008), 377–378. It should not be surprising that New Media studies of narrative do not find much to use in narratology. For such studies, see Noah Wardrip-Fruin and Pat Harrigan, eds., *First Person: New Media as Story, Performance, and Game* (Cambridge, MA: MIT Press, 2006); and the follow-up volumes, Wardrip-Fruin and Harrigan, eds., *Second Person: Role-Playing and Story in Games and Playable Media* (Cambridge, MA: MIT Press, 2007), Wardrip-Fruin and Harrigan, eds., *Third Person: Authoring Vast Narratives* (Cambridge, MA: MIT Press, 2009).

88. Robert Miles, "What Is a Romantic Novel?," *Novel* 34, no. 2 (2001): 180–201. See also Scott Black, *Without the Novel: Romance and the History of Prose Fiction* (Charlottesville: University of Virginia Press, 2019).

89. See D. A. Miller, *Jane Austen, or The Secret of Style* (Princeton, NJ: Princeton University Press, 2003).

90. Garrett Stewart, *Dear Reader: The Conscripted Audience in Nineteenth-Century British Fiction* (Baltimore: Johns Hopkins University Press, 1996), 109.

91. Virginia Woolf, "Modern Fiction," in *The Common Reader* (London: Hogarth, 1925), 153, cited in Wayne C. Booth, *The Rhetoric of Fiction* (Chicago: University of Chicago Press, 1961), 91. See also Woolf, "Middlebrow," in *The Death of the Moth and Other Essays* (New York: Harcourt, Brace, 1942), 176–186.

92. Fredric Jameson, *The Antinomies of Realism* (New York: Verso, 2013), 154.

CHAPTER 2 — THE REFORM OF THE RAKE FROM ROCHESTER TO INCHBALD

1. Gilbert Burnet, *Some Passages of the Life and Death of the Right Honourable John, Earl of Rochester* (1680; London: E. Stock, 1875). Subsequent citations refer to this edition and appear parenthetically in the text. Burnet's book was frequently reprinted: The *English Short Title Catalogue* lists five editions up to 1700 (in 1680, 1681, 1692, 1693, and 1700) and regular printings throughout the eighteenth century (1724, 1727, 1741, 1752, 1765, 1782, 1787, 1791, and 1795), not including American editions.

2. Gustav Ungerer, "Thomas Shadwell's *The Libertine* (1675): A Forgotten Restoration Don Juan Play," *SEDERI: Yearbook of the Spanish and Portuguese Society for English Renaissance Studies* 1 (1990): 222–239.

3. John Traugott, "The Rake's Progress from Court to Comedy: A Study in Comic Form," *Studies in English Literature, 1500–1900* 6, no. 3 (1966): 381–407; Harold Weber, *The Restoration Rake-Hero: Transformations in Sexual Understandings in Seventeenth-Century England*

(Madison: University of Wisconsin Press, 1986); Erin Mackie, *Rakes, Highwaymen, and Pirates: The Making of the Modern Gentleman in the Eighteenth Century* (Baltimore: Johns Hopkins University Press, 2009); Aparna Gollapudi, *Moral Reform in Comedy and Culture, 1696–1747* (Burlington, VT: Ashgate, 2011).

4. Elaine McGirr, *Eighteenth-Century Characters: A Guide to the Literature of the Age* (New York: Palgrave Macmillan, 2007), 27–38.

5. Later eighteenth-century novel titles that reflect this interest include the anonymous *The Libertine Husband Reclaimed; and Virtuous Love Rewarded* (1774) and Charlotte Dacre's *The Libertine* (1807). For these and others, see Peter Garside, James Raven, and Rainer Schowerling, eds., *The English Novel, 1770–1829: A Bibliographical Survey of Prose Fiction Published in the British Isles*, 2 vols. (Oxford: Oxford University Press, 2000).

6. Robert D. Hume, *The Rakish Stage: Studies in English Drama, 1660–1800* (Carbondale: Southern Illinois University Press, 1983).

7. Erin Mackie cites the widespread assumption that Etheredge's Dorimant, the rake of *The Man of Mode* (1767), stood in for Rochester in *Rakes, Highwaymen, and Pirates: The Making of the Modern Gentleman in the Eighteenth Century* (Baltimore: Johns Hopkins University Press, 2010), 44. The presence of Rochester in Thomas Otway's *Venice Preserv'd* (1682) is observed by Graham Greene in *Lord Rochester's Monkey: Being the Life of John Wilmot, Second Earl of Rochester* (London: Bodley Head, 1974), 188–189; and affirmed by Christopher Hill in *The Collected Essays of Christopher Hill*, vol. 1, *Writing and Revolution in 17th-Century England* (Brighton, UK: Harvester, 1985), 310.

8. Green, *Lord Rochester's Monkey*, 10; Hill, *Collected Essays*, 309–310.

9. Quoted in Hill, *Collected Essays*, 310. See also John Wilmot, *The Works of John Wilmot, Earl of Rochester*, ed. Harold Love (Oxford: Oxford University Press, 1999), 241.

10. Michael McKeon, *Origins of the English Novel, 1600–1740* (Baltimore: Johns Hopkins University Press, 1987), 25–64; Lennard J. Davis, *Factual Fictions: The Origins of the English Novel* (New York: Columbia University Press, 1983); Douglas Lane Patey, *Probability and Literary Form: Philosophic Theory and Literary Practice in the Augustan Age* (New York: Cambridge University Press, 1984).

11. Michael McKeon, *Origins of the English Novel*, 46.

12. McKeon on "strange, therefore true" as a device used to validate truth-telling claims in apparition narratives in *Origins of the English Novel*, 84-85.

13. See Love's introduction to Wilmot, *Works of Rochester*, xxix. Nicholas Fisher points out that Rochester's best-known work, *A Satyr against Reason and Mankind*, supposed to have been written before 1674, reached print in an unauthorized broadside in 1679, in "The Contemporary Reception of Rochester's *A Satyr against Reason and Mankind*," *Review of English Studies* 57, no. 229 (2006): 185.

14. Other stories associated with Rochester were circulated widely in 1697, when Charles Gildon published *Familiar Letters*, vol. 2, featuring some of Rochester's correspondence, and again in 1714, when the *Mémoires de la vie du comte de Grammont* (1713) by Anthony Hamilton was translated into English.

15. The fact that Colley Cibber played Tom, Bevil Jr.'s servant, in the initial production of Steele's *Conscious Lovers* brings out the interdependence of the roles of the rake and the fop in the devolution of the rake onstage, a process that I discuss in greater detail later in this chapter.

16. Ronald Paulson, *Hogarth: His Life, Art and Times*, abridged ed. (New Haven, CT: Yale University Press, 1971), 146.

17. Joseph Addison and Sir Richard Steele, *The Tatler*, vol. 1, ed. Donald F. Bond (Oxford: Oxford University Press, 1987).

18. Mackie, *Rakes, Highwaymen, and Pirates*, 35–50.

19. Kristina Straub, *Domestic Affairs: Intimacy, Eroticism and Violence between Servants and Masters in Eighteenth-Century Britain* (Baltimore: Johns Hopkins University Press, 2009), 110–177.

20. Tom Jones is not a servant, but putting him in the trajectory of rakes lets us recognize Fielding's self-conscious separation of Tom's sexcapades from his social privilege. This separation provides the grounds of traditional criticism's celebration of his "natural sexuality," which has licensed the turning of a blind eye to his novels' social politics, but it also clarifies that these cannot be equated with his gender politics.

21. Performed regularly, with a marked uptick between 1714 and 1720 but thereafter with diminishing frequency, up to around 1750, *The Man of Mode* was performed once in 1755 and once more in 1766, with no more recorded performances for the rest of the century. *The Conscious Lovers*, *The Careless Husband*, and *The Provoked Husband* were performed significantly more frequently throughout the century. Revived at Covent Garden in the 1760s, *Love's Last Shift* disappeared from the stage after 1773.

22. Daniel Gustafson, "The Rake's Revival: Steele, Dennis, and the Early Eighteenth-Century Repertory," *Modern Philology* 112, no. 2 (2014): 358–380.

23. For accounts of the rake's decline, see J. Douglas Canfield, "Shifting Tropes of Ideology in English Serious Drama, Late Stuart to Early Georgian," in *Cultural Readings of Restoration and Eighteenth-Century Theater*, ed. J. Douglas Canfield and Deborah Payne (Athens: University of Georgia Press, 1995), 195–227; Laura Brown, *English Dramatic Form, 1660–1760: An Essay in Generic History* (New Haven, CT: Yale University Press, 1981); and Susan Staves, *Players' Sceptors: Fictions of Authority in the Restoration* (Lincoln: University of Nebraska Press, 1979).

24. Gustafson, "Rake's Revival," 380, 361.

25. Christopher Tilmouth, "After Libertinism: The Passions of the Polite Christian Hero," in *Emergent Nation: Early Modern British Literature in Transition 1660–1714*, ed. Elizabeth Sauer (Cambridge: Cambridge University Press, 2019), 240-257. The key texts by Dennis are the 1694 *Usefulness of the Stage* and the 1701 *Advancement and Reformation of Modern Poetry*.

26. John Dennis, *A Defence of Sir Fopling Flutter* (London, 1722), ECCO, accessed July 24, 2017, https://quod.lib.umich.edu/e/ecco/004801509.0001.000/1:2?rgn=div1;view=fulltext.

27. See Nancy Armstrong, *Desire and Domestic Fiction: A Political History of the Novel* (Oxford: Oxford University Press, 1987), 108–134; and McKeon, *Origins of the English Novel*, 411.

28. Tony Claydon, *William III and the Godly Revolution* (New York: Cambridge University Press, 1996), 31.

29. Alan Hunt, *Governing Morals: A Social History of Moral Regulation* (New York: Cambridge University Press, 1999), 28–56.

30. Andrew Starkie, "Contested Histories of the English Church: Gilbert Burnet and Jeremy Collier," *Huntington Library Quarterly* 68, nos. 1–2 (2005): 335–351.

31. Robert Hume, "Jeremy Collier and the Future of London Theater in 1698," *Studies in Philology* 96, no. 4 (1999): 480–511; Matthew J. Kinservik, "Censorship and Generic Change: The Case of Satire on the Early Eighteenth-Century London Stage," *Philological Quarterly* 78, no. 3 (1999): 259–282; Mark Dawson, *Gentility and the Comic Theatre of Late Stuart London* (New York: Cambridge University Press, 2005), 205–216; Lisa A. Freeman, "Jeremy Collier and the Politics of Theatrical Representation," in *Players, Playwrights, Playhouses: Investigating Performance, 1660–1800*, ed. Michael Cordner and Peter Holland (New York: Palgrave Macmillan, 2007), 135–153.

32. Lisa Freeman, *Antitheatricality and the Body Public* (Philadelphia: University of Pennsylvania Press, 2017).

33. Jeremy Collier, *A Short View of the Immorality and Profaneness of the English Stage* (London, 1698), reprinted in *The English Stage: Attack and Defense, 1577–1730*, ed. Arthur Freeman (New York: Garland, 1972), 1–2.

34. See the entry for *Dangerous Connections* in Garside, Raven, and Schowerling, *English Novel*, 1:339.

35. Michael McKeon, *The Secret History of Domesticity* (Baltimore: Johns Hopkins University Press, 2005), 100.

36. See also Catherine Gallagher, *Nobody's Story: The Vanishing Act of Women Writers in the Marketplace, 1670–1820* (Berkeley: University of California Press, 1994), 88–144.

37. Michael McKeon, "What Was an Early Modern Public, and How Was It Made?," *History Compass* 10, no. 9 (2012): 723–724. See also my "Drama Theory, the Division of Knowledge and the Emergence of the Aesthetic" *History Compass* 10, no. 9 (2012): 667–676.

38. Oscar Wilde, *The Importance of Being Earnest: And Other Plays,* ed. Terrence McNally (New York: Random House, 2003), 206.

39. Elaine McGirr, "Rethinking Reform Comedies: Colley Cibber's Desiring Women," *Eighteenth-Century Studies* 46, no. 3 (2013): 385–397; and McGirr, *Partial Histories: A Reappraisal of Colley Cibber* (London: Palgrave Macmillan, 2016).

40. Matthew J. Kinservik, *Disciplining Satire: The Censorship of Satiric Comedy on the Eighteenth-Century London Stage* (Lewisburg, PA: Bucknell University Press, 2002).

41. Julia Fawcett, "Creating Character in '*Chiaro Oscuro*': Sterne's Celebrity, Cibber's *Apology*, and the Life of *Tristram Shandy*," *Eighteenth-Century: Theory and Interpretation* 53, no. 2 (2012): 141–161.

42. Darryl P. Domingo, *The Rhetoric of Diversion in English Literature and Culture, 1690–1760* (Cambridge: Cambridge University Press, 2016), 75.

43. Susan Staves, "A Few Kind Words for the Fop," *Studies in English Literature, 1500–1900,* 22, no. 3 (1982): 413–428.

44. John Vanbrugh, *The Relapse*, act 2, scene 2, lines 46–53 in *The Relapse and Other Plays*, ed. Brean S. Hammond (New York: Oxford University Press, 2004), 24.

45. Collier, *Short View*, 231.

46. In *Antitheatricality and the Body Public,* 121–130, Lisa Freeman describes Collier's objections to Vanbrugh as flowing from his critique of Vanbrugh's support for the Glorious Revolution in an account that is more invested in the political referentiality of the plays involved in the controversy than in their aesthetics.

47. McKeon, *Secret History of Domesticity*, 347–388; Catherine Gallagher, "The Rise of Fictionality," in *The Novel*, vol. 1, *History, Geography, and Culture*, ed. Franco Moretti (Princeton, NJ: Princeton University Press, 2006), 336–363.

48. Harry Glicksman, "The Stage History of Colley Cibber's *The Careless Husband*," *PMLA* 36, no. 2 (1921): 245–250.

49. Kinservik, *Disciplining Satire*, 37–42.

50. Elizabeth Kowaleski Wallace, "Reading the Surfaces of Coley Cibber's *The Careless Husband*," *SEL: Studies in English Literature, 1500–1900* 40, no. 3 (2000): 483; McGirr, "Rethinking Reform Comedies," 391.

51. David Roberts, "Sleeping Beauties: Shakespeare, Sleep and the Stage," *Cambridge Quarterly* 35, no. 3 (2006): 231–254.

52. Brean S. Hammond observes, "It is too often overlooked that Cibber was Fielding's invention, not Pope's," in "Politics and Cultural Politics: The Case of Henry Fielding," *Eighteenth-Century Life* 16 (February 1992): 87.

53. Hammond has proposed that "we can situate later seventeenth-century drama as a transitional phase in the emergence of novelistic realism" ("Politics and Cultural Politics," 80).

54. Allen Michie, *Richardson and Fielding: The Dynamics of a Critical Rivalry* (Lewisburg, PA: Bucknell University Press, 1999), 38.

55. In the persona of Charles Easy, Cibber writes, "I will not, I must not say, how often I was melted with some moving expressions, put in the mouth of a meek, innocent girl.—But to wave this *tritibus* part, I must tell you that the Editor has robbed me of my merry scheme of limited marriages, on which subject I used so often to rattle—he has given it to his *Robin Rattle*, or rather wicked witty *Bob Lovelace*, with this difference only, that he has reduced my term of seven years down to *one year*." Quoted in Florian Stuber and Margaret Anne Doody, "The Clarissa Project and *Clarissa*'s Reception," *Text* 12 (1999): 132–133.

56. Christopher Bollas, "The Transformational Object," in *The Shadow of the Object: Psychoanalysis of the Unthought Known* (London: Free Association Books, 1987), 13–29.

57. Examples from the 1660s would include Wellbred in James Howard's *The English Mounsieur* (1663–1664), Philidor in James Howard's *All Mistaken* (1665–1672), and Celadon in John Dryden's *Secret Love* (1667). Later examples would include Sir Harry Wildair in George Farquhar's *The Constant Couple* (1699) and Aimwell from *The Beaux' Stratagem* (1707).

58. Nancy Armstrong, *Desire and Domestic Fiction: A Political History of the Novel* (Oxford: Oxford University Press, 1987); Michael McKeon, *The Secret History of Domesticity: Public, Private, and the Division of Knowledge* (Baltimore: Johns Hopkins University Press, 2009).

59. Samuel Richardson, *Clarissa; or, The History of a Young Lady*, ed. Angus Ross (New York: Penguin, 1985), 444.

60. Michie, *Richardson and Fielding*.

61. William Warner, *Reading Clarissa: The Struggles of Interpretation* (New Haven, CT: Yale University Press, 1979); Tassie Gwilliam, *Samuel Richardson's Fictions of Gender* (Stanford, CA: Stanford University Press, 1993), 45–46.

62. James Grantham Turner, "Novel Panic: Picture and Performance in the Reception of Richardson's *Pamela*," *Representations* 48 (Fall 1994): 70–96. In *Actions and Objects from Hobbes to Richardson* (Stanford, CA: Stanford University Press, 2010), 194–232, Jonathan Kramnick has persuasively shown that Richardson is as interested in his characters' minds as in their bodies.

63. Henry Fielding, *Joseph Andrews and Shamela*, ed. Douglas Brooks-Davies and Thomas Keymer (New York: Oxford University Press, 1999), 347.

64. Thomas Lockwood, "Theatrical Fielding," *Studies in the Literary Imagination* 32, no. 2 (1999): 105–114.

65. Fielding, *Joseph Andrews and Shamela*, 347.

66. See Katherine Mannheimer on Alexander Pope's theatricalization of print in the four-book *Dunciad* in *Print, Visuality, and Gender in Eighteenth-Century Satire: "The Scope in Ev'ry Page"* (New York: Routledge, 2011) 152–180.

67. Vanbrugh, *Relapse*, act 5, scene 1, line 49, p. 77

68. Thomas Keymer and Peter Sabor, *"Pamela" in the Marketplace: Literary Controversy and Print Culture in Eighteenth-Century Britain and Ireland* (New York: Cambridge University Press, 2005), 88.

69. On Fielding's "double irony," see William Empson, *Using Biography* (Cambridge, MA: Harvard University Press, 1984), 131–162; on his "extreme skepticism," see McKeon, *Origins of the English Novel*, 382–409.

70. Vanbrugh, *Relapse*, act 5, scene 4, lines 159–165, p. 91.

71. Vanbrugh, act 4, scene 3, line 77, p. 65.

72. Henry Fielding, *Joseph Andrews*, ed. Martin Battestin (Middletown, CT: Wesleyan University Press, 1967), 343.

73. Claude Rawson observes that narrative interruptions and dramatic frame breaking are versions of each other in his "Henry Fielding," in *The Cambridge Companion to the Eighteenth-Century Novel*, ed. John Richetti (New York: Cambridge University Press, 1996), 143. Ronald Paulson argues that the active form of meaning-making that Fielding elicits from readers derives from his critical deism, in *The Beautiful, Novel, and Strange: Aesthetics and Heterodoxy* (Baltimore: Johns Hopkins University Press, 1996), 98–114.

74. Lynn Festa, "Sentimental Bonds and Revolutionary Characters: Richardson's *Pamela* in England and France," in *The Literary Channel: The Inter-national Invention of the Novel*, ed. Margaret Cohen and Carolyn Dever (Princeton, NJ: Princeton University Press, 2002), 73–105.

75. See Tom Keymer on Richardson's use of vernacular speech in *Pamela* and the critique of his representation of the idiom of the gentry emanating from his aristocratic lady friends in *Richardson's "Clarissa" and the Eighteenth-Century Reader* (New York: Cambridge University Press, 2004), 15–23.

76. Elizabeth Inchbald, *Wives as They Were, and Maids as They Are* (London: G. G. and J. Robinson, 1797), 45.

77. Paula Backscheider, introduction to *The Plays of Elizabeth Inchbald* (New York: Garland, 1980), xxxii, cited in Misty Anderson, *Female Playwrights and Eighteenth-Century Comedy: Negotiating Marriage on the London Stage* (New York: Palgrave Macmillan, 2002), 193.

78. Daniel O'Quinn, "Scissors and Needles": Inchbald's *Wives as They Were, Maids as They Are* and the Governance of Sexual Exchange," *Theatre Journal* 51, no. 2 (1999): 105–125.

79. Terry Castle, *Masquerade and Civilization: The Carnivalesque in Eighteenth-Century Culture and Fiction* (Stanford, CA: Stanford University Press, 1986), 303.

80. Elizabeth Inchbald, *A Simple Story*, ed. Anna Lott (Peterborough, ON: Broadview, 2007), 157.

81. See Elizabeth Inchbald, *The Diaries of Elizabeth Inchbald*, 3 vols., ed. Ben Robertson (London: Pickering and Chatto, 2007), 1:260; Castle, *Masquerade and Civilization*, 321–323; and Annibel Jenkins, *I'll Tell You What: The Life of Elizabeth Inchbald* (Lexington: University Press of Kentucky, 2003).

82. On the mother-daughter resemblance, see Jenny Davidson, "Why Girls Look like Their Mothers: David Garrick Rewrites *The Winter's Tale*," in *Shakespeare and the Eighteenth Century*, ed. Peter Sabor and Paul Yachnin (Burlington, VT: Ashgate, 2008), 165–180; and Jill Campbell, "Women Writers and the Woman's Novel: The Trope of Maternal Transmission," in *The Cambridge Companion to Fiction of the Romantic Period*, ed. Richard Maxwell and Katie Trumpener (New York: Cambridge University Press, 2008), 159–176.

83. Inchbald, *Simple Story*, 294.

84. Patricia Mayer Spacks notices the Fieldingesque qualities of Inchbald's ending, in *On Rereading* (Cambridge, MA: Harvard University Press, 2011), 179–180.

85. Inchbald, *Simple Story*, 288–289.

86. Emily Anderson, "Revising Theatrical Conventions in *A Simple Story*: Elizabeth Inchbald's Ambiguous Performance," *Journal for Early Modern Cultural Studies* 6, no. 1 (2006): 5–30; Diane Osland, "Heart-Picking in *A Simple Story*," *Eighteenth-Century Fiction* 16, no. 1 (2003): 79–101.

87. Inchbald, *Wives as They Were*, 77–78.

88. Dominique Godineau, *The Women of Paris and Their French Revolution*, trans. Katherine Streip (Berkeley: University of California Press, 1998), xviii–xix, 158–75.

89. Elizabeth Inchbald, *The British Theatre; or, A Collection of Plays Selected by Elizabeth Inchbald* (1808), 25 vols. (New York: Georg Olms Verlag, 1970), 9:5 (B3).

90. Denis Diderot, "Éloge de Richardson," in *Collection complette des oeuvres philosophiques, littéraires et dramatiques de M. Diderot*, vol. 1 (London, 1773), 384–405.

91. Christina Lupton, *Reading and the Making of Time* (Baltimore: Johns Hopkins University Press, 2018), 132–136.

92. Franco Moretti, *Graphs, Maps, Trees: Abstract Models for Literary History* (London: Verso, 2007).

93. On the direct address and Brontë's novel, see Garrett Stewart, *Dear Reader: The Conscripted Audience in Nineteenth-Century British Fiction* (Baltimore: Johns Hopkins University Press, 1996), 267.

CHAPTER 3 — PERFORMING READING IN RICHARDSON AND FIELDING

1. Denis Diderot, "Éloge de Richardson," in *Collection complette des oeuvres philosophiques, littéraires et dramatiques de M. Diderot*, vol. 1 (London, 1773), 386. The translation is mine.

2. Mark Kinkead-Weekes, *Samuel Richardson, Dramatic Novelist* (Ithaca, NY: Cornell University Press, 1973), 396.

3. Though Kinkead-Weekes observes that Richardson's dramatic epistolarity results in his characters coming to be more fully known than any earlier fictional creations (424–432), reading through Richardson's realism, many critics take the characters of *Clarissa* as the vehicle for various issues including gender roles, rape laws, or philosophy of mind, without recognizing the role of drama in his narrative. In "Why Lovelace Must Die," *Novel: A Forum on Fiction*, 37, nos. 1–2 (2004): 5–23, Elaine McGirr produces the apotheosis of this approach, fusing a character-driven reading with the assertion of Richardson's antitheatricality that treats the characters of Lovelace and Clarissa as the embodiments of the literary genres of drama and novel and reading out of Lovelace's death Richardson's declaration of the generic independence of the novel.

4. Tom Keymer, *Richardson's "Clarissa" and the Eighteenth-Century Reader* (New York: Cambridge University Press, 1992), 145.

5. Ros Ballaster, "Rivals for the Repertory: Theatre and Novel in Georgian London," *Restoration and 18th-Century Theatre Research* 27, no. 1 (2012): 5–24. She quotes *Pamela*: "I think the stage, by proper regulation, may be a profitable amusement. But nothing more convinces one of the truth of the common observation, that the best things, corrupted, prove the worst, than these representations. The terror and compunction from evil deeds, the compassion for a just distress, and the general beneficence, which those lively exhibitions are so capable of raising in the human mind, might be of great service, when directed to right ends, and induced by proper motives." Samuel Richardson, *Pamela or Virtue Rewarded*, ed. Thomas Archer (London: Routledge, 1873) vol. 2, 408, letter LXXXIV.

6. Jenny Davidson points out that Richardson's descriptions of characters' gestures may be indebted to newspaper reports on the theater, in "The 'Minute Particular' in Life-Writing and the Novel," *Eighteenth-Century Studies* 48, no. 3 (2015): 269, 276.

7. Albert J. Rivero, *The Plays of Henry Fielding: A Critical Study of His Dramatic Career* (Charlottesville: University of Virginia Press, 1989), ix.

8. Robert D. Hume, "Fielding at 300: Elusive, Confusing, Misappropriated, or (Perhaps) Obvious?," *Modern Philology* 108, no. 2 (2010): 224–262.

9. Michael McKeon, *Origins of the English Novel, 1600–1740* (Baltimore: Johns Hopkins University Press, 1987), 22.

10. Henry Fielding to James Harris, Bath, 8 September 1741, in *The Correspondence of Henry and Sarah Fielding*, ed. Martin C. Battestin and Clive T. Probyn (Oxford, UK: Clarendon, 1993), 11, quoted in Martin C. Battestin, "Life-Writing without Letters: Fielding and

the Problem of Evidence," in *Writing the Lives of Writers*, ed. Warwick Gould and Thomas F. Stanley (New York: St. Martin's, 1998), 91.

11. Battestin, "Life-Writing without Letters," 91.

12. The first five volumes of the projected twelve of the *Cambridge Edition of the Correspondence of Samuel Richardson* under the general editorship of Tom Keymer and Peter Sabor appeared in 2014–2016. For the most recent critical account of Richardson's letters, see Louise Curran, *Samuel Richardson and the Art of Letter Writing* (New York: Cambridge University Press, 2016).

13. Alan Stewart, *Shakespeare's Letters* (New York: Oxford University Press, 2008), 39–74.

14. Henry Fielding, *The Old Debauchees*, in *The Wesleyan Edition of the Works of Henry Fielding: Plays*, 3 vols. ed. Thomas Lockwood (Oxford, UK: Clarendon, 2004), 2:317; hereafter cited as *Fielding Plays*.

15. Henry Fielding, *Love in Several Masques*, in *Fielding Plays*, 1:45, 61–63.

16. Tiffany Potter, *Honest Sins: Georgian Libertinism and the Plays and Novels of Henry Fielding* (Montreal: McGill-Queen's University Press, 1999), 40.

17. See Potter, 34–73.

18. Lovemore is the rake of Thomas Southerne's 1691 play *The Wives' Excuse*, as well as the rake/hero of Thomas Betterton's *The Amorous Widow* (1710); Lovegirlo is the name of the rake/hero in Fielding's *The Covent Garden Tragedy* (1732). As Lockwood points out, just as *The Tragedy of Tragedies* parodies the language of the older heroic drama, so the situations of *The Covent Garden Tragedy* parody those of pseudoclassical tragedies like Ambrose Phillips's *The Distrest Mother* (1712). *Fielding Plays*, 2:344–345.

19. Henry Fielding, *Joseph Andrews* ed. Martin Battestin (Middletown CT.: Wesleyan University Press, 1967), 5.

20. Judith Frank, "The Comic Novel and the Poor: Fielding's Preface to *Joseph Andrews*," *Eighteenth-Century Studies* 27, no. 2 (1993–1994): 219.

21. Roger D. Lund, "Augustan Burlesque and the Genesis of *Joseph Andrews*," *Studies in Philology* 103, no. 1 (2006): 119.

22. Lund discusses Gay in "Augustan Burlesque" on 116–117; Lockwood discusses Fielding's allusions to Gay in *The Covent Garden Tragedy*, in *Fielding Plays*, 2:344.

23. It played for four nights as the afterpiece with *The Tragedy of Tragedies*, when it was replaced by *The Author's Farce*, which as Lockwood observes, "mean[t] probably just 'The Pleasures of the Town,'" the puppet-show play within the play written by Luckless, the hapless author. See *Fielding Plays*, 1:616.

24. Though as Lockwood observes, the topicality of *The Letter-Writers*, like that of *The Old Debauchees*, takes advantage of a news story to give the "racy impression of currency" without depending on it as a source. See *Fielding Plays*, 2:293.

25. *Fielding Plays*, 1:611.

26. Henry Fielding, *The Letter-Writers*, act 2, scene 10, in *Fielding Plays*, 1:649.

27. Fielding, 1:666.

28. Keymer, *Richardson's "Clarissa,"* 8–14.

29. Ian Watt, *The Rise of the Novel: Studies in Defoe, Richardson, and Fielding* (Harmondsworth, UK: Penguin, 1974), 222.

30. William B. Warner, *Licensing Entertainment: The Elevation of Novel Reading in Britain, 1684–1750* (Berkeley: University of California Press, 1998), 176–230. For the adaptations, see Thomas Keymer and Peter Sabor, *The Pamela Controversy: Criticisms and Adaptations of Samuel Richardson's "Pamela," 1740–1750* (London: Pickering and Chatto, 2001), 6 vols. On the international reception of *Pamela*, see also Lynn Festa, "Sentimental Bonds and Revolutionary Characters: Richardson's *Pamela* in England and France," in *The Literary*

Channel: The Inter-national Invention of the Novel, ed. Margaret Cohen and Carolyn Dever (Princeton, NJ: Princeton University Press, 2002), 73–105.

31. Thomas Keymer and Peter Sabor, *"Pamela" in the Marketplace: Literary Controversy and Print Culture in Eighteenth-Century Britain and Ireland* (New York: Cambridge University Press, 2005), 118.

32. Henry Giffard, *Pamela, a Comedy*, in *The Pamela Controversy: Criticisms and Adaptations of Samuel Richardson's "Pamela," 1740–1750*, eds. Tom Keymer and Peter Sabor (London: Pickering and Chatto, 2001), vol. 6, 55.

33. Giffard, 59.

34. Peter Sabor, introduction to Anonymous, *Pamela or Virtue Triumphant* in *The Pamela Controversy: Criticisms and Adaptations of Samuel Richardson's "Pamela," 1740–1750*, eds. Tom Keymer and Peter Sabor (London: Pickering and Chatto, 2001), vol. 6, xvi.

35. David A. Brewer, *The Afterlife of Character, 1726–1825* (Philadelphia: University of Pennsylvania Press, 2005), 121–153. Brewer is attentive to Richardson's attempts to retain authorial control over the adaptations.

36. Brewer, 1.

37. James Grantham Turner, "Novel Panic: Picture and Performance in the reception of Richardson's *Pamela*," *Representations* 48 (Fall 1994): 73, 83. For Brooks's argument, see *The Melodramatic Imagination: Balzac, Henry James, Melodrama, and the Mode of Excess* (New Haven, CT: Yale University Press, 1976).

38. Turner, 78.

39. Brewer, *Afterlife of Character*, 6. On the novel's negotiation between actual and virtual embodiment in women writers of the eighteenth century, see Catherine Gallagher, *Nobody's Story: The Vanishing Acts of Women Writers in the Marketplace, 1670–1820* (Berkeley: University of California Press, 1994).

40. George Colman the Elder, *The Rivals and Polly Honeycombe*, ed. David A. Brewer (Peterborough, ON: Broadview, 2012).

41. See Robert Porrett, *Clarissa; or, The Fatal Seduction, a Tragedy in Prose*, in *Clarissa: the Eighteenth-Century Response, 1747–1804*, vol. 2, *Rewriting Clarissa*, ed. Lois Bueler (New York: AMS Press, 2010), 171–228.

42. See David A. Brewer, "Print, Performance, Personhood, Polly Honeycombe," *Studies in Eighteenth-Century Culture* 41 (2012): 185–194.

43. Colman, *Rivals and Polly Honeycombe*, 10.

44. Colman, 9.

45. See Brewer, *Afterlife of Character*, 4–5. For Deidre Lynch on character, see *The Economy of Character: Novels, Market Culture, and the Business of Inner Meaning* (Chicago: University of Chicago Press, 1998); for Lisa Freeman, see *Character's Theater: Genre and Identity on the Eighteenth-Century English Stage* (Philadelphia: University of Pennsylvania Press, 2001).

46. Brewer reads the scene of Jack Smatter reading Colebrand's letter in Giffard's *Pamela* as reflecting the relationship between Giffard and Ralph Allen as readers of Richardson: according to Brewer, Giffard's scene answers Allen's question of why Mrs. Jewkes was dismissed. But this emphasis on readers' interactions need not come at the expense of an appreciation of the scene as performance. Brewer, *Afterlife of Character*, 129–130.

47. On the history of sociable reading more generally, see Abigail Williams, *The Social Life of Books: Reading Together in the Eighteenth-Century Home* (New Haven, CT: Yale University Press, 2017).

48. Kinkead-Weekes, *Samuel Richardson*.

49. Jill Campbell, "Fielding's Style," *ELH* 72, no. 2 (2005): 407–428.

50. Jeffrey Williams, "The Narrative Circle: The Interpolated Tales in *Joseph Andrews*," *Studies in the Novel* 30, no. 4 (1998): 482. See also Hume, "Fielding at 300," 225–227.

51. A. D. McKillop, *The Early Masters of English Fiction* (Lawrence: University of Kansas Press, 1956), 125. See Stephen B. Dobranski, "What Fielding Doesn't Say in *Tom Jones*," *Modern Philology* 107, no. 4 (2010): 632–653.

52. See R. S. Crane, "The Concept of Plot and the Plot of *Tom Jones*," in *Critics and Criticism*, ed. R. S. Crane et al. (Chicago: University of Chicago Press, 1952), 119–139.

53. See Stephanie Insley Hershinow, "When Experience Matters: *Tom Jones* and 'Virtue Rewarded,'" *Novel: A Forum on Fiction* 47, no. 3 (2014): 363–382.

54. Henry Fielding, *The History of Tom Jones, a Foundling*, ed. Martin C. Battestin and Fredson Bowers (Middleton CT: Wesleyan University Press, 1975), vol. 2, 874. Subsequent citations refer to this edition and appear parenthetically in the text.

55. Terry Castle, *Masquerade and Civilization: The Carnivalesque in Eighteenth-Century English Culture and Fiction* (Stanford, CA: Stanford University Press, 1986), 246.

56. Henry Fielding, *Amelia*, ed. Martin C. Battestin (Middletown, CT: Wesleyan University Press, 1983), 416.

57. Castle, *Masquerade*, 239.

58. Fielding, *Amelia*, 442.

59. I use "close third-person" narration rather than the more familiar term, "limited third-person" narration to emphasize that it is distance from the action that is a significant and overlooked source of meaning. In *Narrative Discourse: An Essay in Method*, trans. Jane E. Lewin (Ithaca, NY: Cornell University Press, 1980), Gérard Genette replaced point of view by focalization in order to emphasize information flows, but his vocabulary, though it sought to avoid the psychological orientation of "persons," nevertheless, with its use of "internal" and "external," still gives greater priority to character than it may need to have.

60. Fielding, *Joseph Andrews*, 315.

61. Campbell, "Fielding's Style," 422.

62. Campbell, 416–417.

63. Angus Fletcher and Michael Benveniste, "Defending Pluralism: The Chicago School and the Case of *Tom Jones*," *New Literary History* 41, no. 3 (2010): 653–667; Wayne Booth, "Telling as Showing: Dramatized Narrators Reliable and Unreliable," in *The Rhetoric of Fiction* (Chicago: University of Chicago Press, 1961), 94–96. See also Campbell on Booth in "Fielding's Style," 411, 425n7.

64. Fletcher and Benveniste, "Defending Pluralism," 661. They argue that these omissions place the emphasis on the narrator rather than the author, who, instead of imposing his authority, engages readers in a "process of plural problem solving" that Fletcher and Benveniste then associate with Dewey (662).

65. Scott Black, "Anachronism and the Uses of Form in *Joseph Andrews*," *Novel: A Forum on Fiction* 38, nos. 2–3 (2005): 147–164. See also Black, "The Adventures of Love in *Tom Jones*," in *Henry Fielding in Our Time: Papers Presented at the Tercentenary Conference*, ed. J. A. Downie (Newcastle-upon-Tyne, UK: Cambridge Scholars, 2008), 45–46.

66. Frances Burney, *Evelina*, ed. Edward A. Bloom and Lillian Bloom (New York: Oxford University Press, 1982), 257.

67. Jane Austen, *Pride and Prejudice*, ed. Pat Rogers (New York: Cambridge University Press, 2006), 227.

68. Michael McKeon, *Secret History of Domesticity: Public, Private, and the Division of Knowledge* (Baltimore: Johns Hopkins University Press, 2009), 692–717; see also Felicia Bonaparte, "Conjecturing Possibilities: Reading and Misreading in Jane Austen's *Pride and Prejudice*," *Studies in the Novel* 37, no. 2 (2005): 141–161.

69. Campbell, "Fielding's Style," 409–410; D. A. Miller, *Jane Austen; or, The Secret of Style* (Princeton, NJ: Princeton University Press, 2003), 31–32.

70. Jane Austen, *Persuasion*, ed. Janet Todd and Antje Blank (New York: Cambridge University Press, 2006), 43.

71. In *Dear Reader: The Conscripted Audience in Nineteenth-Century British Fiction* (Baltimore: Johns Hopkins University Press, 1996), Garrett Stewart recognizes Austen's debt to Fielding but is more interested in what comes after Austen in the development of a new footing for the novel that he wittily describes this way: "You are no longer in the text; it is in you" (109).

72. Virginia Woolf, "Modern Fiction," In *The Common Reader* (London: Hogarth, 1925), 153, cited in Booth, *Rhetoric of Fiction*, 91. See also Virginia Woolf, "Middlebrow," in *The Death of the Moth and Other Essays* (New York: Harcourt, Brace, 1942), 176–186.

CHAPTER 4 — THE PROMISE OF EMBARRASSMENT

1. D. A. Miller, *Jane Austen; or, The Secret of Style* (Princeton, NJ: Princeton University Press, 2003), 84.

2. Miller, 59.

3. Jane Austen, *Sense and Sensibility*, ed. Edward Copeland (New York: Cambridge University Press, 2006), 326.

4. Although Janet Todd is persuaded that Austen's admiration for Burney fell off after *Evelina*, Jocelyn Harris has proposed that Austen's reading of *The Wanderer* and its hostile reviews had an effect on her defense of fiction in *Northanger Abbey* and possibly on the composition of *Persuasion* as well. See Todd's introduction to *Persuasion* (New York: Cambridge University Press, 2006), l–li, lviii; Jocelyn Harris, *A Revolution Almost beyond Expression: Jane Austen's Persuasion* (Newark: Delaware University Press, 2007), 20–22, 24–25.

5. See Devoney Looser, review of *Women in Revolutionary Debate: Female Novelists from Burney to Austen*, by Stephanie Russo, *Modern Philology* 112, no. 4 (2015): 327–329. See also Jillian Heydt-Stevenson and Charlotte Sussman, eds., *Recognizing the Romantic Novel: New Histories of British Fiction, 1780–1830* (Liverpool, UK: Liverpool University Press, 2011), for some recent approaches to the novels of this period.

6. Jane Austen, *The Visit*, in *Juvenilia*, ed. Peter Sabor (New York: Cambridge University Press, 2006), 63–68.

7. Emily Hodgson Anderson, *Eighteenth-Century Authorship and the Play of Fiction: Novels and the Theater, Haywood to Austen* (New York: Routledge, 2009), 48.

8. On Austen and theater, see Penny Gay, *Jane Austen and the Theatre* (Cambridge: Cambridge University Press, 2002); and Daniel O'Quinn, "Jane Austen and Performance: Theatre, Memory, and Enculturation," in *A Companion to Jane Austen*, ed. Claudia Johnson and Clara Tuite (Chichester, UK: Wiley Blackwell, 2009), 377–388.

9. Miller, *Jane Austen*, 71.

10. On the connections between shame, theatricality, and vicarious experience, see Eve Kosofsky Sedgwick, "Shame, Theatricality and Queer Performativity: Henry James's *The Art of the Novel*," in *Touching Feeling: Affect, Pedagogy, Performativity* (Durham, NC: Duke University Press, 2003), 35–66.

11. On Burney's natural ear for dialogue and requests from Garrick and Sheridan for her to write a comedy, see Joyce Hemlow, *The History of Fanny Burney* (Oxford: Clarendon Press, 1958), 96.

12. On the history of Burney's playwriting, see Peter Sabor, "General Introduction," in *The Complete Plays of Frances Burney*, 2 vols., ed. Peter Sabor (Montreal: McGill-Queen's University Press, 1995), 1:xii–xvii. On the importance of her two daddies' responses, see Cath-

erine Gallagher, *Nobody's Story: The Vanishing Act of Women in the Marketplace, 1670–1820* (Berkeley: University of California Press, 1994), 203–256.

13. Burney's *Edwy and Elgiva* (1795) failed after one night. For an account, see Sabor's introduction to *Complete Plays*, 1:xii–xvii; as well as Emily Hodgson Anderson, "Staged Insensibility in Burney's *Cecilia, Camilla*, and *The Wanderer*: How a Playwright Writes Novels," *Eighteenth-Century Fiction* 17, no. 4 (2005): 629–648.

14. Nora Nachumi, *Acting like a Lady: British Women Novelists and the Eighteenth-Century Theater* (New York: AMS Press, 2008), 116–146; Anderson, *Eighteenth-Century Authorship*, 46–76.

15. On Burney's provision of a catalogue of Georgian entertainments, see Deidre Lynch, *The Economy of Character: Novels, Market Culture, and the Business of Inner Meaning* (Chicago: University of Chicago Press, 1998), 168. For the view that Burney abandoned theatricality because she had discovered the genre of the novel, see Emily Allen, "Staging Identity: Frances Burney's Allegory of Genre," *Eighteenth-Century Studies* 31, no. 4 (1998): 433–451. For a semiological account of Burney's theatricality, see Francesca Saggini, *Backstage in the Novel: Frances Burney and the Theater Arts*, trans. Laura Kopp (Charlottesville: University of Virginia Press, 2012).

16. Frances Burney, *Evelina*, ed. Edward A. Bloom and Lillian Bloom (New York: Oxford University Press, 1982), 26. Subsequent citations refer to this edition and appear parenthetically in the text. Matthew Kinservik discusses Evelina's response to Garrick in *Disciplining Satire: The Censorship of Satiric Comedy on the Eighteenth-Century London Stage* (Lewisburg, PA: Bucknell University Press, 2002), 212.

17. Anja Muller-Muth discussed this scene in a conference paper, "Transformations of Theatricality in Frances Burney's *Evelina*" (paper presented at the Dramatic Aspects of Frances Burney conference, McGill University, Montreal, 2004).

18. Silvan Tomkins, *Shame and Its Sisters: A Silvan Tomkins Reader*, ed. Eve Kosofsky Sedgwick and Adam Frank (Durham, NC: Duke University Press, 1995), 136.

19. Brean S. Hammond has proposed that Fielding "invented" the Cibber whom Pope elaborated, in "Politics and Cultural Politics: The Case of Henry Fielding," *Eighteenth-Century Life* 16 (February 1992): 87.

20. Ronald Firbank, *Valmouth*, Notebook 4, fol. 12v, with permission of the Harry Ransom Research Center, University of Texas at Austin. In an extended footnote to the final version of *The Dunciad* (1744), Pope notes that the wig was brought onto the stage in a sedan chair. See John Vanbrugh, *The Relapse* (London, 1696), reprinted in *The Relapse and Other Plays*, ed. Brean Hammond (New York: Oxford University Press, 2004), 122n18.

21. Graham Greene, *Brighton Rock* (New York: Vintage Classics, 2004).

22. Elaine McGirr, *Partial Histories: A Reappraisal of Colley Cibber* (London: Palgrave Macmillan, 2016); Darryl Domingo, *The Rhetoric of Diversion in English Literature and Culture, 1690–1760* (Cambridge: Cambridge University Press, 2016).

23. According to *The London Stage*, *The Provok'd Husband*, which premiered January 10, 1728, was performed at least 547 times before 1800. E. L. Avery, William Van Lennep, Arthur H. Scouten, George Winchester Stone, and Charles B Hogan, eds., *The London Stage: 1660–1800*, 5 vols. (Carbondale: Southern Illinois University Press, 1968).

24. Henry Fielding, *The History of Tom Jones, a Foundling*, ed. Martin Battestin, 2 vols. (Middletown CT: Wesleyan University Press, 1975), vol. 2, 640.

25. Fielding, vol. 2, 640–641. Fielding had explored the generativity of puppets in the conclusion to *The Author's Farce* (1728, 1731) in which the puppet King of Bantam declares that the human poet Luckless is his son and heir. See *The Wesleyan Edition of the Works of Henry Fielding: Plays*, 3 vols., ed. Thomas Lockwood (Oxford, UK: Clarendon, 2004), vol. 1, 1.

26. See appendix 6, "*The Provok'd Husband*," in *The Wanderer; or, Female Difficulties*, by Frances Burney, ed. Margaret Doody, Robert L. Mack, and Peter Sabor (New York: Oxford University Press, 2001), 901–905.

27. Fielding, *Tom Jones*, vol. 2, 855.

28. Frances Burney, *Early Journals and Letters of Fanny Burney*, vol. 3, *The Streatham Years, Part I, 1778–1779*, ed. Lars E. Troide and Stewart J. Cooke (Montreal: McGill-Queen's University Press, 1994), 10, 28–29, 90, 115, 157, 201, 233. Burney records that Samuel Johnson said, "Henry Fielding would have been afraid of Evelina" (109). See also Burney, *Early Journals and Letters of Fanny Burney*, vol. 5, ed. Lars E. Troide and Stewart J. Cooke (Montreal: McGill-Queen's University Press, 2012), in which Burney reports, "If Fielding or Richardson could rise from the grave, I should bid fair for supplanting them in the popular Eye, for being a fair female, I am accounted quelque chose extraordinaire, as dear Kitty says" (132).

29. Burney, *Early Journals and Letters*, vol. 5, 397.

30. Fanny Burney, *Early Journals and Letters of Fanny Burney*, vol. 4, *The Streatham Years: Part II, 1780–1781*, ed. Betty Rizzo (Montreal: McGill-Queen's University Press, 2003), 16–20.

31. Frances Burney, *The Early Diary of Frances Burney, 1768–1778, with a Selection from the Journals of Her Sisters Susan and Charlotte Burney*, 2 vols., ed. Annie Raine Ellis (London: George Bell and Sons, 1889), 2:241, 1: lviii.

32. Frances Burney, *Early Journals and Letters of Fanny Burney*, vol. 2, *1774–1777*, ed. Lars E. Troide (Montreal: McGill-Queen's University Press, 1991), 236, 263; on her stage fright, see also Anderson, *Eighteenth-Century Authorship*, 49–50.

33. Margaret Doody, *Frances Burney: The Life in the Works* (New Brunswick, NJ: Rutgers University Press, 1988), 39–40; Elizabeth Kowaleski-Wallace, *Their Fathers' Daughters: Hannah More, Maria Edgeworth, and Patriarchal Complicity* (New York: Oxford University Press, 1991), vii–ix.

34. Francesca Saggini suggests that this recognition scene resembles Garrick's performance of King Lear cursing his daughter in *King Lear*, act 1, scene 4, providing one chart of his gestures and another of those described in the novel's recognition scene that illustrate acting conventions (*Backstage*, 86, 88).

35. In *Realizations: Narrative, Pictorial, and Theatrical Arts in Nineteenth-Century England* (Princeton, NJ: Princeton University Press, 1983), Martin Meisel analyzes a more sacrificial version of the father-daughter tableau in *The Grecian Daughter* (1772) by Arthur Murphy, a play with which Burney was familiar, as Saggini notes in her appendix (*Backstage*, 236).

36. For a different argument about the abandonment of epistolary form, see Rachael Scarborough King, "The Pleasures of 'the World': Rewriting Epistolarity in Burney, Edgeworth and Austen," *Eighteenth-Century Fiction* 29, no. 1 (2016): 67–89.

37. Blakey Vermeule, *Why Do We Care about Literary Characters?* (Baltimore: Johns Hopkins University Press, 2011), 75–77.

38. Franco Moretti, "Serious Century," in *The Novel*, vol. 1, ed. Franco Moretti (Princeton, NJ: Princeton University Press, 2006), 369. Moretti speculates that the didacticism of novelists like Burney leads them to turn off the free indirect style, thus inhibiting the sophistication of the technique. But as the frequency of free indirect discourse in Burney suggests, this understanding of didacticism as the direct provision of moral judgment coming from the narrator is too restrictive.

39. Ann Banfield, *Unspeakable Sentences: Narration and Representation in the Language of Fiction* (Boston: Routledge and Kegan Paul, 1982).

40. Frances Burney, *Cecilia; or, Memoirs of an Heiress*, ed. Peter Sabor and Margaret Doody (New York: Oxford University Press, 1988), 351–352.

NOTES TO PAGES 108–119

41. On this example, see also Jane Spencer, "*Evelina* and *Cecilia*," in *The Cambridge Companion to Frances Burney*, ed. Peter Sabor (New York: Cambridge University Press, 2007), 34–35.
42. Burney, *Cecilia*, 97.
43. Margaret Doody, introduction to *Cecilia*, xxv.
44. Miller, *Jane Austen*, 31–32.
45. François Hédelin, abbé d'Aubignac, *The Whole Art of the Stage*, cited in James Hirsh, *Shakespeare and the History of Soliloquies* (Madison, NJ: Fairleigh Dickinson University Press, 2003), 281.
46. Hirsh, 280–285. Congreve's rationalization of the device in his dedicatory epistle to *The Double Dealer* (1694) supports Hirsh's equation of Restoration soliloquy and interior monologue: "We ought not to imagine that this Man either talks to us or to himself; he is only thinking, and thinking such matters as were inexcusable Folly in him to speak." Quoted in Hirsh, 284.
47. I identified asides both by stage directions and by observing when characters speak though they find themselves alone on the stage.
48. McGirr has observed that Cibber's numerous asides contributed to the immediacy of his performance style, in "Rethinking Reform Comedies: Colley Cibber's Desiring Women," *Eighteenth-Century Studies* 46, no. 3 (2013): 385–397. Frances Burney, *Love and Fashion*, in *The Complete Plays of Frances Burney*, vol. 1, *Comedies*, ed. Peter Sabor with Geoffrey Sill (Montreal: McGill Queens University Press, 1995), 103–190. Subsequent citations refer to this edition and appear parenthetically in the text.
49. On Sheridan's career, see David Francis Taylor, *Theatres of Opposition: Empire, Revolution and Richard Brinsley Sheridan* (Oxford: Oxford University Press, 2012).
50. On the reception of *Camilla*, see Edward and Lillian Bloom's introduction (Oxford: Oxford University Press, 1999), xx. On the hostile reception of *The Wanderer* by John Wilson Croker, William Hazlitt, and others, see Margaret Doody's introduction (Oxford: Oxford University Press, 2001), xxxiii. In a letter from Burney to her brother James of July 10–12, 1815, she observed that Godwin, along with other critics including Sir James Macintosh, Mme. de Stael, and Lord Byron, received the first volume of *The Wanderer* with "almost unbounded applause," even though they came to be disappointed when they recognized that the rest of the novel was set in England instead of returning to the scene of "the political bustle" of "The Continent." Burney, *The Journals and Letters of Fanny Burney*, vol. 8, 1815, ed. Peter Hughes, with Joyce Hemlow, Althea Douglas, and Patricia Hawkins (Oxford, UK: Clarendon, 1980), 317.
51. Frances Burney, *Camilla; or, A Picture of Youth*, ed. Edward Bloom and Lillian Bloom (Oxford: Oxford University Press, 1999), 681. Subsequent citations refer to this edition and appear parenthetically in the text.
52. Lynch, *Economy of Character*, 178.
53. Lynch, 169.
54. "Shopping" is Burney's coinage. See Burney, *Evelina*, 27.
55. Lynch, *Economy of Character*, 181.
56. Lynch emphasizes the continuities between *Camilla* and *The Wanderer* insofar as both "make visible the gap between what we think we do and what we really do" (204).
57. Hemlow, *History of Fanny Burney*, 272–273.
58. In a diary entry for February 16, 1805, Burney records taking her son Alex "to a Comedy at les Delassemens," where they saw "a pretty likely piece of Marmontel, Lucile and a mock tragedy by Maitre Andre, perruquier—too profoundly absurd for much laughter, though comically within bounds of burlesque now and then for a little." Burney, *The Journals and Letters of Fanny Burney*, vol. 6, *France 1803–1812*, ed. Joyce Hemlow, with George G. Falle, Althea Douglas, and Jill. A. Bourdais de Charbonnière (Oxford, UK: Clarendon, 1976),

746. Other entries for theater visits include March 14, 1805, when she took Alex to "les Francais, to see le Bourgeois Gentilhomme," which she finds "too long, too monotonous, and altogether fatiguing to see, though amusing and excellent to read" (748). A list of public places visited in 1807 included in the notebooks she kept for that year records a visit in January to Theatre Louvois to see "Les 3 Rivaux," an adaptation of Sheridan's *The Rivals*, which Burney notes was "Mediocre et Rampant," and in February to Théâtre National de L'Opéra Comique to see "Don Quichotte; L'Intrigue au Fenetre les 3 Hussards" (803).

59. See Helen Thompson, "How *The Wanderer* Works: Reading Burney and Bourdieu," *ELH* 68, no. 4 (2001): 965–989.

60. Frances Burney, *The Wanderer; or, Female Difficulties*, ed. Margaret Doody, Robert L. Mack, and Peter Sabor (New York: Oxford University Press, 1991), 357. Subsequent citations refer to this edition and appear parenthetically in the text.

61. Patrick McDonagh, "The Mute's Voice: The Dramatic Transformations of the Mute and Deaf-Mute in Early-Nineteenth-Century France," *Criticism* 55, no. 4 (2013): 655–675.

62. The climactic scene of *The 39 Steps* begins with various perspectives on a theatrical performance, showing the stage from the point of view of the wings and then staging the main action in the audience as Robert Hannay (Robert Donat) realizes that the state secrets about to be smuggled out of the country are stored in the memory of the man onstage. We hear a gunshot and see Mr. Memory collapse just as he is about to reveal the name of the country that has employed the spies; then we see the reverse shot of the pinkieless villain, Professor Jordan (Godfrey Tearle), who jumps up to put away his gun. A cut to a side view of the theater reveals the professor jumping off the balcony and leaping onto the stage, from which he makes his escape (the police having cut off all other avenues of egress from the theater). The sequence of shot-reverse-shot followed by the killer jumping onto the stage and then off camera and out of the hands of the police altogether functions to explode the proscenium insofar as it divides the performers from their audience. At arguably analogous experimental phases in the evolution of a new medium or genre, both Burney and Hitchcock exploit the familiarity of the theater as a cultural venue, capitalizing on its repertory of representational and thematic strengths, in order to anchor their formal experiments with point of view or perspective. Both rely on an opposition between recessive performance onstage (the fainting or dying star) and action in the audience that projects itself onto center stage. The interpretive vocabulary of spectatorship must ultimately prove unsatisfying in analyzing these works because both Burney and Hitchcock are intent on giving precisely those perspectives on performance that one cannot have in the theater.

63. Anderson, *Eighteenth-Century Authorship*, 72.

CHAPTER 5 — MELODRAMA IN INCHBALD AND AUSTEN

1. Walter Benjamin, "By the Fireside," trans. Rodney Livingstone, *New Left Review* 96 (Nov/Dec 2015): 56.

2. Walter Benjamin, "The Storyteller: Reflections on the Works of Nikolai Leskov," trans. Harry Zohn, in *Theory of the Novel: An Historical Approach*, ed. Michael McKeon (Baltimore: Johns Hopkins University Press, 2000), 88.

3. Benjamin, 79.

4. Benjamin, 53.

5. It is worth recalling that for Benjamin in "The Storyteller," "The Bildungsroman does not deviate in any way from the basic structure of the novel" (80).

6. One exception is Paula Byrne, "*A Simple Story* from Inchbald to Austen," *Romanticism* 5, no. 2 (1999): 161–171, which establishes that Austen knew Inchbald's novel.

7. Paula Backscheider, "Retrieving Elizabeth Inchbald," in *The Oxford Handbook of Georgian Theatre, 1737–1832*, ed. Julia Swindells and David Francis Taylor (Oxford: Oxford University Press, 2014), 603, 614–615.

8. Patricia Michaelson, *Speaking Volumes: Women Reading and Speech in the Age of Austen* (Stanford, CA: Stanford University Press, 2002), 180–215; see also Abigail Williams, *The Social Life of Books: Reading Together in the Eighteenth-Century Home* (New Haven, CT: Yale University Press, 2017), 280n9.

9. Penny Gay, *Jane Austen and the Theatre* (Cambridge: Cambridge University Press, 2002). Daniel O'Quinn describes Austen's investments in theater, in "Jane Austen and Performance: Theatre, Memory, and Enculturation," in *A Companion to Jane Austen*, ed. Claudia Johnson and Clara Tuite (Chichester, UK: Wiley Blackwell, 2009), 377–388. For Clara Tuite, however, the family theatricals encode the children's rebellion against the absent father in the terms of the French Revolution that Austen does not support. See Tuite, *Romantic Austen: Sexual Politics and the Literary Canon* (Cambridge: Cambridge University Press, 2002), 113–115. For a summary of the criticism, see Deidre Lynch's introduction to *Mansfield Park: An Annotated Edition* (Cambridge, MA: Harvard University Press, 2016), which suggests that Austen investigates what her genre can accommodate by contrast to the theater (6).

10. On the amateur theatricals in *Mansfield Park*, see O'Quinn, "Jane Austen and Performance," 377–388; and Ros Ballaster, "Rivals for the Repertory: Theatre and Novel in Georgian London," *Restoration and 18th-Century Theatre Research* 27, no. 1 (2012): 5–24. On the dovetailing of Austen with novel studies of the past forty years, see Melina Moe, "Charlotte and Elizabeth: Multiple Modernities in Jane Austen's *Pride and Prejudice*," *ELH* 83, no. 4 (2016): 1075–1103.

11. On free indirect discourse and the novel itself, see Franco Moretti, "Serous Century," in *The Novel*, vol. 1, ed. Franco Moretti (Princeton, NJ: Princeton University Press, 2006), 364–400. On free indirect discourse and the novel itself in Austen, see D. A. Miller, *Jane Austen, or The Secret of Style* (Princeton, NJ: Princeton University Press, 2003); and Frances Ferguson, "Jane Austen, *Emma*, and the Impact of Form," *MLQ: Modern Language Quarterly* 61, no. 1 (2000): 157–180. For Austen critics who link her sophistication of free indirect discourse with her contributions to the elevation of the novel, see Tuite, *Romantic Austen*, 62–71; and Lynch, introduction to *Mansfield Park*, 27–28.

12. Michaelson, *Speaking Volumes*, 180–182.

13. Ann Banfield gives an account of the grammar of free indirect discourse in *Unspeakable Sentences: Narration and Representation in the Language of Fiction* (Boston: Routledge and Kegan Paul, 1982).

14. Emily Hodgson Anderson, "Revising Theatrical Conventions in *A Simple Story*: Elizabeth Inchbald's Ambiguous Performance," *Journal for Early Modern Cultural Studies* 6, no. 1 (2006): 5–30; Diane Osland, "Heart-Picking in *A Simple Story*," *Eighteenth-Century Fiction* 16, no. 1 (2003): 79–101.

15. On the possibility of Austen's having seen *Lovers' Vows* in Bath, see Carlotta Farese, "The Strange Case of Herr Von K: Further Reflections on the Reception of Kotzebue's Theatre in Britain," *DQR: Studies in Literature* 55 (2015): 76.

16. Jean-Marie Thomasseau, *Le mélodrame* (Paris: Presses Universitaires de France, 1984), 16.

17. See Monique Rooney, *Living Screens: Melodrama and Plasticity in Contemporary Film and Television* (Lanham, MD: Rowman and Littlefield, 2015), 7–11.

18. See Jeffrey Ravel, *The Contested Parterre: Public Theater and French Political Culture, 1680–1791* (Ithaca, NY: Cornell University Press, 1999).

19. See George Taylor, *The French Revolution and the London Stage, 1789–1805* (New York: Cambridge University Press, 2000).

20. Jane Moody, *Illegitimate Theatre in London, 1770–1840* (New York: Cambridge University Press, 2000); Matthew S. Buckley, "The Formation of Melodrama," in Swindells and Taylor, *Oxford Handbook of the Georgian Theatre*, 457–478.
21. See Robert D. Hume, "Drama and Theater in the Mid and Later Eighteenth Century," in *The Cambridge History of English Literature, 1660–1780*, ed. John Richetti (Cambridge: Cambridge University Press, 2005), 316–339.
22. Richard Bevis, quoted in Hume, 330.
23. On the proximity of Gothic drama to melodrama, see Aubrey S. Garlington Jr., "'Gothic' Literature and Dramatic Music in England, 1781–1802," *Journal of the American Musicological Society* 15, no. 1 (1962): 59; and G. Taylor, *French Revolution*, 148.
24. Farese, "Strange Case," 76–77.
25. Inchbald also adapted Koztebue's *The Wise Men of the East* (1800). See Farese, 79.
26. On *The Stranger*, see Farese, 76. See also David O'Shaugnessy, "Koztebue and Thompson's *The Stranger*: A New Source for Godwin's *St Leon*," *Notes and Queries* 52, no. 4 (2005): 452.
27. Farese, "Strange Case," 79–80.
28. At the same time as Brooks was describing melodrama as a mode in *The Melodramatic Imagination: Balzac, Henry James, Melodrama, and the Mode of Excess* (New Haven, CT: Yale University Press, 1976), Thomas Elsaessar was analyzing its effects, though he worked in film rather than literature. See Elsaessar, "Tales of Sound and Fury: Observations on the Family Melodrama," in *Film Theory and Criticism: Introductory Readings*, ed. Gerald Mast, Marshall Cohen, and Leo Braudy (New York: Oxford University Press, 1992), 512–535. See Rooney, *Living Screens*, 7–11, for a synthesis. Brooks was not alone in seeing stage melodrama as influenced by Gothic novels. See also Jean-Marie Thomasseau, *Le mélodrame*, 2, who himself followed Charles Nodier.
29. Pixérécourt's *Le château des Appenins, ou le fantôme vivant* (Paris, 1799) adapted for the stage the 1797 French translation of Ann Radcliffe's *The Mysteries of Udolpho* (1794) by Victorine de Chastenay. William Godwin's *Caleb Williams* (1794) was translated into French by Garnier in 1796 and was twice adapted for the French stage: as *Falkland, ou la conscience* by Jean Louis Laya, first staged in 1798 with Talma as Falkland and then restaged and printed in 1821, and as *La tete de mort* by Pixérécourt in 1827.
30. Thomas Holcroft, *Alwyn; or, The Gentleman Comedian*, 2 vols. (London: Fielding and Walker, 1780) I: vi.
31. Elizabeth Inchbald, "To the Artist" (1807), originally published in the periodical *The Artist*, ed. Prince Hoare, reprinted in *Nature and Art*, by Inchbald, ed. Shawn Lisa Maurer (Peterborough, ON: Broadview, 2004), 165. Subsequent citations of both the essay and the novel refer to the 2004 edition and appear parenthetically in the text. For a fascinating discussion of Hoare's project and his inclusion of Inchbald within it, see Jon Klancher, *Transfiguring the Arts and Sciences: Knowledge and Cultural Institutions in the Romantic Age* (New York: Cambridge University Press, 2013), 115–117.
32. Patrice Pavis, *Dictionary of the Theatre: Terms, Concepts, and Analyses*, trans. Christine Shantz (Toronto: University of Toronto Press, 1998), 102.
33. Samuel Taylor Coleridge, *Collected Letters*, vol. 1, *1785–1800*, ed. Earl Leslie Griggs, (Oxford, UK: Clarendon, 1956), 378–379 (emphasis in original). Michael Gamer discusses Coleridge's response to Lewis's play, in "Authors in Effect: Lewis, Scott, and the Gothic Drama," *ELH* 66, no. 4 (1999): 831–861.
34. Edward Mayhew, *Stage Effect; or, The Principles Which Command Dramatic Success in the Theatre* (London: C. Mitchell, 1840), 44, quoted in Martin Meisel, *Realizations: Narrative, Pictorial, and Theatrical Arts in Nineteenth-Century England* (Princeton, NJ: Princeton University Press, 1983), 351.

35. David O'Shaughnessy, "William Godwin and the Politics of Playgoing," in Swindells and Taylor, *Oxford Handbook of the Georgian Theatre*, 515.
36. For different accounts of the status of reading in the eighteenth century with special regard to temporal relations, see Christina Lupton, *Reading and the Making of Time* (Baltimore: Johns Hopkins University Press, 2018); and Emily Rohrbach, *Modernity's Mist: British Romanticism and the Poetics of Anticipation* (New York: Fordham University Press, 2016).
37. "The moral of any work may be defined to be, that ethical sentence to the illustration of which the work may most aptly be applied. The tendency is the actual effect it is calculated to produce upon the reader, and cannot be completely ascertained but by experiment. The selection of one, and the character of the other, will in a great degree depend upon the previous state of mind of the reader." William Godwin, "Of Choice in Reading," in *The Enquirer: Reflections on Education, Manners, and Literature, in a Series of Essays* (Philadelphia, 1797), 109.
38. Godwin, 110.
39. Klancher, *Transfiguring the Arts and Sciences*, 160–161.
40. David O'Shaughnessy, *William Godwin and the Theatre* (London: Routledge, 2015), and "William Godwin and the Politics of Playgoing," 514–531. See also David Duff, *Romanticism and the Uses of Genre* (New York: Oxford University Press, 2009), 8, 11–12.
41. Backscheider, "Retrieving Elizabeth Inchbald," 603.
42. Dorothy Wordsworth's diary entry for April 15, 1802, cited in A. Williams, *Social Life of Books*, 1.
43. On the similarity of Miss Milner and Matilda, see Jenny Davidson, "Why Daughters Look like Their Mothers: David Garrick Rewrites *The Winter's Tale*," in *Shakespeare and the Eighteenth Century*, ed. Peter Sabor and Paul Yachnin (Burlington, VT: Ashgate, 2008), 165–180.
44. Terry Castle rehearses the textual history of the novel, which suggests that the novel's two halves may originally have been unrelated, and points to reasons for reading them together anyway, in *Masquerade and Civilization: The Carnivalesque in Eighteenth-Century English Culture and Fiction* (Stanford, CA: Stanford University Press, 1986), 321–323. A survey of responses that see the second half as an apology for the first have is provided by Eun Kyung Min, who sees Dorriforth/Elmwood as central, in "Giving Promises in Elizabeth Inchbald's *A Simple Story*," *ELH* 77, no. 1 (2010): 125n1.
45. Meisel's treatment in *Realizations* of melodrama across the media of the stage, the novel, panting, print serial narratives, and the illustrated chapbook includes as its two most significant formal features the frozen moment, or the tableau vivant; and serial discontinuity, the presentation of characters' subordination to circumstance in which the repetition or recurrence of their situations invited a revisionary recasting of what had appeared to be contingency as necessity.
46. See, for examples, E. Anderson, "Revising Theatrical Conventions"; Osland, "Heart-Picking in *A Simple Story*"; and Nora Nachumi, "'Those Simple Signs': The Performance of Emotion in Elizabeth Inchbald's *A Simple Story*," *Eighteenth-Century Fiction* 11, no. 3 (1999): 317–338.
47. Elizabeth Inchbald, *A Simple Story*, ed. Anna Lott (Peterborough, ON: Broadview, 2007), 152.
48. Osland, "Heart-Picking in *A Simple Story*," 97; E. Anderson, "Revising Theatrical Conventions," 7–8.
49. The narration of a similar set of alternatives under moments of emotional intensity can also be found in Aphra Behn's *The History of the Nun* (1689). On Behn's management of character in *The Fair Jilt* and her distinctive "or," see Aaron Kunin, "Facial Composure and Management in Behn's Novels," *Modern Philology* 107, no. 1 (2009): 72–95.
50. Lytton Strachey, ed. Introduction to Elizabeth Inchbald, *A Simple Story* (London: Henry Frowde 1908), Project Gutenburg, released July 5, 2007, n.p., accessed May 27, 2014.

51. On the compatibility between the visual resources of print and the theater, see Katherine Mannheimer, *Print, Visuality, and Gender in Eighteenth-Century Satire: "The Scope in Ev'ry Page"* (New York: Routledge, 2011), 169–174.
52. Moretti, "Serious Century."
53. William Godwin, *Fleetwood or The New Man of Feeling*, in the second edition of Bentley's "Standard Novels" (London: 1832), 352.
54. John Bender, "Impersonal Violence: The Penetrating Gaze and the Field of Narration in *Caleb Williams*," in *Vision and Textuality*, ed. Stephen Melville and Bill Readings (Durham, NC: Duke University Press, 1995), 270; and Blakey Vermeule, *Why Do We Care about Literary Characters?* (Baltimore: Johns Hopkins University Press, 2011), 118.
55. Pamela Clemit, introduction to *Caleb Williams*, by William Godwin (Oxford: Oxford University Press, 2009), ix, xxi. Subsequent citations of the novel refer to this edition and appear parenthetically in the text.
56. Perhaps Godwin here responded to an undated letter from Inchbald in which she complained that the first volume lagged. Clemit quotes Elizabeth Inchbald's letter in her introduction to *Caleb Williams*, viii. Shawn Lisa Maurer notes that the occasion of the letter was Inchbald's reading the proofs to Godwin's novel. See appendix A in Inchbald, *Nature and Art*, 158.
57. Ronald Paulson, *Representations of Revolution (1789–1820)* (New Haven, CT: Yale University Press, 1983), 230; see Gary Kelly, *The English Jacobin Novel, 1780–1805* (New York: Oxford University Press, 1976), 12–14.
58. Robert Kiely, *The Romantic Novel in England* (Cambridge, MA: Harvard University Press, 1972), 7, cited in Robert Miles, "What Is a Romantic Novel?," *Novel* 34, no. 2 (2001): 192.
59. Samuel Taylor Coleridge, *Biographia Literaria; or, Biographical Sketches of My Literary Life and Opinions* (Princeton, NJ: Princeton University Press, 1983), 207–233.
60. On the discretion of Austen's narrator, see Tuite, *Romantic Austen*, 61–71.
61. Jane Austen, *Sense and Sensibility*, ed. Edward Copeland (New York: Cambridge University Press, 2006), 22. Subsequent citations refer to this edition and appear parenthetically in the text.
62. Jane Austen, *Persuasion*, ed. Janet Todd and Antje Blank (New York: Cambridge University Press, 200g), 202. Subsequent citations refer to this edition and appear parenthetically in the text.
63. Rohrbach, *Modernity's Mist*, 117.
64. Julie Park, "What the Eye Cannot See: Interior Landscape in *Mansfield Park*," *The Eighteenth Century* suppl. 54:2 (Summer 2013), 173–175.
65. Jane Austen, *Mansfield Park*, ed. John Wiltshire (New York: Cambridge University Press, 2005), 306. Subsequent citations refer to this edition and appear parenthetically in the text.
66. D.W. Harding, "Regulated Hatred: An Aspect of the Works of Jane Austen," *Scrutiny* 8 (1940) 346–362.
67. Michaelson, *Speaking Volumes*, 180; A. Williams, *Social Life of Books*, 205, 207–208.
68. See Tuite, *Romantic Austen*, 67, 95.
69. Mary Favret, *Romantic Correspondence: Women, Politics and the Fiction of Letters*, 166, quoted in Deidre Lynch, introduction to *Persuasion*, (New York: Oxford University Press, 2004) xxxiii. For John Guillory, Wentworth's letter, because he writes it as Anne speaks to correct their former failed communication, illustrates the condition that enables letters to become a medium of communication in the first instance. Guillory, "Genesis of the Media Concept," *Critical Inquiry* 36, no. 2 (2010): 357n60.
70. Michael McKeon, *The Secret History of Domesticity: Public, Private, and the Division of Knowledge* (Baltimore: Johns Hopkins University Press, 2005), 701.

71. Penny Gay discusses Wentworth's being a naval hero and Anne's virtual muteness as points at which the novel shares features with melodrama, observing that "Austen's narration takes the place of musical accompaniment in drawing our attention to each moment" in the novel's climactic chapter, in which the narration operates like stage directions. Gay, *Jane Austen and the Theatre*, 155. See also Penny Gay, "Jane Austen's Stage," in Swindells and Taylor, *Oxford Handbook of the Georgian Theatre*, 532–547.
72. The concept of novelization runs across the essays collected in Mikhail Bahktin, *The Dialogic Imagination: Four Essays*, edited by M. Holquist and C. Emerson, translated by M. Holquist (Austin: University of Texas Press, 1981).
73. Benjamin, "Storyteller," 93.

CODA

1. Jenny Davidson, "The 'Minute Particular' in Life-Writing and the Novel," *Eighteenth Century Studies* 48, no. 3 (2015): 269; Ian Watt formulated his classic account of formal realism in *The Rise of the Novel: Studies in Defoe, Richardson, and Fielding* (Harmondsworth, UK: Penguin, 1974).
2. Mark McGurl, *The Novel Art: Elevations of American Fiction after Henry James* (Princeton, NJ: Princeton University Press, 2001).
3. On the theatrical history of the Victorian novel, see Joseph Litvak, *Caught in the Act: Theatricality in the Nineteenth-Century English Novel* (Berkeley: University of California Press, 1992); Emily Allen, *Theater Figures: The Production of the Nineteenth-Century British Novel* (Columbus: Ohio State University Press, 2003); and David Kurnick, *Empty Houses: Theatrical Failure and the Novel* (Princeton, NJ: Princeton University Press, 2011).
4. Charles Dickens, *Dombey and Son*, ed. Dennis Walder (Oxford: Oxford University Press, 2008), 488.
5. Elizabeth Inchbald, *Nature and Art,* ed. Shaun Lisa Maurer (Peterborough, ON: Broadview, 2004), 110.
6. Garrett Stewart, *Dear Reader: The Conscripted Audience in Nineteenth-Century British Fiction* (Baltimore: Johns Hopkins University Press, 1996), 147.
7. As Garrett Stewart observes, "Not only does *Can You Forgive Her?* defer by title to the reader's ethical sense even while tacitly presuming upon the outcome of text-long deliberations . . . but it chastis[es] itself for the premature posing of the question. Nearing the close of the first volume, the narrator once again asks: 'But can you forgive her, delicate reader? Or am I asking this question too early in the story?' (I, 37: 384)" (147). For Stewart, when Trollope reminds us that we read the book of human nature alongside the characters, "our activity borrows conviction from this epistemological archetype" (147).
8. Anthony Trollope, *An Autobiography*, ed. David Skilton (New York: Penguin, 1996), 59.
9. Difficult but not impossible, as the Stage Manager in Thornton Wilder's *Our Town* (New York: Harper and Row, 1938) suggests, with his ability to address separately characters and the audience.
10. Catherine Gallagher, "Telling It like It Wasn't," *Pacific Coast Philology* 45 (2010): 12–25; see also Gallagher, "What Would Napoleon Do? Historical, Fictional, and Counterfactual Characters," *New Literary History* 42, no. 2 (2011): 315–336.
11. Catherine Gallagher, "The Rise of Fictionality," in *The Novel*, vol. 1, ed. Franco Moretti (Princeton, NJ: Princeton University Press, 2006), 336–363.
12. Gallagher's perception that counterfactual novels offer something between reparation for social injustice on a massive scale and revenge fantasy is congruent with my account of the pathos of counterfictional address.

13. Charles Dickens, *Little Dorrit*, ed. Harvey Peter Sucksmith (New York: Penguin, 2003), 490. Martin Meisel observes the connections between *Little Dorrit* and Arthur Murphy's play *The Grecian Daughter* (1772), in *Realizations: Narrative, Pictorial, and Theatrical Arts in Nineteenth-Century England* (Princeton, NJ: Princeton University Press, 1983), 307–308.

14. Dickens, *Little Dorrit*, 490.

15. Dickens, 490.

16. See Robyn Warhol-Down, "'What Might Have Been Is Not What Is': Dickens's Narrative Refusals," *Dickens Studies Annual* 41 (2010): 45–59.

17. Contemporary fiction writers, including Richard Powers, Lorrie Moore, and David Foster Wallace, have published second-person narratives that have received some attention from narratology as well as from new media theory. For a narratological account, see Joshua Parker, "In Their Own Words: On Writing in the Second Person," *Connotations* 21, nos. 2–3 (2011–2012): 165–176, and the debates it inspired on the journal's website: "On Writing in Second Person," *Connotations*, https://www.connotations.de/debate/on-writing-in -second-person/, accessed June 22, 2016. For an account from new media theory, see Noah Wardrip-Fruin and Pat Harrigan, eds., *Second Person: Role-Playing and Story in Games and Playable Media* (Cambridge, MA: MIT Press, 2007).

18. On the playfulness of the second person, see John Emil Vincent, who observes the flexibility of John Ashbery's direct address, the ways "the labile second person, often undecidedly singular or plural," tethers readers to his difficult poetry by producing a range of intimacy effects, including disguising the gender of the addressee. Vincent, *John Ashbery and You: His Later Books* (Athens: University of Georgia Press, 2007), 145.

19. Julia Straub briefly discusses Hardy in "Melodrama and Narrative Fiction: Towards a Typology," *Anglia* 132, no. 2 (2014): 225–241.

20. Frances Burney, *Cecilia; or, Memoirs of an Heiress*, ed. Peter Sabor and Margaret Doody (Oxford: Oxford University Press, 1988), 351–352.

21. Thomas Hardy, *The Mayor of Casterbridge: The Life and Death of a Man of Character* (New York: Penguin, 2003), 308, 318.

22. Hardy, 330.

23. Linda Williams, "Melodrama Revised," in *Refiguring American Film Genres*, ed. Nick Browne (Berkeley: University of California Press, 1998), 74.

24. D. A. Miller, "The Novel as Usual: Trollope's *Barchester Towers*," in *Sex, Politics, and Science in the Nineteenth-Century Novel*, ed. Ruth B. Yeazell (Baltimore: Johns Hopkins University Press, 1986), 1–38.

25. "A novel should give a picture of common life enlivened by humour and sweetened by pathos. To make that picture worthy of attention the canvas should be crowded with real portraits,—not of individuals known to the world or to the author,—but of created personages impregnated with traits of character which are known. To my thinking the plot is a vehicle for all this; and when you have the vehicle without the passengers, you have but a wooden show. There must however be a story. You must provide a vehicle of some sort" (Trollope, *Autobiography*, 84).

26. Anthony Trollope, *Barchester Towers* (New York: Modern Library, 1936), 482.

27. Trollope, 492.

28. Trollope, 509.

29. Amanda Anderson, "Trollope's Modernity," *ELH* 74 (2007): 511–512.

30. Anderson, 515.

Addison, Joseph, and Sir Richard Steele. *The Tatler*. Vol. 1. Edited by Donald F. Bond. Oxford: Oxford University Press, 1987.

———. *The Spectator*. Vol. 3. Edited by Donald F. Bond. Oxford: Clarendon Press, 1965.

Allen, Emily. "Staging Identity: Frances Burney's Allegory of Genre." *Eighteenth-Century Studies* 31, no. 4 (1998): 433–451.

———. *Theater Figures: The Production of the Nineteenth-Century British Novel*. Columbus: Ohio State University Press, 2003.

Anderson, Amanda. "Trollope's Modernity." *ELH* 74 (2007): 509–534.

Anderson, Emily Hodgson. *Eighteenth-Century Authorship and the Play of Fiction: Novels and the Theater, Haywood to Austen*. New York: Routledge, 2009.

———. "Revising Theatrical Conventions in *A Simple Story*: Elizabeth Inchbald's Ambiguous Performance." *Journal for Early Modern Cultural Studies* 6, no. 1 (2006): 5–30.

———. "Staged Insensibility in Burney's *Cecilia*, *Camilla*, and *The Wanderer*: How a Playwright Writes Novels." *Eighteenth-Century Fiction* 17, no. 4 (2005): 629–648.

Anderson, Misty. *Female Playwrights and Eighteenth-Century Comedy: Negotiating Marriage on the London Stage*. New York: Palgrave Macmillan, 2002.

Aravamudan, Srivinas. *Enlightenment Orientalism: Resisting the Rise of the Novel*. Chicago: University of Chicago Press, 2012.

Armstrong, Nancy. *Desire and Domestic Fiction: A Political History of the Novel*. Oxford: Oxford University Press, 1987.

Auerbach, Erich. *Mimesis: The Representation of Reality in Western Literature*. Translated by Willard R. Trask. 1953. Reprint, Princeton, NJ: Princeton University Press, 1974.

Austen, Jane. *Emma*. Edited by Richard Cronin and Dorothy McMillan. New York: Cambridge University Press, 2006.

———. *Mansfield Park*. Edited by John Wiltshire. New York: Cambridge University Press, 2005.

———. *Persuasion*. Edited by Janet Todd and Antje Blank. New York: Cambridge University Press, 2006.

———. *Pride and Prejudice*. Edited by Pat Rogers. New York: Cambridge University Press, 2006.

———. *Sense and Sensibility*. Edited by Edward Copeland. New York: Cambridge University Press, 2006.

———. *The Visit*. In *Juvenilia*. Edited by Peter Sabor, 61–68. New York: Cambridge University Press, 2006.

Austin, Gilbert. *Chironomia; or, A Treatise on Rhetorical Delivery*. London, 1806.

Avery, E. L., William Van Lennep, Arthur H. Scouten, George Winchester Stone, and Charles B. Hogan, eds. *The London Stage: 1660–1800*. 5 vols. Carbondale: Southern Illinois University Press, 1968.

Backscheider, Paula. Introduction to *The Plays of Elizabeth Inchbald*, ix–xlv. New York: Garland, 1980.

————. "Retrieving Elizabeth Inchbald." In *The Oxford Handbook of Georgian Theatre, 1737–1832*, edited by Julia Swindells and David Francis Taylor, 601–620. Oxford: Oxford University Press, 2014.

Baker, David Erskine, Isaac Reed, and Stephen Jones. *Biographia Dramatica; or, A Companion to the Playhouse*. Vol. 2. London: Longman, Hurst, Rees, Orme, and Brown, 1812.

Bakhtin, Mikhail M. *The Dialogic Imagination: Four Essays*. Edited by M. Holquist and C. Emerson. Translated by M. Holquist. Austin: University of Texas Press, 1981.

Ballaster, Ros. "Rivals for the Repertory: Theatre and Novel in Georgian London." *Restoration & 18th Century Theatre Research* 27, no. 1 (2012): 5–24.

————. *Seductive Forms: Women's Amatory Fiction from 1684–1740*. Oxford: Oxford University Press 1998.

Banfield, Ann. *Unspeakable Sentence: Narration and Representation in the Language of Fiction*. Boston: Routledge and Kegan Paul, 1982.

Barrett, Daniel. "Play Publication, Readers, and the 'Decline' of Victorian Drama." *Book History* 2, no. 1 (1999): 173–187.

Battestin, Martin C. "Life-Writing without Letters: Fielding and the Problem of Evidence." In *Writing the Lives of Writers*, edited by Warwick Gould and Thomas F. Stanley, 90–106. New York: St. Martin's, 1998.

Baudry, Jean-Louis. "The Apparatus: Metapsychological Approaches to the Impression of Reality in Cinema." In *Narrative, Apparatus, Ideology: A Film Theory Reader*, edited by Philip Rosen, 299–318. New York: Columbia University Press, 1986.

Behn, Aphra. *The Fair Jilt*. In *The Works of Aphra Behn*, vol. 3, edited by Janet Todd, 1–49. London: William Pickering, 1995.

————. *Oroonoko*. In *The Works of Aphra Behn*, vol. 3, edited by Janet Todd, 50–119. London: William Pickering, 1995.

Bender, John. "Impersonal Violence: The Penetrating Gaze and the Field of Narration in *Caleb Williams*." In *Vision and Textuality*, edited by Stephen Melville and Bill Readings, 256–281. Durham, NC: Duke University Press, 1995.

Bender, John, and Michael Marrinan. *The Diagrammatic Imagination*. Palo Alto: Stanford University Press, 2010.

Benjamin, Walter. "By the Fireside." Translated by Rodney Livingstone. *New Left Review* 96 (November–December 2015): 53–57.

————. "The Storyteller: Reflections on the Works of Nikolai Leskov." Translated by Harry Zohn. In *Theory of the Novel: A Historical Approach*, edited by Michael McKeon, 77–93. Baltimore: Johns Hopkins University Press, 2000.

Betterton, Thomas. *The Amorous Widow; or, The Wanton Wife: A Comedy*. London, 1710.

Black, Scott. "The Adventures of Love in *Tom Jones*." In *Henry Fielding in Our Time: Papers Presented at the Tercentenary Conference*, edited by J. A. Downie, 27–50. Newcastle-upon-Tyne, UK: Cambridge Scholars, 2008.

————. "Anachronism and the Uses of Form in *Joseph Andrews*." *Novel: A Forum on Fiction* 38, nos. 2–3 (2005): 147–164.

————. *Without the Novel: Romance and the History of Prose Fiction*. Charlottesville: University of Virginia Press, 2019.

Bloom, Edward, and Lillian Bloom. Introduction to *Camilla; or, A Picture of Youth*, by Frances Burney, ix–xxvi. Oxford: Oxford University Press, 1999.

Boaden, James. *Fountainville Forest, a Play, in Five Acts*. Dublin: P. Wogan, 1794.

Bollas, Christopher. *The Shadow of the Object: Psychoanalysis of the Unthought Known*. London: Free Association Books, 1987.

Bonaparte, Felicia. "Conjecturing Possibilities: Reading and Misreading Texts in Jane Austen's *Pride and Prejudice*." *Studies in the Novel* 37, no. 2 (2005): 141–161.

Booth, Michael. "Theater History and the Literary Critic." *Yearbook of English Studies* 9 (1979): 15–27.

Booth, Wayne C. *The Rhetoric of Fiction*. Chicago: University of Chicago Press, 1961.

Brewer, David A. *The Afterlives of Character, 1726–1825*. Philadelphia: University of Pennsylvania Press, 2005.

———. "Print, Performance, Personhood, Polly Honeycombe." *Studies in Eighteenth-Century Culture* 41, no. 1 (2012): 185–194.

Brewer, John. *The Pleasures of the Imagination: English Culture in the Eighteenth Century*. New York: HarperCollins, 1997.

Brooks, Peter. *The Melodramatic Imagination: Balzac, Henry James, Melodrama, and the Mode of Excess*. New Haven, CT: Yale University Press, 1976.

Brown, Laura. *English Dramatic Form, 1660–1760: An Essay in Generic History*. New Haven, CT: Yale University Press, 1981.

———. "The Romance of Empire: *Oroonoko* and the Trade in Slaves." In *The New Eighteenth Century: Theory, Politics, English Literature*, edited by Felicity Nussbaum and Laura Brown, 41–61. New York: Methuen, 1987.

Buckley, Matthew S. "The Formation of Melodrama." In *The Oxford Handbook of the Georgian Theatre, 1737–1832*, edited by Julia Swindells and David Francis Taylor, 457–478. Oxford: Oxford University Press, 2014.

Bullard, Rebecca, and Rachel Carnell, eds. *The Secret History in Literature, 1660–1820*. New York: Cambridge University Press, 2017.

Burnet, Gilbert. *Some Passages of the Life and Death of the Right Honourable John, Earl of Rochester*. 1680. London: E. Stock, 1875.

Burney, Frances. *Camilla; or, A Picture of Youth*. Edited by Edward Bloom and Lillian Bloom. Oxford: Oxford University Press, 1999.

———. *Cecilia; or, Memoirs of an Heiress*. Edited by Peter Sabor and Margaret Doody. Oxford: Oxford University Press, 1988.

———. *Complete Plays of Frances Burney*. 2 vols. Edited by Peter Sabor. Montreal: McGill-Queen's University Press, 1995.

———. *The Early Diary of Frances Burney, 1768–1778, with a Selection from Her Correspondence, and from the Journals of Her Sisters Susan and Charlotte Burney*. 2 vols. Edited by Annie Raine Ellis. London: George Bell and Sons, 1889.

———. *Early Journals and Letters of Fanny Burney*. Vol. 2, *1774–1777*. Edited by Lars E. Triode. Montreal: McGill-Queen's University Press, 1991.

———. *Early Journals and Letters of Fanny Burney*. Vol. 3, *The Streatham Years, Part I, 1778–1779*. Edited by Lars E. Triode and Stewart J. Cooke. Montreal: McGill-Queen's University Press, 1994.

———. *Early Journals and Letters of Fanny Burney*. Vol. 4, *The Streatham Years: Part II, 1780–1781*. Edited by Betty Rizzo. Montreal: McGill-Queen's University Press, 2003.

———. *Early Journals and Letters of Fanny Burney*. Vol. 5, *1782–1783*. Edited by Lars E. Triode and Stewart J. Cooke. Montreal: McGill-Queen's University Press, 2012.

———. *Evelina*. Edited by Edward A. Bloom and Lillian Bloom. New York: Oxford University Press, 1982.

———. *The Journals and Letters of Fanny Burney*. Vol. 6, *France 1803–1812*. Edited by Joyce Hemlow, with George G. Falle, Althea Douglas, and Jill. A. Bourdais de Charbonnière. Oxford, UK: Clarendon, 1976.

———. *The Journals and Letters of Fanny Burney*. Vol. 8, *1815*. Edited by Peter Hughes, with Joyce Hemlow, Althea Douglas, and Patricia Hawkins. Oxford, UK: Clarendon, 1980.

———. *Love and Fashion*. In *The Complete Plays of Frances Burney*, vol. 1, *Comedies*, edited by Peter Sabor with Geoffrey Sill, 103–190. Montreal: McGill Queens University Press, 1995.

————. *The Wanderer; or, Female Difficulties*. Edited by Margaret Doody, Robert L. Mack, and Peter Sabor. Oxford: Oxford University Press, 1991.

Byrne, Paula. "*A Simple Story* from Inchbald to Austen." *Romanticism* 5, no. 2 (1999): 161–171.

Campbell, Jill. "Fielding's Style." *ELH* 72, no. 2 (2005): 407–428.

————. "Women Writers and the Woman's Novel: The Trope of Maternal Transmission." In *The Cambridge Companion to Fiction in the Romantic Period*, edited by Richard Maxwell and Katie Trumpener, 159–176. New York: Cambridge University Press, 2008.

Canfield, J. Douglas. "Shifting Tropes of Ideology in English Serious Drama, Late Stuart to Early Georgian." In *Cultural Readings of Restoration and Eighteenth-Century Theater*, edited by J. Douglas Canfield and Deborah Payne, 195–227. Athens: University of Georgia Press, 1995.

Canfield, J. Douglas, and Deborah Payne, eds. *Cultural Readings of Restoration and Eighteenth-Century Theater*. Athens: University of Georgia Press, 1995.

Carnell, Rachel. *Partisan Politics, Narrative Realism, and the Rise of the British Novel*. London: Palgrave Macmillan, 2006.

Castle, Terry. *Masquerade and Civilization: The Carnivalesque in Eighteenth-Century English Culture and Fiction*. Stanford, CA: Stanford University Press, 1986.

Cibber, Colley. *Apology for the Life of Colley Cibber*. Edited by Bryne Fone. Ann Arbor: University of Michigan Press, 1968.

————. *The Careless Husband*. London, 1704.

————. *Love's Last Shift*. London, 1696.

Claydon, Tony. *William III and the Godly Revolution*. New York: Cambridge University Press, 1996.

Clemit, Pamela. Introduction to *Caleb Williams*, by William Godwin, vii–xvii. Oxford: Oxford University Press, 2009.

Coleridge, Samuel Taylor. *Biographia Literaria; or, Biographical Sketches of My Literary Life and Opinions*. Princeton, NJ: Princeton University Press, 1983.

————. *Collected Letters*. Vol. 1, *1785–1800*. Edited by Earl Leslie Griggs. London: Oxford University Press, 1956.

Colie, Rosalie. "Genre Systems and the Functions of Literature." In *Modern Genre Theory*, edited by David Duff, 148–166. London: Longman, 2000.

Collier, Jeremy. *A Short View of the Immorality and Profaneness of the English Stage*. London, 1698. Edited by Arthur M. Freeman. New York: Garland, 1972.

Colman, George, the Elder. *The Rivals and Polly Honeycombe*. Edited by David A. Brewer. Peterborough, ON: Broadview, 2012.

Colman, George, the Younger. *The Iron Chest: A Play; in Three Acts*. Dublin: Thomas Burnside, 1796.

Congreve, William. *Incognita and The Way of the World*. Edited by A. Norman Jeffares, 31–86. Columbia SC: University of South Carolina Press, 1966.

Cowan, Brian. "The History of Secret Histories." *Huntington Library Quarterly* 81, no. 1 (2018): 121–151.

Crane, R. S. "The Concept of Plot and the Plot of Tom Jones." In *Critics and Criticism*, edited by R. S. Crane et al., 119–139. Chicago: University of Chicago Press, 1952.

Crocker, John Wilson, ed. *Noctes Ambrosianae*. Vol. 1. New York: Worthington, 1863.

Curran, Louise. *Samuel Richardson and the Art of Letter Writing*. New York: Cambridge University Press, 2016.

Dames, Nicholas. "Theories of the Novel." In *The Cambridge History of Literary Criticism*, vol. 6, edited by M.A.R. Habib, 506–523. New York: Cambridge University Press, 2013.

Davidson, Jenny. "The 'Minute Particular' in Life-Writing and the Novel." *Eighteenth-Century Studies* 48, no. 3 (2015): 269, 263–281.

————. "Why Girls Look like Their Mothers: David Garrick Rewrites *The Winter's Tale*." In *Shakespeare and the Eighteenth Century*, edited by Peter Sabor and Paul Yachnin, 165–180. Burlington, VT: Ashgate, 2008.

Davis, Lennard J. *Factual Fictions: The Origins of the English Novel*. New York: Columbia University Press, 1983.

Davis, Tracy C. "Nineteenth-Century Repertoire." *Nineteenth Century Theatre and Film* 36, no. 2 (2009): 6–28.

Dawson, Mark Stanley. *Gentility and the Comic Theatre of Late Stuart London*. New York: Cambridge University Press, 2005.

DeMaria, Robert, Jr. *Samuel Johnson and the Life of Reading*. Baltimore: Johns Hopkins University Press, 1997.

Dickens, Charles. *Dombey and Son*. Edited by Dennis Walder. Oxford: Oxford University Press, 2008.

————. *Little Dorrit*. Edited by Harvey Peter Sucksmith. New York: Penguin, 2003.

Diderot, Denis. "Éloge de Richardson." In *Collection complette des oeuvres philosophiques, littéraires et dramatiques de M. Diderot*, vol. 1, 384–405. London, 1773.

Dobranski, Stephen B. "What Fielding Doesn't Say in *Tom Jones*." *Modern Philology* 107, no. 4 (2010): 632–653.

Dobson, Michael. "Becoming Uncut: Enlightenment Hamlets and the Ontology of Performance." Plenary lecture at Shakespeare Association of America conference, Vancouver, 3 April 2015.

Domingo, Darryl P. *The Rhetoric of Diversion in English Literature and Culture, 1690–1760*. Cambridge: Cambridge University Press, 2016.

Doody, Margaret Anne. *Frances Burney: The Life in the Works*. New Brunswick, NJ: Rutgers University Press, 1988.

————. Introduction to *Cecilia; or, Memoirs of an Heiress*, by Frances Burney, xi–xxxix. Oxford: Oxford University Press, 1988.

————. Introduction to *The Wanderer; or, Female Difficulties*, vii–xxxvii. Oxford: Oxford University Press, 2001.

————. *The True Story of the Novel*. New Brunswick, NJ: Rutgers University Press, 1997.

Dryden, John. *The Works of John Dryden*. Vol. 11. Edited by John Loftis, David Stuart Rodes, and Vinton A. Dearing. Berkeley: University of California Press, 1978.

Duff, David. Introduction to *Modern Genre Theory*, edited by David Duff, 1–24. New York: Longman, 2000.

————. *Romanticism and the Uses of Genre*. New York: Oxford University Press, 2009.

Dugas, Don-John. *Marketing the Bard: Shakespeare in Performance and Print, 1660–1740*. Columbia: University of Missouri Press, 2006.

Dugas, Don-John, and Robert Hume. "The Dissemination of Shakespeare's Plays circa 1714." *Studies in Bibliography* 56 (2003–2004): 261–275.

Eliot, Simon. "Some Trends in British Book Production, 1800–1919." In *Literature in the Marketplace: Nineteenth-Century British Publishing and Reading Practices*, edited by John O. Jordan and Robert L. Patten, 19–43. New York: Cambridge University Press, 1995.

Elsaesser, Thomas. "Tales of Sound and Fury: Observations on the Family Melodrama." In *Film Theory and Criticism: Introductory Readings*, edited by Gerald Mast, Marshall Cohen, and Leo Braudy, 512–535. New York: Oxford University Press, 1992.

Empson, William. *Using Biography*. Cambridge MA: Harvard University Press, 1984.

Etherege, George. *The Man of Mode; or, Sir Fopling Flutter*. London, 1676.

Farese, Carlotta. "The Strange Case of Herr Von K: Further Reflections on the Reception of Kotzebue's Theatre in Britain." *DQR: Studies in Literature* 55 (2015): 71–84.

Fawcett, Julia. "Creating Character in 'Chiaro Oscuro': Sterne's Celebrity, Cibber's *Apology*, and the Life of *Tristram Shandy*." *Eighteenth-Century: Theory and Interpretation* 53, no. 2 (2012): 141–161.

Fergus, Jan. *Provincial Readers in Eighteenth-Century England*. New York: Oxford University Press, 2007.

Ferguson, Frances. "Jane Austen, *Emma*, and the Impact of Form." *MLQ: Modern Language Quarterly* 61, no. 1 (2000): 157–180.

Ferguson, Margaret. "News from the New World: Miscegenous Romance in Aphra Behn's *Oroonoko* and *The Widow Ranter*." In *The Production of English Renaissance Culture*, edited by David Lee Miller, Sharon O'Dair, and Harold Weber, 151–189. Ithaca, NY: Cornell University Press, 1994.

Festa, Lynn. "Sentimental Bonds and Revolutionary Characters: Richardson's *Pamela* in England and France." In *The Literary Channel: The Inter-national Invention of the Novel*, edited by Margaret Cohen and Carolyn Dever, 73–105. Princeton, NJ: Princeton University Press, 2002.

Fielding, Henry. *Amelia*. Edited by Martin C. Battestin. Middletown, CT: Wesleyan University Press, 1983.

———. *The History of Tom Jones, a Foundling*. 2 vols. Edited by Martin C. Battestin and Fredson Bowers. Middletown CT: Wesleyan University Press, 1975.

———. *Joseph Andrews*. Edited by Martin C. Battestin. Middletown CT.: Wesleyan University Press, 1967.

———. *Shamela* in *Joseph Andrews and Shamela*. Edited by Douglas Brooks-Davies and Thomas Keymer. New York: Oxford University Press, 1999.

———. *The Wesleyan Edition of the Works of Henry Fielding: Plays*. 3 vols. Edited by Thomas Lockwood. Oxford, UK: Clarendon, 2004.

Firbank, Ronald. *Valmouth*. Notebook 4. Harry Ransom Research Library. University of Texas at Austin.

Fisher, Nicholas. "The Contemporary Reception of Rochester's *A Satyr against Mankind*." *Review of English Studies* 57, no. 229 (2006): 185–220.

Fletcher, Angus, and Michael Benveniste. "Defending Pluralism: The Chicago School and the Case of *Tom Jones*." *New Literary History* 41, no. 3 (2010): 653–667.

Fludernik, Monika. "Narrative and Drama." In *Theorizing Narrativity*, edited by John Pier and José Angel Garcia Landa, 355–383. Berlin: de Gruyter, 2008.

———. "Spectacle, Theatre, and Sympathy in Caleb Williams." *Eighteenth-Century Fiction* 14, no. 1 (2001): 1–30.

———. *Towards a "Natural" Narratology*. New York: Routledge, 2002.

Frank, Judith. "The Comic Novel and the Poor: Fielding's Preface to *Joseph Andrews*." *Eighteenth-Century Studies* 27, no. 2 (1993–1994): 217–234.

Frank, Marcie. "Tragedy, Comedy, Tragicomedy and the Incubation of New Genres." In *Emergent Nation: Early Modern British Literature in Transition 1660–1714*, edited by Elizabeth Sauer, 66–79. Cambridge: Cambridge University Press, 2019.

Freedgood, Elaine. *Worlds Enough: The Invention of Realism in the Victorian Novel*. Princeton, NJ: Princeton University Press, 2019.

Freeman, Lisa A. *Antitheatricality and the Body Public*. Philadelphia: University of Pennsylvania Press, 2017.

———. *Character's Theater: Genre and Identity on the Eighteenth-Century English Stage*. Philadelphia: University of Pennsylvania Press, 2001.

———. "Jeremy Collier and the Politics of Theatrical Representation." In *Players, Playwrights, Playhouses: Investigating Performance, 1660–1800*, edited by Michael Cordner and Peter Holland, 135–151. New York: Palgrave Macmillan, 2007.

Fried, Michael. *Absorption and Theatricality: Painting and Beholder in the Age of Diderot.* Chicago: University of Chicago Press, 1988.

Gallagher, Catherine. *Nobody's Story: The Vanishing Acts of Women Writers in the Marketplace, 1670–1820.* Berkeley: University of California Press, 1994.

———. "The Rise of Fictionality." In *The Novel*, vol. 1, *History, Geography, and Culture*, edited by Franco Moretti, 336–363. Princeton, NJ: Princeton University Press, 2006.

———. "Telling It like It Wasn't." *Pacific Coast Philology* 45 (2010): 12–25.

———. "What Would Napoleon Do? Historical, Fictional, and Counterfactual Characters." *New Literary History* 42, no. 2 (2011): 315–336.

Gamer, Michael. "Authors in Effect: Lewis, Scott, and the Gothic Drama." *ELH* 66, no. 4 (1999): 831–861.

Gardiner, Judith Kegan. "The First English Novel: Aphra Behn's *Love Letters*, the Canon, and Women's Tastes." *Tulsa Studies in Women's Literature* 8, no. 2 (1989): 201–222.

Garlington, Aubrey S., Jr. "'Gothic' Literature and Dramatic Music in England, 1781–1802." *Journal of the American Musicological Society* 15, no. 1 (1962): 48–64.

Garside, Peter, James Raven, and Rainer Schöwerling, eds. *The English Novel, 1770–1829: A Bibliographical Survey of Prose Fiction Published in the British Isles.* 2 vols. Oxford: Oxford University Press, 2000.

Gay, Penny. *Jane Austen and the Theatre.* Cambridge: Cambridge University Press, 2002.

———. "Jane Austen's Stage." In *The Oxford Handbook of the Georgian Theatre 1737–1832*, edited by Julia Swindells and David Francis Taylor, 532–547. Oxford: Oxford University Press, 2014.

Genette, Gérard. *Narrative Discourse: An Essay in Method.* Translated by Jane E. Lewin. Ithaca, NY: Cornell University Press, 1980.

Gentleman, Francis. *The Dramatic Censor.* Vol. 1. London, 1770.

Glicksman, Harry. "The Stage History of Colley Cibber's *The Careless Husband.*" *PMLA* 36, no. 2 (1921): 245–250.

Godineau, Dominique. *The Women of Paris and Their French Revolution.* Translated by Katherine Streip. Berkeley: University of California Press, 1998.

Godwin, William. *Caleb Williams.* Edited by Pamela Clemit. Oxford: Oxford University Press, 2009.

———. *The Enquirer: Reflections on Education, Manners, and Literature, in a Series of Essays.* Philadelphia, 1797.

———. *Fleetwood, or The New Man of Feeling.* London: 1832.

———. *Four Early Pamphlets (1783–1784).* Introduction by Burton R. Pollin. New York: Scholar's Facsimiles and Reprints, 1977

Goethe, Johann Wolfgang von. *Wilhelm Meister's Apprenticeship and Travels.* 2 vols. Translated by Thomas Carlyle. Boston: Dana Estes, 1839.

Goldsmith, Oliver. *She Stoops to Conquer; or, The Mistakes of a Night.* London, 1773.

Gollapudi, Aparna. *Moral Reform in Comedy and Culture, 1696–1747.* Burlington, VT: Ashgate, 2011.

Greene, Graham. *Brighton Rock.* New York: Vintage Classics, 2004.

———. *Lord Rochester's Monkey: Being the Life of John Wilmot, Second Earl of Rochester.* London: Bodley Head, 1974.

Guillory, John. *Cultural Capital: The Problem of Literary Canon Formation.* Chicago: University of Chicago Press, 1993.

———. "Genesis of the Media Concept." *Critical Inquiry* 36, no. 2 (2010): 321–362.

Gustafson, Daniel. "The Rake's Revival: Steele, Dennis, and the Early Eighteenth-Century Repertory." *Modern Philology* 112, no. 2 (2014): 358–380.

Gwilliam, Tassie. *Samuel Richardson's Fictions of Gender*. Stanford, CA: Stanford University Press, 1993.

Hamlin, Cyrus. "Faust in Performance: Peter Stein's Production of Goethe's *Faust*, parts 1 and 2." *Theater* 32, no. 1 (2002): 116–136.

Hammond, Brean S. "Politics and Cultural Politics: The Case of Henry Fielding." *Eighteenth-Century Life* 16 (February 1992): 76–93.

Harding, D.W. "Regulated Hatred: An Aspect of the Works of Jane Austen," *Scrutiny* 8 (1940) 346–362.

Hardy, Thomas. *The Mayor of Casterbridge: The Life and Death of a Man of Character*. New York: Penguin Books, 2003.

Harris, Jocelyn. *A Revolution Almost beyond Expression: Jane Austen's Persuasion*. Newark: University of Delaware Press, 2007.

Hemlow, Joyce. *The History of Fanny Burney*. Oxford, UK: Clarendon, 1958.

Hershinow, Stephanie Insley. "When Experience Matters: *Tom Jones* and 'Virtue Rewarded.'" *Novel* 47, no. 3 (2014): 363–382.

Heydt-Stevenson, Jillian, and Charlotte Sussman. *Recognizing the Romantic Novel: New Histories of British Fiction, 1780–1830*. Liverpool, UK: Liverpool University Press, 2010.

Hill, Christopher. *The Collected Essays of Christopher Hill*. Vol. 1, *Writing and Revolution in 17th-Century England*. Brighton, UK: Harvester, 1985.

Hirsh, James E. *Shakespeare and the History of Soliloquies*. Madison, NJ: Fairleigh Dickinson University Press, 2003.

Hobbes, Thomas. "Answer to Davenant's Preface to *Gondibert*." In *Critical Essays of the Seventeenth Century*, vol. 2, *1650–1685*, edited by Joel Elias Spingarn, 54–67. Oxford, UK: Clarendon, 1908.

Holcroft, Thomas. *Alwyn; or, The Gentleman Comedian*. 2 vols. London: Fielding and Walker, 1780.

———. *A Tale of Mystery, a Melo-Drame*. London: R. Phillips, 1802.

Hume, Robert D. "Drama and Theater in the Mid and Later Eighteenth Century." In *The Cambridge History of English Literature, 1660–1780*, edited by John Richetti, 316–339. Cambridge: Cambridge University Press, 2005.

———. "Fielding at 300: Elusive, Confusing, Misappropriated, or (Perhaps) Obvious?" *Modern Philology* 108, no. 2 (2010): 224–262.

———. "Jeremy Collier and the Future of the London Theater in 1698." *Studies in Philology* 96, no. 4 (1999): 480–511.

———. *The Rakish Stage: Studies in English Drama, 1660–1800*. Carbondale: Southern Illinois University Press, 1983.

Hunt, Alan. *Governing Morals: A Social History of Moral Regulation*. New York: Cambridge University Press, 1999.

Inchbald, Elizabeth. *The British Theatre; or, A Collection of Plays Selected by Elizabeth Inchbald*. 1808. 25 vols. New York: Georg Olms Verlag, 1970.

———. *The Diaries of Elizabeth Inchbald*. 3 vols. Edited by Ben Robertson. London: Pickering and Chatto, 2007.

———. *Nature and Art*. Edited by Shaun Lisa Maurer. Peterborough, ON: Broadview, 2004.

———. *A Simple Story*. Edited by Anna Lott. Peterborough, ON: Broadview, 2007.

———. "To the Artist." 1807. In *Nature and Art*, edited by Shaun Lisa Maurer, 160–166. Peterborough, ON: Broadview, 2004.

———. *Wives as They Were, and Maids as They Are*. London: G. G. and J. Robinson, 1797.

Jameson, Fredric. *The Antinomies of Realism*. New York: Verso, 2013.

Jenkins, Annibel. *I'll Tell You What: The Life of Elizabeth Inchbald*. Lexington: University Press of Kentucky, 2003.

Jennings, Charles, ed. *Hamlet* by William Shakespeare. London: 1770.

Johnson, Samuel. *Lives of the English Poets*. Edited by George Birkbeck Hill. 3 vols. New York: Octagon Books, 1967.

———. *Selected Writings*. Edited by Peter Martin. Cambridge, MA: Harvard University Press, 2009.

Kaufman, Robert. "The Sublime as Super-Genre of the Modern, or 'Hamlet' in Revolution: Caleb Williams and His Problems." *Studies in Romanticism* 36 (1997): 541–574.

Kelly, Gary. *The English Jacobin Novel, 1780–1805*. New York: Oxford University Press, 1976.

Keymer, Thomas, and Peter Sabor. *The Pamela Controversy: Criticisms and Adaptations of Samuel Richardson's "Pamela," 1740–1750*. London: Pickering and Chatto, 2001.

———. *"Pamela" in the Marketplace: Literary Controversy and Print Culture in Eighteenth-Century Britain and Ireland*. New York: Cambridge University Press, 2005.

Keymer, Tom. "Mastering the Art of Understating Your Wealth." Review of *The Literary Correspondence of the Tonsons*, edited by Stephen Bernard. *London Review of Books* 38, no. 9 (2016), 21.

———. *Richardson's "Clarissa" and the Eighteenth-Century Reader*. New York: Cambridge University Press, 2004.

———. "Shakespeare in the Novel." In *Shakespeare in the Eighteenth Century*, edited by Fiona Ritchie and Peter Sabor, 118–140. New York: Cambridge University Press, 2012.

——— and Peter Sabor eds. *The Pamela Controversy: Criticisms and Adaptations of Samuel Richardson's "Pamela," 1740–1750*. 6 vols. London: Pickering and Chatto 2001.

Kiely, Robert. *The Romantic Novel in England*. Cambridge, MA: Harvard University Press, 1972.

King, Rachael Scarborough. "The Pleasures of 'the World': Rewriting Epistolarity in Burney, Edgeworth and Austen." *Eighteenth-Century Fiction* 29, no. 1 (2016): 67–89.

Kinkead-Weekes, Mark. *Samuel Richardson, Dramatic Novelist*. Ithaca, NY: Cornell University Press, 1973.

Kinservik, Matthew J. "Censorship and Generic Change: The Case of Satire on the Early Eighteenth-Century London Stage." *Philological Quarterly* 78, no. 3 (1999): 259–282.

———. "The Dialectics of Print and Performance after 1737." In *The Oxford Handbook of the Georgian Theatre, 1737–1832*, edited by Julia Swindells and David Francis Taylor, 123–139. Oxford: Oxford University Press, 2014.

———. *Disciplining Satire: The Censorship of Satiric Comedy on the Eighteenth-Century London Stage*. Lewisburg, PA: Bucknell University Press, 2002.

Klancher, Jon. "Godwin and the Genre Reformers: On Necessity and Contingency in Romantic Narrative Theory." In *Romanticism, History, and the Possibilities of Genre, 1798–1837*, edited by Tilottama Rajan and Julia Wright, 21–38. New York: Cambridge University Press, 1998.

———. *Transfiguring the Arts and Sciences: Knowledge and Cultural Institutions in the Romantic Age*. New York: Cambridge University Press, 2013.

Kowaleski-Wallace, Elizabeth. "Reading the Surfaces of Colley Cibber's *The Careless Husband*." *SEL: Studies in English Literature, 1500–1900* 40, no. 3 (2000): 473–489.

———. *Their Fathers' Daughters: Hannah More, Maria Edgeworth, and Patriarchal Complicity*. New York: Oxford University Press, 1991.

Kraft, Elizabeth, and Debra Taylor Bourdeau, eds. *On Second Thought: Updating the Eighteenth-Century Text*. Newark: University of Delaware Press, 2007.

Kramnick, Jonathan Brody. *Actions and Objects from Hobbes to Richardson*. Stanford, CA: Stanford University Press, 2010.

———. "Reading Shakespeare's Novels: Literary History and Cultural Politics in the Lennox-Johnson Debate." *Modern Language Quarterly* 55, no. 4 (1994): 429–453. Reprinted in

Eighteenth-Century Literary History: An MLQ Reader, edited by Marshall Brown, 43–67. Durham, NC: Duke University Press, 1999.

Kramnick, Jonathan, and Anaheid Nercessian. "Form and Explanation." *Critical Inquiry* 43 (Spring 2017): 650–669.

Kunin, Aaron. "Facial Composure and Management in Behn's Novels." *Modern Philology* 107, no. 1 (2009): 72–95.

Kurnick, David. *Empty Houses: Theatrical Failure and the Novel*. Princeton, NJ: Princeton University Press, 2011.

Laya, Jean Louis. *Falkland, ou la conscience: Drame en cinq actes et en prose*. Paris: Chez J.-N. Barba, 1821.

Lewis, M. G. *The Castle Spectre: A Drama; In Five Acts*. London: J. Bell, 1798.

Litvak, Joseph. *Caught in the Act: Theatricality in the Nineteenth-Century English Novel*. Berkeley: University of California Press, 1992.

Lockwood, Thomas. General introduction to *The Wesleyan Edition of The Works of Henry Fielding Plays*, vol. 1, xvii–xxviii. Oxford, UK: Clarendon, 2004.

———. "Theatrical Fielding." *Studies in the Literary Imagination* 32, no. 2 (1999): 105–114.

Looser, Devoney. Review of *Women in Revolutionary Debate: Female Novelists from Burney to Austen*, by Stephanie Russo. *Modern Philology* 112, no. 4 (2015): 327–329.

Love, Harold. Introduction to *The Works of John Wilmot, Earl of Rochester*, by John Wilmot, xv–xlvii. Oxford: Oxford University Press, 1999.

Lund, Roger D. "Augustan Burlesque and the Genesis of *Joseph Andrews*." *Studies in Philology* 103, no. 1 (2006): 88–119.

Lupton, Christina. *Reading and the Making of Time*. Baltimore: Johns Hopkins University Press, 2018.

Lynch, Deidre Shauna. *The Economy of Character: Novels, Market Culture, and the Business of Inner Meaning*. Chicago: University of Chicago Press, 1998.

———. Introduction to *Mansfield Park: An Annotated Edition*, by Jane Austen, 1–41. Cambridge MA: Harvard University Press, 2016.

———. Introduction to *Persuasion*, by Jane Austen, vii–xxxiii. New York: Oxford University Press, 2004.

———. *Loving Literature: A Cultural History*. Chicago: University of Chicago Press, 2014.

Mackie, Erin. *Rakes, Highwaymen, and Pirates: The Making of the Modern Gentleman in the Eighteenth Century*. Baltimore: Johns Hopkins University Press, 2010.

Maguire, Nancy Klein. *Regicide and Restoration: English Tragicomedy 1660–1671*. Cambridge: Cambridge University Press 1992.

Mannheimer, Katherine. *Print, Visuality, and Gender in Eighteenth-Century Satire: "The Scope in Ev'ry Page."* New York: Routledge, 2011.

Mayhew, Edward. *Stage Effect; or, The Principles Which Command Dramatic Success in the Theatre*. London: C. Mitchell, 1840.

McDonagh, Patrick. "The Mute's Voice: The Dramatic Transformations of the Mute and Deaf-Mute in Early-Nineteenth-Century France." *Criticism* 55, no. 4 (2013): 655–675.

McGirr, Elaine. *Eighteenth-Century Characters: A Guide to the Literature of the Age*. New York: Palgrave Macmillan, 2007.

———. *Partial Histories: A Reappraisal of Colley Cibber*. London: Palgrave Macmillan, 2016.

———. "Rethinking Reform Comedies: Colley Cibber's Desiring Women." *Eighteenth-Century Studies* 46, no. 3 (2013): 385–397.

———. "Why Lovelace Must Die." *Novel: A Forum on Fiction* 37, nos. 1–2 (2004): 5–23.

McGurl, Mark. *The Novel Art: Elevations of American Fiction after Henry James*. Princeton, NJ: Princeton University Press, 2001.

McKeon, Michael. "The Eighteenth-Century Challenge to Narrative Theory." In *Narrative Concepts in the Study of Eighteenth-Century Literature*, edited by Liisa Steinby and Aino Makikalli, 39–78. Amsterdam: Amsterdam University Press, 2017.

———. *Origins of the English Novel, 1600–1740*. Baltimore: Johns Hopkins University Press, 1987.

———. *The Secret History of Domesticity: Public, Private, and the Division of Knowledge*. Baltimore: Johns Hopkins University Press, 2009.

———, ed. *Theory of the Novel: A Historical Approach*. Baltimore: Johns Hopkins University Press, 2000.

———. "What Was an Early Modern Public, and How Was It Made?" *History Compass* 10, no. 9 (2012): 714–730.

McKillop, A. D. *The Early Masters of English Fiction*. Lawrence: University of Kansas Press, 1956.

Meisel, Martin. *Realizations: Narrative, Pictorial, and Theatrical Arts in Nineteenth-Century England*. Princeton, NJ: Princeton University Press, 1983.

Menke, Christof. *Force: A Fundamental Concept in Aesthetic Anthropology*. New York: Fordham University Press, 2013.

Michaelson, Patricia. *Speaking Volumes: Women, Reading and Speech in the Age of Austen*. Stanford, CA: Stanford University Press, 2002.

Michals, Teresa. "'Like a Spoiled Actress off the Stage': Anti-theatricality, Nature, and the Novel." *Studies in Eighteenth-Century Culture* 39, no. 1 (2010): 191–214.

Michie, Allen. *Richardson and Fielding: The Dynamics of a Critical Rivalry*. Lewisburg, PA: Bucknell University Press, 1999.

Miles, Robert. "What Is a Romantic Novel?" *Novel* 34, no. 2 (2001): 180–201.

Miller, D. A. *Jane Austen, or The Secret of Style*. Princeton, NJ: Princeton University Press, 2003.

———. "The Novel as Usual: Trollope's *Barchester Towers*." In *Sex, Politics, and Science in the Nineteenth-Century Novel*, edited by Ruth B. Yeazell, 1–38. Baltimore: Johns Hopkins University Press, 1986.

Min, Eun Kyung. "Giving Promises in Elizabeth Inchbald's *A Simple Story*." *ELH* 77, no. 1 (2010): 105–127.

Moe, Melina. "Charlotte and Elizabeth: Multiple Modernities in Jane Austen's *Pride and Prejudice*." *ELH* 83, no. 4 (2016): 1075–1103.

Moody, Jane. *Illegitimate Theatre in London, 1770–1840*. New York: Cambridge University Press, 2000.

Moretti, Franco. *Graphs, Maps, Trees: Abstract Models for Literary History*. London: Verso, 2007.

———. "Serious Century." In *The Novel*, vol. 1, edited by Franco Moretti, 364–400. Princeton, NJ: Princeton University Press, 2006.

Muller-Muth, Anja. "Transformations of Theatricality in Frances Burney's *Evelina*." Paper presented at "Dramatic Aspects of Frances Burney," McGill University, Montreal, 2004.

Nachumi, Nora. *Acting like a Lady: British Women Novelists and the Eighteenth-Century Theater*. New York: AMS Press, 2008.

———. "'Those Simple Signs': The Performance of Emotion in Elizabeth Inchbald's *A Simple Story*." *Eighteenth-Century Fiction* 11, no. 3 (1999): 317–338.

Nelson, William. *The Dilemma of the Renaissance Storyteller*. Cambridge, MA: Harvard University Press, 1973.

Nixon, Cheryl L., ed. *Novel Definitions: An Anthology of Commentary on the Novel, 1688–1815*. Peterborough, ON: Broadview, 2009.

Novak, Maximillian E. "The Politics of Shakespeare Criticism in the Restoration and Early Eighteenth Century." *ELH* 81, no. 1 (2014): 115–142.

———. "Some Notes towards a History of Fictional Forms: From Aphra Behn to Daniel Defoe." *Novel: A Forum on Fiction* 6, no. 2 (1973): 120–133.

O'Quinn, Daniel. "Jane Austen and Performance: Theatre, Memory, and Enculturation." In *A Companion to Jane Austen*, edited by Claudia Johnson and Clara Tuite, 377–388. Chichester, UK: Wiley Blackwell, 2009.

———. "Scissors and Needles: Inchbald's *Wives as They Were, Maids as They Are* and the Governance of Sexual Exchange." *Theatre Journal* 51, no. 2 (1999): 105–125.

O'Shaughnessy, David. "Kotzebue and Thompson's *The Stranger*: A New Source for Godwin's *St Leon*." *Notes and Queries* 52, no. 4 (2005): 452–456.

———. "William Godwin and the Politics of Playgoing." In *The Oxford Handbook of the Georgian Theatre, 1737–1832*, edited by Julia Swindells and David Francis Taylor, 514–531. Oxford: Oxford University Press, 2014.

———. *William Godwin and the Theatre*. London: Routledge, 2015.

Osland, Dianne. "Heart-Picking in *A Simple Story*." *Eighteenth-Century Fiction* 16, no. 1 (2003): 79–101.

Park, Julie. *The Self and It: Novel Objects in Eighteenth-Century England*. Stanford, CA: Stanford University Press, 2010.

———. "What the Eye Cannot See: Interior Landscape in *Mansfield Park*." *The Eighteenth Century* suppl. 54, no. 2 (Summer 2013) 169–181.

Parker, Joshua. "In Their Own Words: On Writing in the Second Person." *Connotations* 21, nos. 2–3 (2011–2012): 165–176.

Patey, Douglas Lane. *Probability and Literary Form: Philosophic Theory and Literary Practice in the Augustan Age*. New York: Cambridge University Press, 1984.

Paulson, Ronald. *The Beautiful, Novel, and Strange: Aesthetics and Heterodoxy*. Baltimore: Johns Hopkins University Press, 1996.

———. *Hogarth: His Life, Art, and Times*. New Haven, CT: Yale University Press, 1971.

———. *Representations of Revolution (1789–1820)*. New Haven, CT: Yale University Press, 1983.

Pavel, Thomas. *The Lives of the Novel: A History*. Princeton, NJ: Princeton University Press, 2013.

Pavis, Patrice. *Dictionary of the Theatre: Terms, Concepts, and Analysis*. Translated by Christine Shantz. Toronto: University of Toronto Press, 1998.

Peters, Julie Stone. *Theatre of the Book, 1480–1880: Print, Text, and Performance in Europe*. New York: Oxford University Press, 2000.

Pixérécourt, R.-C. Guilbert de (René-Charles Guilbert). *Le château des Apennins, ou le fantôme vivant, drame en cinq actes, en prose, et à grand spectacle. Imité du roman anglais, les Mystères d'Udolphe*. Paris, 1799.

———. *Théâtre*. 5 vols. Paris: Chez J. N. Barba, 1802.

Porrett, Robert. *Clarissa; or, The Fatal Seduction, a Tragedy in Prose*. In *Clarissa: The Eighteenth-Century Response, 1747–1804*, vol. 2, *Rewriting Clarissa*, edited by Lois E. Bueler, 171–228. New York: AMS Press, 2010.

Potter, Tiffany. *Honest Sins: Georgian Libertinism and the Plays and Novels of Henry Fielding*. Montreal: McGill-Queen's University Press, 1999.

Ravel, Jeffrey S. *The Contested Parterre: Public Theater and French Political Culture, 1680–1791*. Ithaca, NY: Cornell University Press, 1999.

Rawson, Claude. "Henry Fielding." In *The Cambridge Companion to the Eighteenth-Century Novel*, edited by John Richetti, 120–152. New York: Cambridge University Press, 1996.

Richards, Cynthia, and Mary Ann O'Donnell, eds. *Approaches to Teaching Behn's "Oroonoko."* New York: Modern Language Association of America, 2014.

Richardson, Alan. "Byron and the Theatre." In *The Cambridge Companion to Byron*, edited by Drummond Bone, 133–150. New York: Cambridge University Press, 2004.

Richardson, Samuel. *Clarissa; or, The History of a Young Lady*. Edited by Angus Ross. New York: Penguin, 1985.

———. *Pamela, or Virtue Rewarded*. Edited by Tom Keymer. London: Oxford University Press, 2001.

———. *Pamela or Virtue Rewarded*. Edited by Thomas Archer. London: Routledge, 1873.

Richetti, John, ed. *The Cambridge Companion to the Eighteenth-Century Novel*. New York: Cambridge University Press, 1996.

Rivero, Albert J. *The Plays of Henry Fielding: A Critical Study of His Dramatic Career*. Charlottesville: University of Virginia Press, 1989.

Roach, Joseph. *"The God of Our Idolatry": Garrick and Shakespeare*. Exhibition catalog for an exhibition at the Lewis Walpole Library. New Haven, CT: Yale University Press, 2012.

Roberts, David. "Sleeping Beauties: Shakespeare, Sleep and the Stage." *Cambridge Quarterly* 35, no. 3 (2006): 231–254.

Rohrbach, Emily. *Modernity's Mist: British Romanticism and the Poetics of Anticipation*. New York: Fordham University Press, 2016.

Rooney, Monique. *Living Screens: Melodrama and Plasticity in Contemporary Film and Television*. Lanham, MD: Rowman and Littlefield, 2015.

Rutherford, Andrew, ed. *Byron: The Critical Heritage*. London: Routledge and Kegan Paul, 1970.

Sabor, Peter. "General Introduction." In *The Complete Plays of Frances Burney*, vol. 1, xi–xli. Montreal: McGill-Queen's University Press, 1995.

Saggini, Francesca. *Backstage in the Novel: Frances Burney and the Theater Arts*. Translated by Laura Kopp. Charlottesville: University of Virginia Press, 2012.

Schmidgen, Wolfram. "Undividing the Subject of Literary History: From James Thomson's Poetry to Daniel Defoe's Novels." In *Eighteenth-Century Poetry and the Rise of the Novel Reconsidered*, edited by Kate Parker and Courtney Weiss Smith, 87–104. Lewisburg, PA: Bucknell University Press, 2014.

Scott, Walter, Sir. *The Lives of the Novelists*. 1821–1824. Reprint, London: J. M. Dent, 1910.

Sedgwick, Eve Kosofsky. *Touching Feeling: Affect, Pedagogy, Performativity*. Durham, NC: Duke University Press, 2003.

Shakespeare, William. *Hamlet* in *The Riverside Shakespeare*, edited by G. Blakemore Evans. Boston: Houghton Mifflin, 1974.

———. *Hamlet, Prince of Denmark: A Tragedy; As It Is Now Acted by His Majesty's Servants*. London, 1756.

Sheridan, Richard Brinsley. *The School for Scandal, a Comedy in Five Acts*. Berlin: J. F. Unger, 1790.

Sherman, Stuart. "Garrick among Media: The '*Now* Performer' Navigates the News." *PMLA* 126, no. 4 (2011): 966–982.

Siskin, Clifford. *The Work of Writing: Literature and Social Change, 1700–1830*. Baltimore: Johns Hopkins University Press, 1998.

Spacks, Patricia Meyer. *On Rereading*. Cambridge, MA: Harvard University Press, 2011.

Spencer, Jane. "*Evelina* and *Cecilia*." In *The Cambridge Companion to Frances Burney*, edited by Peter Sabor, 23–38. New York: Cambridge University Press, 2007.

Starkie, Andrew. "Contested Histories of the English Church: Gilbert Burnet and Jeremy Collier." *Huntington Library Quarterly* 68, nos. 1–2 (2005): 335–351.

Staves, Susan. "A Few Kind Words for the Fop." *Studies in English Literature, 1500–1900* 22, no. 3 (1982): 413–428.

———. *Players' Scepters: Fictions of Authority in the Restoration*. Lincoln: University of Nebraska Press, 1979.

St. Clair, William. *The Reading Nation in the Romantic Period*. New York: Cambridge University Press, 2004.

Steele, Richard. *The Conscious Lovers: A Comedy*. London, 1760.

Stewart, Alan. *Shakespeare's Letters*. New York: Oxford University Press, 2008.

Stewart, Garrett. *Dear Reader: The Conscripted Audience in Nineteenth-Century British Fiction*. Baltimore: Johns Hopkins University Press, 1996.

Strachey, G. Lytton, Ed. Introduction to Elizabeth Inchbald, *A Simple Story* (London: Henry Frowde 1908), Project Gutenburg, released July 5, 2007, n.p., accessed May 27, 2014.

Straub, Julia. "Melodrama and Narrative Fiction: Towards a Typology." *Anglia* 132, no. 2 (2014): 225–241.

Straub, Kristina. *Domestic Affairs: Intimacy, Eroticism, and Violence between Servants and Masters in Eighteenth-Century Britain*. Baltimore: Johns Hopkins University Press, 2009.

Stuber, Florian, and Margaret Anne Doody. "The Clarissa Project and *Clarissa's* Reception." *Text* 12 (1999): 123–141.

Taylor, David Francis. *Theatres of Opposition: Empire, Revolution and Richard Brinsley Sheridan*. Oxford: Oxford University Press, 2012.

Taylor, Diana. *The Archive and the Repertoire: Performing Cultural Memory in the Americas*. Durham, NC: Duke University Press, 2003.

Taylor, George. *The French Revolution and the London Stage, 1789–1805*. New York: Cambridge University Press, 2000.

Thomasseau, Jean-Marie. *Le mélodrame*. Paris: Presses Universitaires de France, 1984.

Thompson, Helen. "How *The Wanderer* Works: Reading Burney and Bourdieu." *ELH* 68, no. 4 (2001): 965–989.

Tierney-Hynes, Rebecca. *Novel Minds: Philosophers and Romance Readers, 1680–1740*. New York: Palgrave Macmillan, 2012.

Tilmouth, Christopher. "After Libertinism: The Passions of the Polite Christian Hero." In *Emergent Nation: Early Modern British Literature in Transition 1660–1714*, 240–257. Edited by Elizabeth Sauer. Cambridge: Cambridge University Press, 2019.

Todd, Janet, and Derek Hughes, eds. *The Cambridge Companion to Aphra Behn*. New York: Cambridge University Press, 2004.

———. "Tragedy and Tragicomedy." In *The Cambridge Companion to Aphra Behn*, edited by Janet Todd and Derek Hughes, 83–97. New York: Cambridge University Press, 2004.

Tomkins, Silvan. *Shame and Its Sisters: A Silvan Tomkins Reader*. Edited by Eve K. Sedgwick and Adam Frank. Durham, NC: Duke University Press, 1995.

Traugott, John. "The Rake's Progress from Court to Comedy: A Study in Comic Form." *Studies in English Literature, 1500–1900* 6, no. 3 (1966): 381–407.

Trollope, Anthony. *An Autobiography*. Edited by David Skilton. New York: Penguin, 1996.

———. *Barchester Towers*. New York: Modern Library, 1936.

———. *Can You Forgive Her?* New York: Oxford University Press, 2012.

Tuite, Clara. *Romantic Austen: Sexual Politics and the Literary Canon*. Cambridge: Cambridge University Press, 2002.

Turner, James Grantham. "Novel Panic: Picture and Performance in the Reception of Richardson's *Pamela*." *Representations* 48 (Fall 1994): 70–96.

Tynyanov, Yury. "The Literary Fact." In *Modern Genre Theory*, edited by David Duff, 29–49. New York: Longman, 2000.

Ungerer, Gustav. "Thomas Shadwell's *The Libertine* (1675): A Forgotten Restoration Don Juan Play." *SEDERI: Yearbook of the Spanish and Portuguese Society for English Renaissance Studies* 1 (1990): 222–239.

Vanbrugh, John. *The Relapse* in *The Relapse and Other Plays*. Edited by Brean S. Hammond, 1–100. New York: Oxford University Press, 2004.

Vanbrugh, John, and Colley Cibber. *The Provoked Husband*. Edited by Peter Dixon. Lincoln: University of Nebraska Press, 1973.

Vermeule, Blakey. *Why Do We Care about Literary Characters?* Baltimore: Johns Hopkins University Press, 2011.

Vickers, Brian. *William Shakespeare: The Critical Heritage.* Vol. 3, *1733–52.* Vol. 4, *1753–1765.* London: Routledge and Kegan Paul, 1976.

Vincent, John Emil. *John Ashbery and You: His Later Books.* Athens: University of Georgia Press, 2007.

Wall, Cynthia. *The Prose of Things.* Chicago: University of Chicago Press, 2006.

Wardrip-Fruin, Noah, and Pat Harrigan, eds., *First Person: New Media as Story, Performance, and Game.* Cambridge, MA: MIT Press, 2006.

———, eds. *Second Person: Role-Playing and Story in Games and Playable Media.* Cambridge, MA: MIT Press, 2007.

———, eds. *Third Person: Authoring Vast Narratives.* Cambridge, MA: MIT Press, 2009.

Warhol-Down, Robyn. "'What Might Have Been Is Not What Is': Dickens's Narrative Refusals." *Dickens Studies Annual* 41 (2010): 45–59.

Warner, William B. *Licensing Entertainment: The Elevation of Novel Reading in Britain, 1684–1750.* Berkeley: University of California Press, 1998.

———. *Reading Clarissa: The Struggles of Interpretation.* New Haven, CT: Yale University Press, 1979.

Watt, Ian P. *The Rise of the Novel: Studies in Defoe, Richardson, and Fielding.* Harmondsworth, UK: Penguin, 1974.

Weber, Harold. *The Restoration Rake-Hero: Transformations in Sexual Understanding in Seventeenth-Century England.* Madison: University of Wisconsin Press, 1986.

Widemayer, Anne F. *Theater and Novel from Behn to Fielding.* Oxford: Oxford University Press, 2015.

Wilde, Oscar. *The Importance of Being Earnest: And Other Plays.* Edited by Terrence McNally. New York: Random House, 2003.

Wilder, Thornton. *Our Town.* New York: Harper and Row, 1938.

Williams, Abigail. *The Social Life of Books: Reading Together in the Eighteenth-Century Home.* New Haven, CT: Yale University Press, 2017.

Williams, Jeffrey. "The Narrative Circle: The Interpolated Tales in *Joseph Andrews.*" *Studies in the Novel* 30, no. 4 (1998): 473–488.

Williams, Linda. "Melodrama Revised." In *Refiguring American Film Genres,* edited by Nick Browne, 42–88. Berkeley: University of California Press, 1998.

Wilmot, John. *The Works of John Wilmot, Earl of Rochester.* Edited by Harold Love. Oxford: Oxford University Press, 1999.

Woolf, Virginia. "Middlebrow." In *The Death of the Moth and Other Essays,* 176–186. New York: Harcourt, Brace, 1942.

———. "Modern Fiction." In *The Common Reader,* 146–154. London: Hogarth, 1925.

Wordsworth, William. *Lyrical Ballads, and Other Poems, 1797–1800.* Edited by James Albert Butler. Ithaca, NY: Cornell University Press, 1992.

adaptation, 10, 12, 21, 28, 30, 44, 65, 76, 155; of *Clarissa*, 84; of *The Monk*, 119, 133; of *Pamela*, 81–86; of Shakespeare, 33–34

Addison, Joseph, 33; *Cato*, 25, 30

aesthetic theory, 37, 51–52, 56, 63

amateur theatricals, 35, 103–104, 148

Anderson, Amanda, 165, 198n29

Anderson, Emily Hodgson, 3, 28, 101, 122, 137, 171n10, 175n43, 189n13, 195n46

anonymity, 11, 80–83

asides, 2, 8, 11, 24, 54, 85, 105, 127; and Austen, 144, 146, 148, 150, 153; and Burney, 11, 114; and direct address, 140; and free indirect discourse, 109–114; and soliloquy, 109–110

Austen, Jane, 4–6, 8, 73; and Burney, 97–98, 144; and comedy of manners, 44, 65–66, 102; *Emma*, 99; and free indirect discourse, 107, 109, 127; *Juvenilia*, 98; *Mansfield Park*, 11–12, 34–36, 119, 128, 144, 148–149, 151–153; and melodrama, 126, 129, 148, 151; *Northanger Abbey*, 144, 188; *Persuasion*, 12, 41, 94–98, 114, 128, 144, 147–148, 152–153; *Pride and Prejudice*, 93, 127, 151–152; *Sense and Sensibility*, 12, 45, 98, 144–145, 148–149, 151–152; and theater, 97, 127

Austin, Gilbert, 36

Ballaster, Ros, 3, 28, 76, 127, 171n4, 173n6, 184n5

Behn, Aphra, 4–5, 27, 39, 41, 80; *Fair Jilt*, 18–19, 22–24, 195n49; *Oroonoko*, 8, 17–25

Benjamin, Walter, 12–13, 135; *The Storyteller*, 125–126, 155

bildungsroman, 4–5, 8; female, 5, 8, 11, 12, 46, 66, 73, 156

Black, Scott, 93, 178n88

book history, 16

Brewer, David A., 83–85, 186n39

Burnet, Gilbert, 9, 50, 58; *Life and Death of Rochester*, 43, 46–48

Burney, Frances, 4–5, 8, 10–12, 19, 35, 45, 62, 65–66, 73, 93; and Austen, 97–98, 144, 153; *Camilla*, 11, 62, 97, 100, 103–105, 112, 114–124; *Cecilia*, 11, 97, 100, 104–105, 107–108, 120, 161; and Cibber, 58–59, 97, 102–104, 109–110; *Evelina*, 11, 45, 93, 100–101, 103–107, 117, 120, 136; and Fielding, 11, 103–104, 190n38; and free indirect discourse, 97, 161–162; and Godwin, 11; and Inchbald, 136, 153; *Journals*, 103–104; *Love and Fashion*, 105, 109, 111, 119; *The Wanderer*, 10–11, 59, 97–98, 103–105, 114–115, 119, 188

Byron, George Gordon, Lord, 29

Campbell, Jill, 86, 92, 94, 183n82, 186n49

Cibber, Colley, 9–11, 43, 179n15; *Apology for the Life of Colley Cibber*, 53, 58; and Burney, 97, 102–104; *The Careless Husband*, 56–58, 71, 102–104, 109–110, 113; *The Comic Lovers*, 22; as Lord Foppington, 55, 62, 102; *Love's Last Shift*, 49–50, 53–56, 60, 62; *The Provoked Husband*, 102–103, 119; as transformational object, 58

Coleridge, Samuel Taylor, 5, 134; on *Bertram*, 143–144; on *Castle Spectre*, 133

Colman, George, the Elder, 30, 34; *Polly Honeycomb*, 84–86

Colman, George, the Younger, 119

comedy, 2, 20, 56, 66, 68, 92, 100, 113, 119; in drama theory, 21, 26; new comedy, 25

comedy of manners, 73; and Austen, 12, 44, 59, 66, 98, 102, 126, 144–145, 151–153; and Inchbald, 139, 144; *Love and Fashion*, 105, 111; migration from stage to novel, 4–5, 8–9, 15, 41, 44, 65–66, 98, 156

Congreve, William, 78, 135, 191n46; *Incognita*, 2, 26; *Love for Love*, 101; *Way of the World*, 111

Davidson, Jenny, 157, 183n82, 184n2
Dickens, Charles, 12, 95, 126, 157, 164; *Dombey and Son*, 158; *Little Dorrit*, 160–161, 163
Diderot, Denis, 37, 86, 91; *Eloge de Richardson*, 71–72, 75
domestic novel, 8, 19–20, 24, 38, 46, 49, 71–73
Doody, Margaret, 103, 108
drama theory, 7, 20, 21, 26, 39, 133
dramatization, 10, 83, 88, 92, 123, 146, 148
dramaturgy, 98, 123, 146–147
Dryden, John, 32; *Marriage a la Mode*, 21–22

elocutionary movement, 35–37, 127, 150–151

Fergus, Jan, 3, 32–33
fictionality, 5, 19, 31, 38–39, 56, 86, 157
Fielding, Henry, 2–4, 39, 43, 153; *Amelia*, 10, 76–77, 89–92; and Burney, 103–104; and Cibber, 11, 55, 58–59, 62, 102–103; *Joseph Andrews*, 2, 10, 26, 48, 64–65, 76–77, 79–80, 86–87, 91; and letters, 8, 10–11, 76–78, 86–91, 92–94; *The Letter Writers*, 10, 80–82, 185; and narration, 41, 64–65, 69, 73; and Richardson, 59–60, 75–77, 94; *Shamela*, 10, 55, 58, 60–65, 86–87, 92, 102; *Tom Jones*, 10–11, 59, 65, 76–77, 87–88, 90–92, 103
film studies, 8, 39, 107, 120–121; shot-reverse-shot, 9, 120, 192
Firbank, Ronald, 102
Fludernik, Monika, 39, 173n28, 174n26, 178n87
fop, 22, 54–56, 82, 101, 115, 179n15
Freedgood, Elaine, 39, 177n81, 178n83
free indirect discourse, 8, 39, 95, 104, 123, 140, 157, 159–163; and Austen, 97–98, 127–128, 143–144, 147, 149, 153, 154; and Burney, 11, 107–109, 112–114, 161, 190n38
Freeman, Lisa, 3, 28, 50, 85–86, 177n10, 180n32
Fried, Michael, 3, 41

Gallagher, Catherine, 5, 18–19, 31, 38, 56, 84–86, 159–160
Garrick, David, 2, 33–34, 82, 100–103
Gay, Penny, 127, 188n8, 193n9
Gender, 4–5, 17, 45, 59, 79, 101, 115, 119, 126, 151–153
genre: classification of, 15, 21, 26–28, 46, 84; and media, 5–9, 13, 15–19, 38, 40, 126, 134
Godwin, William, 4–5, 73, 124, 126, 128; *Caleb Williams*, 11–12, 73, 134, 141–143, 173; and theater, 130, 134–135
Goethe, Johann Wolfgang von, 27, 29, 129, 175–176, 205–206
Goldsmith, Oliver, 39, 111
gothic novel, 5, 9, 40–41, 69, 130–131
Greene, Graham, 46, 102
Guillory, John, 6, 27, 37–40

Hardy, Thomas, 12, 48, 126, 157; *Mayor of Casterbridge*, 161–163
Holcroft, Thomas, 32, 62, 119–120, 124, 149; *Alwyn*, 131; *Anna St. Ives*, 1; *The Tale of Mystery*, 5, 120, 129
Hume, Robert D., 6, 32–33, 45–46, 77, 129

imitation, 26, 37, 48, 51, 55, 60, 64, 86, 143. *See also* mimesis
Inchbald, Elizabeth, 2–6, 59, 69, 98, 101–102, 155; and Austen, 6, 11, 124–128, 153; and Godwin, 124, 141, 143–144; and Kotzebue, 128, 130; *Nature and Art*, 73, 128, 136, 139, 141, 157–158; "Remarks," 2, 29, 66, 71–72, 127, 135; *A Simple Story*, 9, 12, 44, 66–68, 72–73, 128, 135–136, 139, 141, 143; "To the Artist", 27, 131, 134, 194; *Wives as They Were* [. . .], 9, 44, 67–69, 72–73

Johnson, Samuel, 2, 26, 35

Keats, John, 66
Keymer, Tom, 30, 62, 78, 81–82, 183, 185
Kinservik, Matthew, 54, 56
Kotzebue, Alexander von, 128–130; *Lovers Vows*, 34, 128, 130, 152

letters: and Fielding, 8, 10–11, 76–78, 86–91, 92–94; in novels, 101, 105–106, 152–153; and Richardson, 10, 76, 81

Lewis, Matthew, 119, 129–130, 133
Lupton, Christina, 72–73, 195n36
Lynch, Deidre, 85–86, 115–117

McGirr, Elaine, 45–46, 54, 57, 102, 181n39, 184n3
McKeon, Michael, 19–20, 37–38, 52–56, 59–60, 77, 93, 152, 154
media: concepts of, 15–17, 36–38; and genre, 3–7, 9, 12–13, 18–19, 27, 35, 134–135; intermedia, 30, 34, 58, 60, 67, 126–127, 154; media blindness, 16, 20, 35; media difference, 36, 124, 126; media opposition, 30, 32; multimedia, 5, 7–9, 28, 32, 126, 156; *Pamela* media event, 82–85
melodrama, 4, 9, 12, 15, 28, 157–165; in Austen, 144–145, 146–153; in Godwin, 141–143; history of, 5, 32, 128–131; in Inchbald, 125–126, 135–140; and situation, 133–134; on stage, 5, 130–131, 133; in *The Wanderer*, 98, 114–120, 123
Miller, D.A., 41, 94, 97, 99, 109, 164
mimesis, 37–39, 76. *See also* imitation
Moretti, Franco, 107, 140, 190n38

narrative technique, 11, 13, 76; and affective distance, 93, 94, 99, 104, 107–108, 114, 126, 133, 139, 154; and affective involvement, 4, 91, 114, 137, 161; and backstory, 23; and Burney, 97–98, 115–118
narratology, 39–40, 178n87
Noctes Ambrosianae, 28–29, 31, 36
novel theory, 3, 15–16, 19–20, 26–31, 36–37, 84

O'Quinn, Daniel, 67, 72, 127–128, 171
O'Shaughnessy, David, 130, 134

parody, 11, 24, 26–27, 58, 82, 87
performance, 1, 52–54, 180, 192; female, 101, 119, 122, 151; history, 53; as medium, 3, 6, 15, 19, 20, 25, 36–37, 40–41, 44–46; versus print, 6–7, 9, 15–17, 28–33, 83–85, 131, 154–155; versus reading, 2, 67, 127; of reading, 34–35, 36, 85, 154; as setting, 100–101, 117; as spectacle, 117–119; studies, 3, 6, 16, 40
Pixérécourt, Guilbert de, 5, 32, 120, 128
poetry, 27, 29, 31, 37–38, 40, 79, 126, 131, 134
Pope, Alexander, 32, 58, 61, 81; and Cibber, 102, 104, 130; *The Dunciad*, 11, 102

rake, in novels, 87–88, 101, 140, 143, 158; in plays, 5, 9, 10, 43–74; social decline of, 48–49; types of plays featuring, 43–44, 48–49
reading, 4, 6, 9, 78, 139; aloud, 16, 34–36, 62, 135; and imitation, 59–60; immersive versus interruptive, 10, 65, 87; interrupted, 76, 80, 122; letters, 93–94, 152–155; versus performance, 2–3, 30–36, 127–128; and performance, 30, 134–135; performances of, 34–35, 36, 85, 154; plays, 29–36; rereading, 1, 92–94; sociable, 2, 36, 85, 135, 154; "tendency" in, 134, 136, 195n37
repertory, 49, 66, 68; concepts of, 6–7, 45–46; logic of, 72, 129
Richardson, Samuel, 10, 98, 103, 106; adaptions of, 82–86; and antitheatricality, 76, 172n24, 184n3; *Clarissa*, 1–2, 5, 33–34, 71, 76, 91; influence of, 59, 93–95, 143–144; and Lovelace, 48; and Mr. B, 10, 47, 60; *Pamela*, 9–10, 43–44, 55, 57, 59; and reading, 59, 86; *Vade Mecum*, 25–26, 76

Schmidgen, Wolfram, 3–4, 16
Shakespeare, William, 21, 25, 98, 127, 134; read aloud, 150–151; read versus performed, 29, 32–35
shame, and Austen, 102; and Burney, 11, 99–101; in *Camilla*, 116–117; and Cibber, 10–11, 102, 104; in *Evelina*, 104–105, 120; in *Love and Fashion*, 111–113; and Silvan Tomkins, 102; in *The Wanderer*, 119, 122–123
Sheridan, Richard Brinsley, 30–31, 66, 100, 130; *School for Scandal*, 111
Southerne, Thomas, 21, 25
Steele, Richard, 30; *Conscious Lovers*, 48, 179n15; debate with John Dennis, 48–49, 51
Stewart, Garrett, 41, 158, 178n90, 188n71, 197n7
stock character, 45–46

theater, and copyright, 31–32; experience of, 16, 71, 75–76, 86, 135, 148, 155; as fictional space, 61, 93; history, 6–7, 29–30, 95; library classification of, 31–32; mental, 2, 15, 76; and/or novel, 26–27, 153–156; as setting, 120–122

theatricality, and absorption, 3; and
    antitheathricality, 34, 52, 148, 172n24,
    184n3; and Burney, 99–103, 105–114, 119,
    123–124; and Inchbald, 67, 73, 141, 153;
    and narration, 11, 90, 136, 141, 162
39 Steps, The, 121, 192n62
tragedy, 5, 34, 79, 129, 130–131; in drama
    theory, 20, 39, 111
tragicomedy, 4–5, 15, 17–25, 41, 80, 123
Trollope, Anthony, 12, 109, 126, 197; *An
    Autobiography*, 159, 163–164; *Barchester
    Towers*, 163, 165; Can *You Forgive Her?*,
    158–159

Vanbrugh, Sir John, 9, 43, 189n20; *The
    Relapse*, 48–50, 54–56, 58, 60–64

Walpole, Horace, 5, 94
Wilmot, John, Earl of Rochester, 9, 43,
    46–50, 53, 58, 73
Wordsworth, William, 27, 29, 36, 131,
    133, 135

Marcie Frank is a professor of English at Concordia University in Montreal. She has previously published two books, *Gender, Theatre, and the Origins of Criticism from Dryden to Manley* (2003) and *How to Be an Intellectual in the Age of TV: The Lessons of Gore Vidal* (2005), and coedited a collection of essays, *This Distracted Globe: Worldmaking in Early Modern Literature* (2016), with Jonathan Goldberg and Karen Newman. Recent essays include "Cooper's Queer Objects," in *Angelaki* 23, no. 1 (2018), and "Tragedy, Comedy, Tragicomedy and the Incubation of New Genres," in *Emergent Nation: Early Modern Literature in Transition*, edited by Elizabeth Sauer (2019).

Printed in the United States
By Bookmasters